# Personal Best

Student's Book

**B1+**
Intermediate

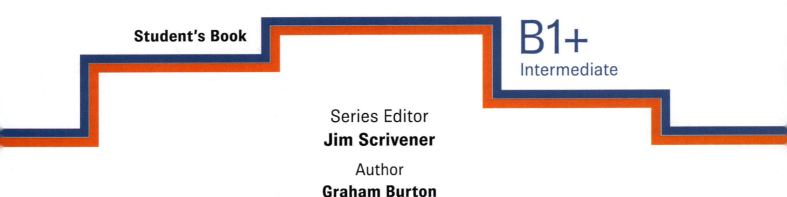

Series Editor
**Jim Scrivener**

Author
**Graham Burton**

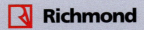

# CONTENTS

| | | LANGUAGE | | | SKILLS | |
|---|---|---|---|---|---|---|
| | | GRAMMAR | PRONUNCIATION | VOCABULARY | | |
| **1** Communication | | ▪ simple present and present continuous; action and state verbs ▪ question forms | ▪ sentence stress ▪ question intonation | ▪ communication ▪ *say*, *tell*, *speak*, and *talk* | READING ▪ a text about surviving without a smartphone ▪ skimming a text ▪ *actually*, *in fact* | SPEAKING ▪ making small talk ▪ keeping a conversation going **PERSONAL BEST** ▪ having an informal conversation |
| 1A Connected | p4 | | | | | |
| 1B Smart living? | p6 | | | | | |
| 1C Liar, liar | p8 | | | | | |
| 1D Small talk | p10 | | | | | |
| **2** Tell me a story | | ▪ narrative tenses ▪ *used to* and *usually* | ▪ /d/ sound in the past perfect ▪ sentence stress | ▪ *-ed* and *-ing* adjectives ▪ phrasal verbs | LISTENING ▪ a video looking at the role of luck in our lives ▪ listening for the main idea ▪ linking consonants and vowels | WRITING ▪ making a narrative interesting ▪ time linkers **PERSONAL BEST** ▪ a blog post about a memorable event |
| 2A What a coincidence! | p12 | | | | | |
| 2B Do we make our own luck? | p14 | | | | | |
| 2C Radical changes | p16 | | | | | |
| 2D It happened to me | p18 | | | | | |
| **1** and **2** REVIEW and PRACTICE | p20 | | | | | |
| **3** People | | ▪ future forms: present continuous, *be going to*, and *will* ▪ defining and non-defining relative clauses | ▪ *going to* ▪ pausing in relative clauses | ▪ personality adjectives ▪ relationships | READING ▪ an article about birth order and personality ▪ reading for specific information ▪ linkers of reason and result | SPEAKING ▪ giving and responding to news ▪ giving bad news **PERSONAL BEST** ▪ exchanging news with a friend |
| 3A It's a plan | p22 | | | | | |
| 3B Born to rebel | p24 | | | | | |
| 3C Good neighbors, bad neighbors | p26 | | | | | |
| 3D I have some news | p28 | | | | | |
| **4** Places and homes | | ▪ quantifiers ▪ comparatives and superlatives, *as ... as* | ▪ sentence stress ▪ /ə/ sound | ▪ compound nouns ▪ common verb phrases ▪ describing homes | LISTENING ▪ a video looking at how we feel about where we live ▪ understanding key points ▪ linking similar consonant sounds | WRITING ▪ writing an informal e-mail ▪ informal discourse markers **PERSONAL BEST** ▪ an e-mail catching up with a friend |
| 4A What makes your city great? | p30 | | | | | |
| 4B City or country? | p32 | | | | | |
| 4C A place to stay in NYC | p34 | | | | | |
| 4D Hope to hear from you soon! | p36 | | | | | |
| **3** and **4** REVIEW and PRACTICE | p38 | | | | | |
| **5** Money and shopping | | ▪ zero and first conditional; future time clauses ▪ predictions: *will*, *be going to*, *may/might* | ▪ intonation ▪ word stress | ▪ money ▪ shopping | READING ▪ an article about the Black Friday shopping phenomenon ▪ identifying opinions ▪ *even*, *just* | SPEAKING ▪ explaining what's wrong ▪ taking something back to a store **PERSONAL BEST** ▪ getting a refund or exchange |
| 5A Spend, spend, spend | p40 | | | | | |
| 5B Black Friday | p42 | | | | | |
| 5C Tomorrow's world of shopping | p44 | | | | | |
| 5D It's not working | p46 | | | | | |
| **6** Work and education | | ▪ present perfect and simple past, *already*, *yet*, *recently* ▪ present perfect continuous and present perfect | ▪ present perfect and simple past ▪ weak form of *been* | ▪ work and careers (1) ▪ work and careers (2) ▪ education | LISTENING ▪ a video looking at how we feel about our jobs ▪ understanding specific information ▪ sentence stress | WRITING ▪ writing a cover letter ▪ prepositions after verbs, nouns, and adjectives **PERSONAL BEST** ▪ an e-mail to apply for a job |
| 6A Career change | p48 | | | | | |
| 6B Dream job | p50 | | | | | |
| 6C School days | p52 | | | | | |
| 6D I am writing to apply ... | p54 | | | | | |
| **5** and **6** REVIEW and PRACTICE | p56 | | | | | |

Language App, unit-by-unit grammar and vocabulary games

# CONTENTS

| | | LANGUAGE | | | SKILLS | |
|---|---|---|---|---|---|---|
| | | GRAMMAR | PRONUNCIATION | VOCABULARY | | |
| **7** Entertainment | | ■ the passive <br> ■ modals of ability and possibility | ■ past participles <br> ■ /eɪ/ and /ʊ/ sounds | ■ movies <br> ■ TV and music | **READING** <br> ■ an article about Vic Armstrong, stunt performer <br> ■ guessing the meaning of words from context <br> ■ referencing: *this* and *that* | **SPEAKING** <br> ■ giving directions <br> ■ asking for information <br> **PERSONAL BEST** <br> ■ asking a stranger for directions |
| **7A** Lights, camera, action! | p58 | | | | | |
| **7B** Action man | p60 | | | | | |
| **7C** Got talent | p62 | | | | | |
| **7D** Could you tell me where it is? | p64 | | | | | |
| **8** Sport and health | | ■ tag questions <br> ■ modals of obligation and advice | ■ intonation <br> ■ sentence stress | ■ sports, places, and equipment <br> ■ health and fitness verb phrases | **LISTENING** <br> ■ a video about what we do to get in shape <br> ■ understanding facts and figures <br> ■ intonation | **WRITING** <br> ■ writing a report <br> ■ adding information <br> **PERSONAL BEST** <br> ■ a report about sports in your country |
| **8A** On the field, in the pool | p66 | | | | | |
| **8B** So many ways to get in shape | p68 | | | | | |
| **8C** Is there an app for that? | p70 | | | | | |
| **8D** Sports in my country | p72 | | | | | |
| **7 and 8** ■ REVIEW and PRACTICE | p74 | | | | | |
| **9** Food | | ■ uses of *like* <br> ■ *-ing* forms and infinitives | ■ /dʒ/ sound <br> ■ *-ing* | ■ food and cooking <br> ■ eating out | **READING** <br> ■ an article about the benefits of chocolate <br> ■ reading for detail <br> ■ substitution: *one, ones* | **SPEAKING** <br> ■ making and responding to suggestions <br> ■ making a group decision <br> **PERSONAL BEST** <br> ■ having a group discussion and making a decision |
| **9A** Chefs at home | p76 | | | | | |
| **9B** Chocolate – the world's favorite superfood | p78 | | | | | |
| **9C** Eating out | p80 | | | | | |
| **9D** Why don't you try the curry? | p82 | | | | | |
| **10** Right and wrong | | ■ reported speech <br> ■ second conditional, *would, could,* and *might* | ■ sentence stress <br> ■ conditionals | ■ crime <br> ■ making nouns from verbs | **LISTENING** <br> ■ a video about our experiences with emergency services <br> ■ listening in detail <br> ■ final /t/ and /d/ sounds | **WRITING** <br> ■ writing a for-and-against essay <br> ■ useful phrases for topic sentences <br> **PERSONAL BEST** <br> ■ a for-and-against essay |
| **10A** Smooth criminals? | p84 | | | | | |
| **10B** Emergency! | p86 | | | | | |
| **10C** Do the right thing | p88 | | | | | |
| **10D** For and against | p90 | | | | | |
| **9 and 10** ■ REVIEW and PRACTICE | p92 | | | | | |
| **11** The natural world | | ■ articles <br> ■ third conditional | ■ *the* <br> ■ weak form of *have* | ■ the natural world <br> ■ extreme adjectives | **READING** <br> ■ an article about living near one of the world's most dangerous volcanoes <br> ■ understanding the writer's purpose <br> ■ understanding noun phrases | **SPEAKING** <br> ■ making recommendations <br> ■ checking and clarifying information <br> **PERSONAL BEST** <br> ■ recommending the best natural places to visit in your country |
| **11A** Nature goes viral | p94 | | | | | |
| **11B** A disaster waiting to happen | p96 | | | | | |
| **11C** I will survive | p98 | | | | | |
| **11D** The great outdoors | p100 | | | | | |
| **12** Getting away | | ■ *So/Neither do I* <br> ■ modals of deduction | ■ auxiliary verbs and stress <br> ■ sentence stress | ■ phrases with *go* and *get* <br> ■ air travel | **LISTENING** <br> ■ a video looking at how we feel about flying <br> ■ identifying agreement between speakers <br> ■ linking: /w/ and /y/ sounds | **WRITING** <br> ■ writing an online review <br> ■ adverbs of attitude <br> **PERSONAL BEST** <br> ■ an online review of a hotel, restaurant or service |
| **12A** Dream destinations | p102 | | | | | |
| **12B** Fly away | p104 | | | | | |
| **12C** Around the world | p106 | | | | | |
| **12D** Five-star review | p108 | | | | | |
| **11 and 12** ■ REVIEW and PRACTICE | p110 | | | | | |

**Grammar practice** p112    **Vocabulary practice** p136    **Communication practice** p156    **Irregular verbs** p175

Language App, unit-by-unit grammar and vocabulary games

3

# UNIT 1

# Communication

**LANGUAGE** simple present and present continuous; action and state verbs ■ communication

## 1A Connected

**1** How do you keep in touch with people? Order the communication phrases from 1 (I do this less often) to 6 (I do this most often). Compare your answers in pairs.

☐ get a text message ☐ share a photo ☐ give someone a call ☐ reply to an e-mail ☐ check your phone ☐ comment on a post

Go to Vocabulary practice: communication, page 136

**2** Think of three people in your life. Tell your partner how you keep in touch with these people.

**3 A** Are sentences 1–6 true (T) or false (F)? Discuss your answers in pairs.

1 We speak to each other face-to-face more often nowadays. _____
2 Our phone calls are longer today compared to ten years ago. _____
3 These days, it seems we prefer text messages to phone calls. _____
4 People in the U.S. send more letters and packages nowadays. _____
5 We are sending a million e-mails per second, now. _____
6 More than half of the Internet pages we visit are social media sites. _____

**B** Read the text and check your answers in 3A. Correct the false sentences.

## THE CHANGING FACE OF COMMUNICATION

The way we communicate has never changed so much in such a short period of time. We look at the results of recent surveys that tell us about the changing face of communication.

### We talk to each other less.
Ten years ago, 80% of our communication was face-to-face. Now, it's only 60%. Even our phone calls are shorter – on average, each call now lasts one minute, compared to three minutes ten years ago. It seems that people prefer texting to calling.

### We use traditional postal services less.
In the U.S., over 200 billion letters and packages were sent in 2008, compared to 150 billion last year. These days, we usually write to people by text, messaging app, or e-mail. In fact, right now, people are sending two million e-mails per second!

### We love social media.
Sixty percent of the pages we view on the Internet are social media pages, and we share nearly two billion photos on them every day. The average person has five social media accounts and spends about two hours a day looking at them.

### Comments

**Tina**
It's a shame we don't write letters much, but the post office seems so slow nowadays compared to communicating online! I need the Internet to be in immediate contact with people, especially right now because I'm planning my wedding.

**Rob**
I agree with Tina, but I still try to send letters and cards on important occasions, and postcards when I'm on vacation. I don't know how people planned things with just snail mail!

simple present and present continuous; action and state verbs ■ communication **LANGUAGE** **1A**

**4** Which piece of information in the text did you find most surprising? Do you agree with Tina and Rob?

**5** **A** Look at the highlighted verbs in Tina's comment and answer the questions.

1 Which four verbs are in the simple present? Which verb is in the present continuous?

2 Which two verbs describe actions? Which three verbs describe states?

**B** Choose the correct options to complete the rules.

1 We use the *simple present / present continuous* to talk about things that happen regularly or things that are always true.

2 We use the *simple present / present continuous* to talk about actions that are happening now or actions that are temporary.

3 We can't use the present continuous for *action / state* verbs.

**6** Read the Grammar box. Then look at the sentences in exercise 3A again. Do they contain action or state verbs? What tense are they?

---

**📖 Grammar** | **simple present and present continuous; action and state verbs**

**Simple present with action and state verbs:**
*I **call** my brother at least once a week.   I'm so thirsty right now. I **need** some water.* NOT ~~I'm needing some water.~~

**Present continuous with action verbs:**
*I'm **calling** you from New York!   We'**re studying** French this year.*

---

**Go to Grammar practice:** simple present and present continuous; action and state verbs, page 112

**7** **A** ▶1.3 **Pronunciation:** sentence stress Listen to the sentences. Do we stress the auxiliary verbs *be* and *do*?

1 Are you trying to access the Internet?

2 Do you need a new laptop?

3 The Internet doesn't seem slow right now.

4 Why are you using my tablet?

**B** ▶1.3 Listen, check, and repeat.

**8** **A** Complete the sentences with the correct tense of the verbs in parentheses.

1 I _____ (not check) my text messages when I'm having coffee with friends.

2 The price of desktop computers _____ (go) down at the moment.

3 I _____ (like) looking at the selfie photos that my friends post on social media.

4 I'm studying English online, right now, so I _____ (need) the Internet on my phone.

5 I _____ (look) for a new phone because my phone is very old.

6 Most people _____ (have) friends on Facebook that they never talk to face-to-face.

**B** In pairs, discuss the sentences in 8A. Which sentences do you agree with or are true for you?

**Go to Communication practice:** Student A page 156, Student B page 166

**9** Complete the questionnaire and discuss your answers in pairs.

---

## How do you communicate?

**1** When I want to get together with friends, I normally …

message them on Facebook. ☐   text them. ☐
call them. ☐

**2** When I'm feeling happy and I want to share good news with people that live far away, I …

send a text message. ☐   send a letter. ☐
make plans to get together. ☐

**3** When I'm feeling sad, I prefer to speak to people …

on the phone. ☐   on Skype. ☐   face-to-face. ☐

**4** On my best friend's birthday, I usually send …

a message on social media. ☐   a text. ☐   a card. ☐

**5** I usually share important photos …

using a messaging app. ☐   by e-mail. ☐
on social media. ☐

**6** When I want to keep in touch with old friends, I usually …

contact them on social media. ☐   e-mail them. ☐
give them a call. ☐

---

**Personal Best** | Write four sentences with state verbs in the simple present.

5

# 1 SKILLS READING skimming a text ■ *actually, in fact*

## 1B Smart living?

**1** What do you use your smartphone for? What do you think of people who constantly check their phones?

> **Skill** skimming a text
>
> **Before you read a text in detail, get a general idea of the topic of the text and of each paragraph.**
> - Read the title of the text and look at any images. Can you predict what the text is about?
> - Quickly read the first paragraph. This will confirm the topic and can give you an idea of the text content and organization.
> - Read the first sentence of each paragraph. This can give you information about the main idea of each paragraph.

**2** Read the Skill box. Then look at the title of the text, the picture, and the first paragraph on page 7. Do you think the writer had a positive or negative experience without his smartphone?

**3** Read the first sentences of paragraphs 2–6. What is the main idea of each paragraph? Match the paragraphs with ideas a–e.
   a  With no smartphone, he felt less tired.
   b  He worked better.
   c  He communicated more often face-to-face.
   d  There were more advantages than disadvantages.
   e  He found things to do to entertain himself.

**4** Read the complete text. Are the sentences true (T) or false (F)? Correct the false sentences.
   1  The writer stopped using his smartphone because of an article he read.  _____
   2  Normally his smartphone distracts him when he's working.  _____
   3  He has become a better listener when he's with friends.  _____
   4  He doesn't enjoy reading books and newspapers any more.  _____
   5  The light from smartphone screens helps us sleep.  _____
   6  The writer now uses his smartphone differently than before.  _____

**5** Read this sentence from the text. Which word is used to express surprise that something unexpected happened?

"I actually talked to people more and felt more connected to them, although we weren't in constant contact online."

> **Text builder** *actually, in fact*
>
> **To say that something is surprising or unexpected, we can use *actually* or *in fact*:**
> *I was worried that I would be bored without my phone as entertainment, but, **actually**, I enjoyed it.*
> *I thought living without a smartphone would be hard, but, **in fact**, it was pretty easy.*
>
> **Look!** We can use **actually** at the start of a phrase, before a main verb, or after *be*.
> We usually use **in fact** at the start of a phrase.

**6** Read the Text builder. Match 1–4 with a–d.
   1  My friends say I'm addicted to my new smartphone.
   2  My teacher's surprised because
   3  Tim thought the movie was on at 8:30 this evening,
   4  I thought I was going away this weekend,

   a  but it was actually on yesterday, not today.
   b  Actually, I don't use it as much as my old one.
   c  but, in fact, I'm staying at home.
   d  I actually passed the exam!

**7** Could you live without your smartphone for a week? In pairs, discuss what you think the experience would be like.

6

skimming a text ■ actually, in fact   READING    SKILLS    1B

# A WEEK WITHOUT MY *smartphone*

by David Sharpe

**1** When I read that we spend three hours every day checking our smartphones, I was surprised. What was I missing in the real world when walking down the street, lost in a virtual world of social media updates and videos of dogs on bicycles? I promised myself I would use my smartphone less … but it didn't happen. But then my phone died, and I had to wait a week for a new one. Would I survive? I thought it would be hard, but, in fact, it was pretty easy – and surprising, in a good way, for a number of reasons!

**2** The first result was pretty amazing – on the first day in the office without my phone, I was thinking more deeply and concentrating more. I had rediscovered my brain! Not having access to my favorite apps meant that I wasn't interrupted every five minutes by social media alerts, soccer scores, and WhatsApp group messages. Without these distractions, I was more productive and felt satisfied that I'd done a better job.

**3** Another result was that I actually talked to people more and felt more connected to them, although we weren't in constant contact online. At lunch with friends one day, I realized I was being more responsive to their news and sympathetic to their problems because I wasn't constantly checking my phone. Another day I was in a new city and I asked people for directions instead of using an app. Their kindness made me feel welcome, and I discovered my brain has a very good GPS!

**4** I was worried that I would be bored without my phone as entertainment, but, actually, I enjoyed it – I'd forgotten how much I love books and newspapers. I'd also forgotten how much I enjoyed doing Sudoku puzzles. I had an app for that on my smartphone, but never used it. Doing one every day in the newspaper felt a lot more special, and it became part of my morning routine. My brain felt a lot sharper and much more ready for the day ahead as a result.

**5** One completely unexpected result of not having a smartphone was that I slept so much better and felt more awake in the morning. At night, I relaxed with a book before going to sleep, instead of watching Netflix or reading the news on my phone. Apparently, the blue light from smartphone screens makes our brain think it's morning, so it's releasing chemicals to wake us up, just when we're trying to get to sleep. That's not very smart!

**6** Of course, at times, it was extremely inconvenient to have no cell-phone Internet connection, but, all in all, there were a lot of benefits to not being connected 24/7. Although I was jumping for joy when my new smartphone arrived, I'm a lot more careful about how much I use it now. So, if you think you use your smartphone too much, put it away for a few days and see what happens. You never know, you may become smarter!

**Personal Best**  Have you ever lived without something for a period of time? Write two or three sentences about the experience.

# 1 LANGUAGE  question forms ■ *say*, *tell*, *speak*, and *talk*

## 1C Liar, liar

**1** In pairs, answer the questions.
1 What are the people in the pictures lying about?
2 What other things do people often tell lies about? Make a list.

a   b   c   d

Go to Vocabulary practice: *say*, *tell*, *speak*, and *talk*, page 136

**2  A** In pairs, take the quiz "The truth about lying."

## THE TRUTH ABOUT LYING

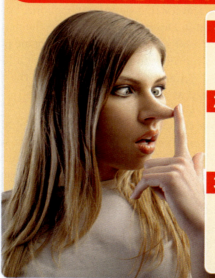

1 How often do people tell lies?
  a twice a month
  b twice a week
  c twice a day

2 What do people lie about most frequently?
  a work
  b money
  c unimportant things

3 How do people usually answer the question, "When did you last tell a lie?"
  a "I never lie."
  b "I can't remember."
  c "Some time today."

4 How can you know when people are lying?
  a They don't look directly at you.
  b They move their hands a lot.
  c They give unnecessary information.

5 Is communication technology making us less honest?
  a yes    b no

6 Do men lie more often than women?
  a yes    b no

7 Do men and women lie about the same things?
  a yes    b no

**B** ▶ 1.5 Listen and check your answers. Which answer surprised you most?

**3** Cover the quiz. Complete the questions from memory. Then check your answers in the quiz.

1 _____ lies?
2 _____ most frequently?
3 _____ last _____ a lie?
4 _____ when people are lying?
5 _____ us less honest?

**4  A** Look at questions 1–5 in exercise 3. How do we form most questions? Choose the correct structure, a or b.

a  (question word/s) + auxiliary verb + subject + main verb

b  (question word/s) + main verb

**B** Look at question 2 in exercise 3. Is the preposition before the question word or after the main verb?

8

question forms ■ say, tell, speak, and talk    LANGUAGE  1C

**5 A** ▶1.6 Listen to people telling a lie in three conversations. What is each person lying about? Write the conversation number (1–3).

a receiving text messages ____   b eating chocolate ____   c liking someone's food ____

**B** ▶1.6 Listen again and complete the questions.
1 Who _____ all of my chocolate?    3 Who _____ more banana and potato sandwiches?
2 What _____ to you last night?

**6** Look at the questions in exercise 5B. Choose the correct options to complete the sentences. Then read the Grammar box about the different question forms.
1 In these questions, we *know / don't know* the subject of the verb.
2 We use the *affirmative / question* form of the verb.

> **Grammar    question forms**
>
> **Object questions:**
> Where do you work?
> What are you doing right now?
> Where did you go to college?
> Have you finished?
>
> **Questions with prepositions:**
> Where do they come **from**?
> Who did you play tennis **with**?
>
> **Subject questions:**
> Who called me? NOT ~~Who did call me~~?
> Who wants coffee? NOT ~~Who does want coffee~~?
> Who invented the telephone? NOT ~~Who did invent the telephone~~?

Go to Grammar practice: question forms, page 113

**7** ▶1.8 **Pronunciation:** question intonation Listen to four of the questions from this lesson. Does the intonation go up (↗) or down (↘) at the end of the questions?
1 Have you finished?        3 What happened to you last night?
2 How often do people tell lies?  4 Do men lie more often than women?

**8 A** Complete the questions with an auxiliary verb from the box if necessary. Which question doesn't need an auxiliary?

    do (x2)   did (x5)   have

1 _____ you usually tell little white lies to protect people's feelings?
2 When _____ you last tell a little white lie? What _____ you lie about?
3 When you were younger, _____ you tell your parents lies? _____ you tell the truth later?
4 Who _____ tells the best jokes in your family?
5 _____ you usually say hello to people you don't know on the street?
6 _____ you ever told someone that he or she can't cook well? What _____ the person say?

**B** In pairs, decide if the intonation goes up (↗) or down (↘) at the end of the questions in 8A. Then ask and answer the questions.

Go to Communication practice: Student A page 156, Student B page 166

**9** Ask and answer the questions in pairs.
1 Who helped you with your homework as a child?
2 Who taught you how to ride a bike?
3 What happened on your first day of school?
4 Who taught you how to drive?
5 Which author wrote your favorite book?
6 What happened on your first day at work?

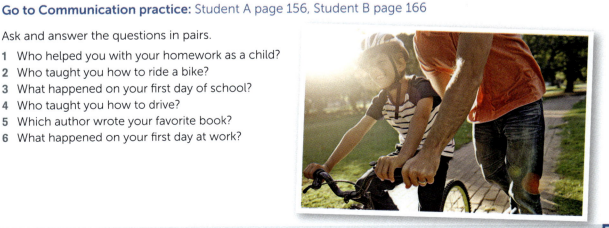

**Personal Best**  Write four questions to ask your partner about his or her life.

# 1 SKILLS
**SPEAKING** making small talk ■ keeping a conversation going

## 1D Small talk

**1 A** Read the definition of *small talk* and look at the topics. Which topics do people typically discuss when they make small talk?

> **small talk** *noun* polite and informal conversation about light topics, often between people who don't know each other well.

- the weather
- politics
- TV, sports, and movies
- relationship problems
- work and family
- the situation (party, trip, etc.)
- your day

**B** In pairs, discuss the questions.
1 When did you last make small talk?
2 Where were you?
3 Who did you talk to?
4 What did you talk about?

**2** ▶1.9 Watch or listen to the first part of a webshow called *Learning Curve*. Ethan catches a train, and a passenger makes small talk with him. Who are sentences 1–6 about? Check (✓) *Ethan* or *passenger*.

|   | Ethan | passenger |
|---|---|---|
| 1 He starts the conversation. | ☐ | ☐ |
| 2 He asks where the other person is going. | ☐ | ☐ |
| 3 He's going to City Island. | ☐ | ☐ |
| 4 He asks where the other person is from. | ☐ | ☐ |
| 5 He's from Pennsylvania. | ☐ | ☐ |
| 6 He asks about the other person's job. | ☐ | ☐ |

**3** ▶1.9 Complete the sentences from the conversation with the words in the box. Watch or listen again and check.

> so   nice   mind   ahead   have   excuse   sounds   living

1 _____ me. Does this train go to the baseball stadium?
2 Would you _____ if I sit here?
3 Uh, no. Go right _____.
4 _____ , where are you going?
5 What do you do for a _____ ?
6 Well, that _____ interesting.
7 Hey, it was _____ talking to you!
8 _____ fun at the game!

### Conversation builder — making small talk

**Starting the conversation**
Excuse me ...
Is anyone sitting here?
Would you mind if I sit here?
Beautiful day, isn't it?

**Asking about the person/situation**
Are you having a good time/trip/day?
Are you from around here?
So, what do you do for a living?
And what does that involve?
I love your phone. Is it new?

**Ending the conversation**
Nice talking to you.
Great to meet you.
Have a nice evening.

**4** Read the Conversation builder. Make small talk with your partner. Imagine it's your first English class and you've never met.

making small talk ■ keeping a conversation going   **SPEAKING**   SKILLS   **1D**

**5** ▶ 1.10  Watch or listen to the second part of the show. Ethan goes to a party and meets Cindy for the first time. Check (✓) the topics that Cindy and Ethan talk about.

1 Penny and Taylor's apartment ☐
2 their families ☐
3 their jobs ☐
4 how they know Penny and Taylor ☐
5 the food at the party ☐
6 the weather ☐

**6** ▶ 1.10  Put sentences (a–i) in order. Watch or listen again and check.

a ☐ **Cindy** So, what do you do on your webshow?
b ☐ **Ethan** Oh, you met at work! So, are you having a good time?
c ☐ **Cindy** Sorry, I don't know Penny that well. By the way, I'm Cindy. I work with Taylor at the gym.
d ☐ **Ethan** Well, I'm a presenter, a co-host, like Penny.
e ☐1 **Cindy** How do you know Penny and Taylor?
f ☐ **Ethan** Mmm! Well, I love carrot cake.
g ☐ **Cindy** It's a great party. I got here early so I could bring my famous carrot cake.
h ☐2 **Ethan** I'm Ethan. I work with Penny on *Learning Curve*. It's a webshow. We're presenters.
i ☐ **Cindy** Hmm, a presenter, that's interesting. And what does that involve?

🔧 **Skill**  keeping a conversation going

When we talk to someone we don't know well, we keep the conversation going so we don't run out of things to say.
• Give extra information when you answer a question, e.g., *"Are you from around here?"* *"No. I moved here from Brazil six months ago."*
• Respond to a statement with a positive comment, e.g., *"That's interesting! I love Brazil. I've been there twice."*
• Ask open questions to find out more information, e.g., *"Really? What were you doing there?"*

**7** Read the Skill box. Answer the questions about the conversation in exercise 6.
1 What extra information does Ethan give when he explains how he knows Penny?
2 What positive comments do Ethan and Cindy make?
3 What open questions does Cindy ask?

**8** In pairs, practice the conversation in exercise 6.

**Go to Communication practice:** Student A page 156, Student B page 166

**9 A** PREPARE  In pairs, choose one of the situations below and think about how you could start a conversation with someone you don't know well.

**B** PRACTICE  Take turns starting a conversation. Make small talk and keep the conversation going.

**C** PERSONAL BEST  Was it easy to start the conversation and keep it going? What could you do differently next time? Choose another situation and have another conversation.

**Personal Best**  You meet someone new at Penny and Taylor's party. Write the conversation.

11

# UNIT 2  Tell me a story

**LANGUAGE** — narrative tenses ■ -ed and -ing adjectives

## 2A What a coincidence!

**1 A** Choose the correct options to complete the questions. Explain why they are correct.
1. In your opinion, what kind of social media posts are *bored / boring*?
2. What kind of social media posts are you *interested / interesting* in?

**B** In pairs, answer the questions in 1A.

Go to Vocabulary practice: *-ed* and *-ing* adjectives, page 137

**2** Tell your partner about the last time you felt shocked or terrified, and about something you find fascinating or amusing.

**3 A** Read the text quickly. What do you think the title *Twinsters* means?

**B** Read the text again. Order the events from 1–6.
a ☐ The twins made a movie about finding each other.
b ☐ Anaïs saw a woman online who looked identical to her.
c ☐ Anaïs found a way of contacting Samantha.
d ☐ Anaïs discovered that they had the same date of birth.
e ☐ They got to know each other online, and then they met in person.
f ☐ A scientific test proved they were twins.

In February 2013, 25-year-old Anaïs Bordier, a fashion design student from Paris, was checking Facebook when she saw a video of a young American actress that a friend had posted. Anaïs couldn't believe it – the actress looked exactly like her! Unfortunately, there was no name on the video, but she was extremely curious and told all her friends about it.

A few months later, while Anaïs was traveling by bus to college, she got a message from the same friend. He had seen the actress in another video, and this time there was a name – Samantha Futerman. When Anaïs googled her, she found out that they were born on the same day, and that, like Anaïs, Samantha had been adopted when she was a baby. Anaïs was so shocked that she got off the bus. Could Samantha be her twin? She decided to contact her to find out.

When Samantha received a friend request from Anaïs on Facebook, she was amazed to see that the face in the profile picture was identical to her own. Anaïs messaged Samantha to explain how she had found her, and to ask her where she was born. Samantha replied and confirmed that she was also born in Busan, South Korea. The girls spoke regularly on Skype after that and discovered that they were not only very similar in appearance, but also had the same mannerisms, found the same things amusing, and both loved cheese!

Anaïs and Samantha were excited to meet for the first time several months later in London, where Anaïs was studying. While Samantha was visiting Anaïs, they received the results of a DNA test which confirmed what they already knew – that they really were identical twins. The sisters then wrote a book and filmed an award-winning documentary, *Twinsters*, about their amazing story.

narrative tenses ■ -ed and -ing adjectives     **LANGUAGE**     **2A**

**4** What did you think of Anaïs and Samantha's story?
*I thought it was an amazing coincidence.*

**5 A** Which forms are the verbs in **bold**? Choose from the simple past, past perfect, and past continuous.
1 He **had seen** the actress in another video. _____
2 While Anaïs **was traveling** by bus to college, she got a message. _____
3 The sisters **wrote** a book about their amazing story. _____

**B** Match the forms with their uses. Then read the Grammar box.
a an action that happened before another action in the past _____
b a completed action in the past _____
c an action in progress at a specific moment in the past _____

---

**Grammar**    narrative tenses

Simple past (for main events):
I **visited** my friend Ana last year.

Past perfect (for actions that happened before other actions):
When we arrived at the theater, the movie **had started**.

Past continuous (for longer actions/background):
At 9 p.m. last night I **was having** dinner.

**Look!** We usually use **when** with the simple past and **when** or **while** with the past continuous:
I was walking in the park **when** I met Jo.    **When/While** I was walking in the park, I met Jo.

---

Go to Grammar practice: narrative tenses, page 114

**6 A** ▶ 2.3 **Pronunciation:** /d/ in the past perfect   Listen to the sentence. Notice the pronunciation of /d/ in the past perfect form. Listen again and repeat.
He'**d** seen the woman before.

**B** ▶ 2.4   Listen to the sentences and choose the verb forms you hear.
1 I bought / I'd bought
2 He asked / He'd asked
3 She caught the bus / She'd caught the bus
4 We realized / We'd realized
5 You watched / You'd watched
6 They lost / They'd lost

Go to Communication practice: Student A page 157, Student B page 167

**7 A** ▶ 2.5   Complete the text with the correct form of the verbs in parentheses. Listen and check.

"Last year, while I ¹_____ (stay) with my grandmother for the weekend in a town a few hours away, I ²_____ (go) to visit my friend Marco, who also lives there. I ³_____ (call) him the day before to arrange a time to get together, but he hadn't answered. I went to his house anyway, but when I ⁴_____ (ring) the doorbell, nobody ⁵_____ (come) to the door, so I ⁶_____ (decide) to leave. Right then, I ⁷_____ (get) a message on my phone. It was Marco! He ⁸_____ (go) to my hometown the evening before to visit his parents, and now he ⁹_____ (knock) on my door! It was such a coincidence!"

**B** Have there been any coincidences in your life or in your friends' lives? Talk about them in pairs.

**8** In pairs, talk about a time when you met someone important in your life. Use the questions to help you.

- Where were you?
- What had happened before you met?
- What were you both doing when you met?
- What happened when you met?
- What did you both say?
- How did your life change after you met him/her?

Read the story about Anaïs and Samantha again. Close your books and retell the story in pairs.

13

## 2 SKILLS  LISTENING listening for the main idea ■ linking consonants and vowels ■ phrasal verbs

### 2B Do we make our own luck?

**1** Do you think these things bring good or bad luck? Can you think of more examples?

a dream catcher

a broken mirror

a fortune cat

a penny

a four-leaf clover

the number 13

**2 A** Were these people lucky or unlucky? Match the verbs in **bold** with the meanings.

> I found a lucky penny on the street, but that day, my car [1]**ran out** of gas and my boyfriend [2]**broke up** with me – we'd been [3]**going out** for ten years. So much for lucky pennies!

> My plane ticket was for seat 13. I [4]**set off** early for the airport to get there on time, but the traffic was terrible, and I [5]**ended up** missing my flight. I was really [6]**looking forward to** that vacation!

a  be excited about something in the future
b  finally be in a situation or place you didn't originally intend
c  have a romantic relationship
d  start a trip
e  finish or use all of something
f  end a relationship

**B** Answer the questions in pairs.
1  Has the battery on your phone ever run out right before an important call?
2  What did you plan to do last weekend? Did you end up doing something different?
3  What are you looking forward to right now?

**Go to Vocabulary practice:** phrasal verbs, page 138

> **Skill**  listening for the main idea
>
> It's important to understand the main idea when someone is speaking.
> • Think about who is speaking and what the topic is.
> • Remember that speakers often repeat the main idea using different words.
> • Listen for key words, which are often stressed.
> • Don't worry if you don't understand all the words or details.

**3 A** ▶ 2.8  Read the Skill box. Watch or listen to the first part of *Learning Curve* and choose the correct option to answer the questions.
1  What does Penny talk about?
   a  a scientific experiment about luck
   b  a book about luck
   c  an unlucky day she had
2  What is the main idea?
   a  Some people are simply unlucky.
   b  Positive people generally see more opportunities in life.
   c  People who believe they are lucky are usually unlucky.

**B** Do you believe in luck? Do you think people make their own luck? Discuss in pairs.

14

listening for the main idea ■ linking consonants and vowels ■ phrasal verbs  LISTENING    SKILLS  2B

**4** ▶ 2.9 Watch or listen to the second part of the show. Complete the sentences about the main ideas with *Herman*, *Winnie*, or *Juan*.

1 _____ considers himself/herself to be very lucky.
2 _____ talks about someone else who believes in bad luck.
3 _____ is having a bit of bad luck, but his/her luck changes.

**5** ▶ 2.9 Watch or listen again. Choose the correct option to answer the questions.

1 What happened to Herman earlier?
  a He slept badly, lost his keys, and left for work late.
  b His motorcycle broke down, he lost his keys, and missed the bus.
  c The shower ran out of hot water, and he lost his key chain.
2 What happened to Winnie?
  a She went out with a dentist and ended up marrying him.
  b She was going out with a mechanic, but broke up with him.
  c She ended up marrying a man she'd met several times by chance.
3 Which sentence about Juan is true?
  a He's looking forward to getting married to Winnie.
  b He's in the city doing a favor for a neighbor.
  c He has to go back home because he forgot his backpack.

**6** Think of a time when you were lucky or unlucky. Describe what happened in pairs.

> **Listening builder** | **linking consonants and vowels**
>
> When a word ends in a consonant sound, we often move the consonant sound to the beginning of the next word if it starts with a vowel sound. This can sometimes mean it's difficult to hear the correct words.
>
> *It all started last night.   She's trying on her wedding dress.*

**7** ▶ 2.10 Read the Listening builder. Look at the sentences from the show and mark where the consonant-vowel links are. Listen and check. Then practice saying the sentences.

1 Do we make our own luck?
2 I ran out of energy.
3 I think Ethan is back.
4 I'm picking up a package.
5 I think it's his backpack.
6 I'm the luckiest person I know.

**8** Discuss the questions in pairs.

1 Who's the luckiest person you know? And the unluckiest?
2 Do you have any lucky charms? What are they? Have they brought you good luck?
3 Is there anything you avoid doing because it might bring bad luck?

**Personal Best** Write a paragraph about things that bring good luck on special occasions, e.g., a wedding, New Year's Eve.

## 2 LANGUAGE  *used to* and *usually*

### 2C Radical changes

**1 A** In pairs, look at the pictures and describe what you see. What are the similarities and differences?

**B** Read the text and choose the best caption for the pictures.

1 Steve Way and his trainer    2 Steve Way: before and after    3 Like father, like son

## Sports interview:
# Marathon Man

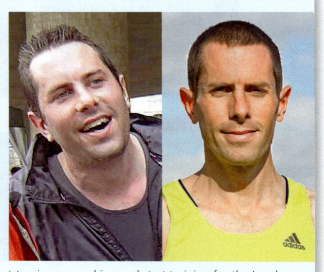

Steve Way, a long-distance runner, has two memorable career highlights: running a marathon in Glasgow in just 2 hours and 15 minutes and finishing the British Ultramarathon (100 km.) in 6 hours and 19 minutes. Both were personal best times for him and broke records. He is a top athlete, but behind the success there is an extraordinary story.

Steve usually runs about 120 km. a week, weighs 67 kg., and like all top athletes, is normally very careful about what he eats. But he hasn't always been so healthy. When Steve was in his thirties, he used to be dangerously overweight because of his addiction to chocolate and junk food. He didn't use to get any exercise, smoked a pack of cigarettes a day, and had a stressful job with long hours.

He felt horrible, "I could hardly sleep at night. I was coughing and waking up because of the smoking," he remembers. "I realized I had to do something radically different to break the cycle." The radical change was to give up smoking and start training for the London Marathon, which he completed in just over three hours despite training for only three weeks!

It soon became clear that Steve was a very talented athlete. Nowadays, he is so enthusiastic about running that he travels to competitions all over the world. So how does an ultra-healthy person celebrate another successful marathon? Steve admits that for 48 hours after a marathon he usually lets the old Steve out of the box and enjoys fast food, steak, and French fries. "I still struggle to see myself as a serious athlete," he says. "I am just a man who got obsessed with his hobby."

*Adapted from theguardian.com*

**2** Read the text again. What do the numbers refer to?

> 100 km.   6 hours 19 minutes   thirties   three weeks   48 hours

**3** In pairs, complete the notes about Steve in the chart with the words in the box.

> overweight   healthy food   67 kg.   runs a lot   junk food   get any exercise

|  | now | before |
|---|---|---|
| amount of exercise | 1 He usually _____. | 2 He didn't use to _____. |
| weight | 3 He weighs _____. | 4 He used to be _____. |
| diet | 5 He usually eats _____. | 6 He used to eat _____. |

**4** Have you made any changes in your life? What changes would you like to make?

*used to* and *usually*  LANGUAGE 2C

**5** Answer the questions and then read the Grammar box. Which sentences in the chart in exercise 3 describe:

1 present habits and states? ___ ___ ___
2 past habits and states? ___ ___ ___

> **Grammar** *used to* and *usually*
>
> **Past habits and states:**
> I **used to** be in shape.
> I **didn't use to** work.
> He never **used to** call me.
> **Did** you **use to** do your homework?
>
> **Present habits:**
> I **usually** walk to work.
> I **don't usually** watch much TV.
> **Do** you **usually** start work so early?
>
> **Look!** We use the simple past for things that happened only once, or to say how many times something happened.
> I broke my leg three times when I was a child. NOT ~~I used to break my leg three times~~.

**Go to Grammar practice:** *used to* and *usually*, page 115

**6** ▶ 2.12 **Pronunciation: sentence stress** Read sentences 1–3. Which syllables are stressed? Listen, check, and repeat.

1 Did they use to play sports?  2 I used to go to the gym.  3 He didn't use to run.

**7 A** Rewrite the sentences with *usually* or a form of *used to*.

1 These days, I have cereal for breakfast.
2 I didn't play volleyball when I was younger.
3 I enjoyed math when I was in school.
4 I go swimming on Saturdays.
5 I ate healthier food as a teenager.
6 I didn't like fruit when I was young.
7 I don't eat much fast food.
8 I didn't work hard in school.

**B** Which of the sentences in 7A are true for you? Change the other sentences so they are true for you. Discuss your answers in pairs.

**Go to Communication practice:** Student A page 157, Student B page 167

**8 A** Use the prompts to make questions with the correct form of *used to*.

1 which TV shows / watch / when you were eight?
_____
2 which candies and snacks / like / when you were young?
_____
3 which toys / play with / when you were a child?
_____
4 which sports / play / in school?
_____
5 where / go on vacation / when you were a child?
_____
6 have / pet / when you were young?
_____
7 which pop group / like / when you were twelve?
_____
8 what / do / after school when you were young?
_____

**B** In pairs, ask and answer the questions in exercise 8A. Say what you do now that is different.

A *Which TV shows did you use to watch when you were eight?*
B *We never used to watch TV during the week, but we watched all the cartoons on Saturday morning.*
A *Do you still watch TV on Saturday morning?*
B *No, I usually meet friends. I watch TV in the evening after work.*

---

**Personal Best** Write about differences between your life now and your parents' lives when they were your age with *usually* and *used to*.  17

## 2 SKILLS  WRITING   making a narrative interesting ■ time linkers

## 2D It happened to me

**1** Read the blog post quickly. Which word is missing from the title: *surprising*, *frustrating*, or *terrifying*?

Home   About   Blog   Contact

### A _____ evening

Yesterday it was my friend Sarah's 21st birthday. My friends and I had planned a surprise party for her at The Firehouse, a [1]small and cozy restaurant that she loves. Sarah's sister was going to bring her to the restaurant at 9 p.m., so we all needed to be there to surprise her when she arrived.

Just before I left my house, I got a text message, but the battery on my phone ran out before I could read it. I didn't have time to charge my phone, so I got in the car and left. [2]It was a horrible, rainy evening, but there wasn't much traffic, and everything was going fine until my car stopped suddenly. I'd run out of gas! [3]I was so angry with myself – [4]why hadn't I gotten some the night before?

I thought my best option would be to find a cab. After waiting for ten minutes, I finally found one. [5]I felt so relieved – I could still get to the restaurant in time. However, on the way, I realized that I'd left my wallet in my car and didn't have any money to pay! I explained this to the driver, [6]a rude and impatient man. He stopped the car and told me to get out.

[7]What a disaster! It was now almost 9 p.m., so I had to run. When I finally got to the restaurant, I was surprised to see that it was completely empty. I waited for an hour, but nobody came. So I walked back to the car, got my wallet, and took a bus home. As soon as I got home, I started charging my phone in the kitchen, but before I could call anyone, I got a message. It said, "Sarah sick, party canceled!" I didn't know whether to laugh or cry.

a ☐

b ☐

c ☐

f ☐

e ☐

d ☐

making a narrative interesting ∎ time linkers  **WRITING**  **SKILLS** **2D**

**2** **A** Read the blog post again. Put the pictures in the correct order from 1–6.

**B** Cover the blog. Look at the pictures and retell the story in pairs.

> 🔧 **Skill**  **making a narrative interesting**
>
> When writing a narrative, make the story more interesting by:
> - describing people, places, and the events
> - describing emotions and feelings
> - including one or two comments about the events.

**3** Read the Skill box. Match the underlined phrases (1–7) in the blog post with the three features of a narrative (a–c).

   **a** descriptions of people, places, and events: _____ _____ _____

   **b** descriptions of emotions and feelings:     _____ _____

   **c** comments about the events:     _____ _____

**4** **A** Choose the correct words to complete the sentences.

> comfortable   surprised   nightmare   luckily   tall   disappointed

   **1** I thought Sue was on vacation, so I was _____ to see her at work.

   **2** _____, I had another pair of glasses in my bag.

   **3** She was _____, blonde, and wearing a beautiful green dress.

   **4** When they told me I'd failed the exam, I felt really _____.

   **5** The hotel room was small, but it was very _____.

   **6** The train had already left, and I had lost my ticket. What a _____!

**B** Which of the features a–c in exercise 3 does each sentence in 4A use?

> 🧩 **Text builder**  **time linkers**
>
> We use time linkers like *before*, *after*, *until*, and *as soon as* to make the order of two past actions clear:
> *Just **before** I left my house, I got a text message.*   *Everything was going fine **until** my car stopped suddenly.*
> ***After** waiting for ten minutes, I finally got a cab.*   ***As soon as** I got home, I started charging my phone.*
>
> **Look!** After *before* and *after*, we can use a verb + *-ing* or a subject and verb. After *until* and *as soon as*, we can only use a subject and verb:
> *As soon as I arrived, I went to bed.* NOT ~~As soon as arriving, I went to bed.~~

**5** **A** Read the Text builder. In each of the four example sentences, which action happened first? Discuss in pairs.

**B** Complete the sentences with the correct time linker.

   **1** It was raining, so I waited in my car *until / as soon as* my sister's train arrived.

   **2** *Before / After* she got off the train, she checked that she had all of her things.

   **3** They sent their parents a text *until / as soon as* their plane landed in Buenos Aires.

   **4** *After / Until* he closed the door, he realized that he had left his keys inside the apartment.

   **5** *Before / As soon as* I got home, I started to cook dinner.

   **6** *As soon as / After* driving him home, she went to get some gas.

**6** **A** **PREPARE** Think about something amazing, surprising, frustrating, or terrifying that happened to you. Make notes about the main events and any descriptions or comments you want to include to make your story more interesting.

**B** **PRACTICE** Write a blog post, using your notes to help you. Include different narrative tenses and time linkers.

**C** **PERSONAL BEST** Exchange your blog post with your partner. Read his/her work and correct any mistakes. How could you improve it? What do you like best about his/her story?

**Personal Best** Read the blog post on page 18 again. Close your book and write a one-paragraph summary of it.

19

# 1 and 2 REVIEW and PRACTICE

## Grammar

**1** Choose the correct options to complete the sentences.

1 I usually _____ my e-mails in the morning.
   a am checking   b check   c was checking
2 What _____ last weekend?
   a did you   b do you do   c did you do
3 While I _____ for my cab, my girlfriend called.
   a waited   b had waited   c was waiting
4 When I lived in London, I _____ ride my bike to work.
   a usually   b used to   c use to
5 Sorry, I can't talk now. We _____ dinner.
   a 're having   b had   c have
6 Who _____ that bar of chocolate?
   a did you give   b gave you   c did give you
7 I couldn't go to the concert because they _____ all the tickets the day before.
   a were selling   b sold   c had sold
8 Where _____ to go on vacation when you were young?
   a did you used   b did you use   c you used

**2** Rewrite the sentences using the tenses or phrases in parentheses.

1 Sam plays tennis in the park with his brother. (present continuous)
   Sam _____ tennis in the park with his brother.
2 The ground is very wet because it rained all night. (simple past, past perfect)
   The ground _____ very wet because it _____ all night.
3 What do you do with your friends on the weekend? (simple past)
   What _____ with your friends on the weekend?
4 Jack was out of shape when he was in school. (used to)
   Jack _____ out of shape when he was in school.
5 He's using his tablet to check Facebook. (simple present)
   He _____ his tablet to check Facebook.
6 At nine o'clock last night, I took a bath. (past continuous)
   At nine o'clock last night, I _____ a bath.
7 Who does she live with? (simple past)
   Who _____ with?
8 Who takes the children to school every day? (used to)
   Who _____ the children to school?

**3** Choose the correct options to complete the text.

## Saved by a kitten

Yuriko Morota is a professional musician from Tokyo in Japan. She ¹*plays / is playing* the piano for a living. Last week, Yuriko ²*had shared / shared* an amazing story about her uncle on her Twitter account. Apparently, her uncle lived in Tokyo and ³*used to have / usually has* a beautiful cat called Nikko. Yuriko ⁴*doesn't like / isn't liking* cats, but she loved Nikko because he ⁵*was saving / had saved* her uncle's life. One day, her uncle ⁶*went / was going* to the airport to catch a plane when he ⁷*was seeing / saw* an abandoned kitten on the street – its owners ⁸*were leaving / had left* it outside. Yuriko's uncle ⁹*was loving / loved* cats, so he ¹⁰*took / had taken* the kitten home with him. Because of this, he ¹¹*missed / was missing* his flight. The following morning he ¹²*listened / was listening* to the radio when he ¹³*was hearing / heard* that his plane ¹⁴*crashed / had crashed* into the mountains 100 km. from Tokyo. He couldn't believe how lucky he was!

## Vocabulary

**1** Circle the word or phrase that is different. Explain your answer.

1 check your e-mails      get a text message
  speak face-to-face      give someone a call
2 a story                 congratulations
  a joke                  the truth
3 go out                  bring up
  break up                pay back
4 excited                 terrified
  depressed               embarrassed
5 a lie                   slowly
  a language              loudly
6 fascinating             amazing
  annoying                exciting

20

**REVIEW and PRACTICE** **1** and **2**

**2** Match the words in the box with definitions 1–8.

> keep in touch with   go up   amusing   try on
> bring up   go back   fascinating   run out of

1   something that makes you smile or laugh  _____
2   care for a child until he/she is an adult  _____
3   return  _____
4   communicate regularly with  _____
5   have no more of  _____
6   very interesting  _____
7   put on clothes before buying them to see if they fit  _____
8   increase  _____

**3** Choose the correct options to complete the sentences.

1   I _____ a lot of my photos on social media.
   a give        b share        c send
2   It was very _____ because I couldn't remember her name.
   a exciting    b disappointing   c embarrassing
3   We ended _____ having dinner at home last night.
   a again       b up           c back
4   My grandpa _____ us a really funny joke last night.
   a told        b said         c talked
5   I think it's polite to _____ to e-mails on the same day.
   a answer      b check        c reply
6   My mother was really _____ because the cab was twenty minutes late.
   a amazed      b amused       c annoyed
7   I didn't know you could _____ Japanese!
   a talk        b speak        c say
8   Hurry _____ ! I don't want to be late for work.
   a off         b on           c up

**4** Complete the e-mail with the words in the box.

> shocking   said   face   told   out   talk   spoke
> depressed   checked   gotten   broken   call

Hi Anna,
When I ¹_____ my phone this morning I saw that I'd ²_____ a text message from Chloe. So I decided to give her a ³_____ . When I ⁴_____ to her she seemed pretty ⁵_____ . She ⁶_____ me that her boyfriend had ⁷_____ up with her, and she wanted to ⁸_____ to someone about it. They've been going ⁹_____ together for three years, so it was very ¹⁰_____ when he ¹¹_____ he'd met someone else. Anyway, we're going to get together for coffee later, as it's always better to speak to someone ¹²_____-to-face.
Hope to see you soon!
Love,
Sophie

## Personal Best

**Lesson 1A**
Describe three things you did yesterday using communication phrases.

**Lesson 2A**
Name five -ed adjectives that describe your feelings today.

**Lesson 1A**
Describe three things that you are/aren't doing now.

**Lesson 2A**
Write a sentence using the simple past and past continuous.

**Lesson 1B**
Write one sentence with *actually* and one with *in fact*.

**Lesson 2A**
Write a sentence using the simple past and past perfect.

**Lesson 1C**
Name five phrases with *say* and *tell*.

**Lesson 2B**
Write two sentences about a friend using phrasal verbs.

**Lesson 1C**
Write two object questions and two subject questions.

**Lesson 2C**
Name something you used to do and something you didn't use to do when you were a teenager.

**Lesson 1D**
Write three questions you can use to make small talk.

**Lesson 2D**
Write four sentences about the past using these time linkers: *before, after, until,* and *as soon as.*

21

# UNIT 3

# People

| LANGUAGE | future forms ■ personality adjectives |

## 3A It's a plan

1 Look at the words in the box. Which adjectives describe your personality?

> kind   sociable   patient   generous   hardworking   organized   responsible

**Go to Vocabulary practice:** personality adjectives, page 139

2 In pairs, think of three adjectives to describe:
   a a good boss   b a good teacher   c a good friend

3 **A** Read the text. <u>Underline</u> the personality adjectives.

## Planning personalities

You can tell a lot about people by the way they organize their social life. Here are four types of planners we probably all know.

The **last-minute** planner is very easygoing, calls you ten minutes before an event, and is surprised when you can't come!

The **disorganized** planner never uses a calendar and often plans to do two things at the same time, sometimes forgetting both!

The **plan-ahead** planner is extremely organized and likes to make detailed plans a long time before the event, expecting everyone else to do the same.

The **unreliable** planner makes plans, but cancels just before you're going to meet and doesn't think this is a problem.

**B** Read the text again. Ask and answer the questions in pairs.
1 Do you have any friends who make plans like this?   2 What kind of planner are you?

4 **A** ▶ 3.3 Listen to four voicemail messages. Which type of planner is each person?
Ben _____   Zoe _____   Eva _____   Jack _____

**B** ▶ 3.3 Who said the sentences: Ben (B), Zoe (Z), Eva (E), or Jack (J)? Listen again and check.
1 I'm going to cook Japanese food for you.    _____
2 I'm going to stay at home and watch TV.    _____
3 How about coffee at 4 p.m. instead? I won't forget, I promise.    _____
4 I have my sister's car – I'll come and get you if you'd like.    _____
5 My friend's band is playing at 9:30.    _____
6 I'm having lunch with my brother tomorrow.    _____

future forms ■ personality adjectives    LANGUAGE  3A

**5** **A** Match the forms with the sentences in exercise 4B.
present continuous ____ ____    future with *be going to* ____ ____    future with *will* ____ ____

**B** Match the sentences in 4B with the correct functions (a–c). Then read the Grammar box.
a  a plan or intention ____ ____    c  a promise ____
b  an offer ____

📖 **Grammar**  future forms: present continuous, *be going to*, and *will*

Future plans and intentions:
We**'re meeting** at the restaurant at eight thirty.    He**'s going to learn** another language.

Promises, offers, and instant decisions:
I**'ll help** you with your homework tomorrow.    I**'ll carry** your bags for you.    I**'ll text** her.

**Go to Grammar practice:** future forms: present continuous, *be going to*, and *will*, page 116

**6** **A** ▶ 3.5  **Pronunciation:** *going to* Listen to the conversation. When is *going to* pronounced "gonna"?
A  Are you going to the beach this weekend?
B  No, I think I'm going to visit my parents. And you?
A  I'm going to take the bus to the beach on Friday night. I can't wait.
B  You're so lucky! I'm going to the beach the weekend after.

**B** In pairs, practice the conversation. Use the two different pronunciations of *going to*.

**7** **A** Match text messages 1–5 with responses a–e.

1  I'_____ (go) away this weekend, but I can't take my dog with me. ☹
2  Help! My tablet has a virus!
3  You ate all my chocolate! ☹
4  I can't believe how terrible the band was last night.
5  I hear you'_____ (get) married next year. Congratulations! ☺

a  I'_____ (come) over right away.
b  Thanks! The wedding _____ _____ (be) in the spring, but we don't have a date yet.
c  Sorry! I _____ _____ (not do) it again …
d  I'_____ (look) after him!
e  I know. I'm never _____ _____ _____ (go) to see them again!

**B** Complete the text messages with the future forms of the verbs in parentheses.

**Go to Communication practice:** Students A and B page 158

**8** In pairs, ask and answer the questions. Use future forms. Give as much information as possible and ask follow-up questions.

New Year's resolutions:
-go to the gym
-work harder
-eat less chocolate

What are your New Year's resolutions for next year?
What are you doing this weekend?
What are you going to do this summer?
What decisions have you made about your future studies or career?
Which future plans are you most excited about?
Which future plans are you not excited about?

**Personal Best**  Imagine you are helping to plan a party. Think of six offers you could make to help.    23

## 3 SKILLS  READING  reading for specific information ■ linkers of reason and result

# 3B Born to rebel

**1** Read the title, introduction, and headings of the text on page 25. In pairs, answer the questions.
1 What are the four different birth orders? Which are you?
2 According to the introduction, which child is typically a rebel? Do you agree?

**2** Read the text quickly. Which people agree that their personality is typical of their birth order? Discuss your answers in pairs.

> **Skill   reading for specific information**
>
> When we want to find specific information in a text, we need to know where to look.
> • Read the question carefully and underline key words.
> • Scan the text, looking for any synonyms or paraphrases of the underlined key words.
> • Read that part in detail.

**3** Read the Skill box. Scan the text and find the information you need to match sentences 1–8 with the people.

Which person ...
1 thinks the experience with her brothers helps with her job now?  _____
2 works hard and doesn't like making mistakes?  _____
3 is certain of his ability to do well and is good at making decisions?  _____
4 used to take care of younger family members, but worried about it?  _____
5 is good at making people agree with her, but can think about herself too much?  _____
6 didn't like people making decisions for her and became a rebel?  _____
7 thinks his parents' behavior made him calm, but bad at planning?  _____
8 is happy that her brothers and sisters received more attention than her?  _____

**4 A** Look at the two sentences. Underline the part of each sentence that gives a reason for something. Circle the part that gives a result of something.
1 Psychologists say that middle children become independent since they get less parental attention.
2 Psychologists say that middle children get less parental attention, so they become independent.

**B** Which two words in the sentences above express reason and result?

> **Text builder   linkers of reason and result**
>
> Reasons (*as* and *since*):
> I'm tired **as I slept badly**.          I took a cab **since it was late**.
> Results (*That's why* and *so*):
> I slept badly. **That's why I'm tired**.    It was late, **so I took a cab**.

**5** Read the Text builder. Rewrite the sentences from the text with the words in parentheses.
1 I wanted to be my own person, so when I was a child I was pretty rebellious. (as)
2 Parents usually pay more attention to their first child. That's why oldest children like me are normally confident. (since)
3 Oldest children are often more responsible and reliable since they look after their younger siblings. (That's why)
4 We tend to be hardworking and mature since we have our parents' full attention and support. (so)

**6** Is your personality typical of your birth order, according to the text? How about your family and friends? Discuss in pairs.

# The birth order effect

Many psychologists agree that your birth order influences your personality more than other factors such as your gender or culture. One belief is that oldest children identify with parents and authority, whereas youngest children often rebel against them. There are many other personality types thought to be typical of youngest, middle, oldest, and only children. But are they true? We interviewed eight people to find out.

## Oldest children

Apparently, parents usually pay more attention to their first child. That's why oldest children like me are normally confident and decisive. I suppose that was true of my parents, and it made me a pretty confident person. I'm definitely not indecisive. Am I a rebel? No, not at all, I work for the police department! *Jack*

I had to help my mother with my two younger sisters. Psychologists believe that oldest children are often more responsible and reliable since they look after their younger siblings, but this can also make us pretty anxious. I'd say that's true for me, and because I've always respected my parents' authority, I accepted the responsibility and the anxiety. *Mick*

## Youngest children

According to research, parents have a relaxed attitude when bringing up their last-born child, and that's why we're easygoing and free-spirited. That describes me perfectly. I don't like discipline, and I'm very relaxed and creative. Being the youngest, I had a lot of help and support, but maybe that stopped me from being independent and made me more disorganized. *Tom*

I grew up with older brothers and sisters who were bigger and smarter than me. They were extremely bossy – always telling me what to do, which I hated. I wanted to be my own person, so when I was a child I was pretty rebellious, which psychologists think is normal for youngest children. *Tina*

## Middle children

My older sister was serious and used to prefer spending time with our parents, and my younger brother always used to get their love and attention. Because of this, I used to spend most of my time alone or with friends. Psychologists say that middle children become independent since they get less parental attention. That's definitely true in my case, and in my opinion, it was good for me. *Sara*

Research has suggested that middle children are often very competitive, but I'm the opposite – I was always trying to keep the peace between my older and younger brothers! I definitely think that's why I have good communication skills now, which helps with my career in Human Resources. *Alice*

## Only children

I don't have any brothers or sisters. According to experts, there are clear advantages and disadvantages to this. On the one hand, we tend to be hardworking and mature as we have our parents' full attention and support, but we also have their expectations on our shoulders, which can be difficult. For this reason, I think I'm a bit of a perfectionist and sensitive to criticism. *Adam*

As we usually got what we wanted when we were growing up, apparently it's difficult for only children to compromise. That's why we can be a bit selfish and impatient. I think that's also why I'm good at persuading people. I remember trying to persuade my parents to give me a sister for my birthday! It didn't work. *Anita*

Underline all the personality adjectives in the text. Do you know what they mean?

# 3 LANGUAGE — defining and non-defining relative clauses ■ relationships

## 3C Good neighbors, bad neighbors

**1** Work in pairs. Explain the difference between:
1. a **close friend** and a **best friend**.
2. a **neighbor** and a **next-door neighbor**.
3. a **colleague** and a **classmate**.
4. a **couple** and a **partner**.
5. a **parent** and a **relative**.

Go to Vocabulary practice: relationships, page 139

**2** Think of a friend, colleague, or neighbor you know well. Ask and answer the questions in pairs.
1. How do you know this person?
2. How long did it take you to get to know each other?
3. Have you ever argued or had a falling out? Why?
4. When did you last get together?
5. What do you have in common?

**3** Read the notice. Do you think events like this are a good idea? Why/Why not?

**4 A** 3.8 Listen to three people answer the question "What makes a good neighbor?" Match the opinions with the speakers: John (J), Mary (M), or Lisa (L).
1. Good neighbors help each other. _____
2. They're not noisy. _____
3. They're kind and try not to annoy other neighbors. _____

**B** 3.8 Listen again and complete the sentences with the words you hear.

> **John** I had a bad experience in the _____ building ¹**where I used to live**. The biggest problem was the people ²**that lived on the first floor**. They played _____ heavy metal music all the time, and their _____ was always loud, too.
>
> **Mary** My neighbor Tony, ³**who works as a travel agent**, is away at the moment. I'm _____ after his apartment. Once, though, another _____ did something ⁴**that made me furious**. I'd given her my keys while I was away, but she _____ with her boyfriend, and when I came home, he was asleep on my sofa!
>
> **Lisa** Most people here are very _____ and considerate. And we have some _____ rules, ⁵**which most people follow**. I get annoyed with some neighbors, though, like the family ⁶**whose children leave bicycles in front of my door** and throw trash on my _____ .

**5** Do you agree with the speakers? What do you think makes a good or bad neighbor?

**6** Look at clauses 1–6 in **bold** in exercise 4B. Which relative pronouns do we use to talk about:
1. things? _____ or _____
2. people? _____ or _____
3. places? _____
4. possessions? _____

defining and non-defining relative clauses ■ relationships          LANGUAGE  3C

**7 A** Look at the two sentences from exercise 4B and answer the questions.
  a  The biggest problem was the people **that lived on the first floor**.
  b  My neighbor Tony, **who works as a travel agent**, is away at the moment.

  1  Which relative clause is essential and identifies who or what we are talking about? _____
  2  Which relative clause gives extra information, although, without it, the sentence still makes sense? _____

**B** Look at clauses 1–6 in exercise 4B again. Which clauses are essential? Which give extra information? Then read the Grammar box.

> **Grammar**  defining and non-defining relative clauses
>
> Defining relative clauses (identifying who or what we are talking about):
> The woman **who lives above me** is a doctor.
> That's the village **where I grew up**.
> Do you know the man **whose car was stolen**?
>
> Non-defining relative clauses (giving extra information):
> I saw the movie, **which was great**.
> That town, **where my mother grew up**, is beautiful.
> My uncle, **whose house is over there**, works as a fire fighter.
>
> **Look!**  When a relative clause gives extra information, we separate it with commas (or a comma and a period).

Go to Grammar practice: defining and non-defining relative clauses, page 117

**8 A** ▶ 3.10  **Pronunciation:** pausing in relative clauses  We usually pause before a clause that gives extra information. Listen to the sentences. Add commas where the pauses are.
  1  The family who lives on my floor is really friendly.
  2  My grandmother lives in Quito which is in the north of Ecuador.
  3  My brother who is a chef works at the hospital.
  4  I get along well with the couple who lives in the apartment next to mine.
  5  I don't see my cousins who live in Argentina.
  6  It's easy to park on the street where I live.

**B** In pairs, change the sentences in 8A so they are true for you. Add extra details if necessary.

*The couple who lives on my floor is really noisy.*

Go to Communication practice: Student A page 158, Student B page 168

**9 A** Choose two places, two objects, and two people that are very important to you.

Places
1 _____
2 _____

Objects
1 _____
2 _____

People
1 _____
2 _____

**B** In pairs, talk about your choices. Ask your partner why each of his/her choices is important, and ask for more information. Use relative clauses in your answers.

  A  *Tell me about one of your places.*
  B  *It's Montevideo.*
  A  *Why is it so important to you?*
  B  *Because it's the place where I met my boyfriend.*
  A  *How did you meet him?*
  B  *We were both in college there.*

**Personal Best**  Write five sentences about your relatives and close friends with non-defining relative clauses.

27

# 3 SKILLS   SPEAKING  giving and responding to news ■ giving bad news

## 3D I have some news

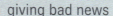

**1 A** Look at the sentences. Which are good news? Which are bad news? Which news do you think the man in the photo has?

1 I'm afraid you didn't get the job.
2 We won the game! We're in the final!
3 I've had a falling out with my best friend.
4 Your rent's going up by 20%.
5 She said "Yes"!
6 I got a promotion.

**B** In pairs, discuss the questions.

1 What good news can you remember receiving in your life? What did you say?
2 Have you ever had to give someone bad news? How did you feel?

**2** ▶ 3.11  Watch or listen to the first part of *Learning Curve*. Answer the questions.

1 What news does Penny give Simon?
2 How do they both feel about the news?

**3** ▶ 3.12  How did Penny give Simon the news? How did Simon respond? Listen and complete the sentences.

1 I'm _____ I have some bad news.

2 _____? What _____?

3 You aren't going to _____ this, _____ our boss is asking me to fire our student workers.

4 _____! That's _____!

### Conversation builder — giving and responding to news

**Giving news**
I'm afraid I have some bad news.
I'm really sorry to say this, but …
You aren't going to believe this, but …
Great news! I'm …
Guess what? I'm …

**Responding to news**
That's a relief.
Oh no, that's terrible!
What a shame! That's too bad!
I'm so happy for you! That's fantastic news!
I'm absolutely thrilled for you! Congratulations!

**4** Read the Conversation builder. Put the phrases in the correct column in the chart.

| giving good news | giving bad news | responding to good news | responding to bad news |
|---|---|---|---|
|  |  |  |  |

giving and responding to news ■ giving bad news  **SPEAKING**  **SKILLS**  **3D**

**5 A** In pairs, complete the conversation with the words in the box.

> awful  thrilled  afraid  shame  that's  wonderful  congratulations

**A** Great news! I've been offered a job writing for a new magazine!
**B** Wow! ¹_____ fantastic news! I'm absolutely ²_____ for you! When do you start?
**A** Next month. I can't wait. It's a really exciting place to work.
**B** That's ³_____ ! ⁴_____ !
**A** How are things with you?
**B** Well, I'm ⁵_____ I have some bad news. I broke my leg last week.
**A** Oh no, that's ⁶_____ ! What a ⁷_____ ! I'm so sorry.

**B** In pairs, practice the conversation. You can change the details.

**6** ▶ 3.13 Watch or listen to the second part of the show.
Answer the questions.

1 What news does Sherry give Penny?
2 How does Penny feel about it?
3 How does Simon feel about it?

Sherry

**7** ▶ 3.13 How did Sherry give Penny her news? Order phrases a–h. Watch or listen again and check.

a ☐ It's in my neighborhood, much closer to my apartment.
b ☐ but it's sort of bad news for you.
c ☐ It's a great opportunity to work with customers.
d ☐ Well, you know that I study fashion at college, right?
e ☐ So, I'm really sorry to say this, but I'm resigning.
f ☐ Well, it's good news for me,
g ☑ I have some news.
h ☐ Well, I got a great job offer to work at a department store that I just love.

---

🔧 **Skill**  **giving bad news**

**When we give someone bad news, we often try to do it in a sensitive way.**
• Prepare the person first – tell him/her you have some bad news.
• Briefly explain the situation behind the bad news.
• Say exactly what the bad news is.
• Be sympathetic – say that you're really sorry.

---

**8** Read the Skill box. What did Sherry do to give Penny the news in a sensitive way?

**Go to Communication practice:** Student A page 158, Student B page 168

**9 A** PREPARE In pairs, look at the situations below. Think about what you will say.

| | situation 1 | situation 2 |
| --- | --- | --- |
| Student A | You've been offered an amazing job in another city, but you're worried your parents will be upset that you're leaving. Tell your mother/father the news. | You're Student B's roommate and close friend. Listen and respond to the news. Ask questions and continue the conversation. |
| Student B | You're Student A's mother/father. Listen and respond to the news. Ask questions and continue the conversation. | Your cousin has just moved into a fantastic apartment and wants you to rent the spare room. You're worried your current roommate will be upset that you're leaving. Tell him/her the news. |

**B** PRACTICE In pairs, take turns giving your news and responding to it.

**C** PERSONAL BEST How could you improve the way you gave the news and responded to your partner's news? Find another partner and give your news again.

**Personal Best**  Imagine what Ethan's news is. Write his conversation with Penny.

29

# UNIT 4 Places and homes

**LANGUAGE** quantifiers ■ compound nouns

## 4A What makes your city great?

**1** What three things make your town or city great? Discuss your answers in pairs.

**2** Look at the text about four cities below. According to each writer, what makes his/her city great?

# I ♥ MY CITY

With Melbourne topping the list of the best cities in the world to live, we celebrate cities everywhere, and invite you to share what you love about your city. #whatmakesyourcitygreat

**David**

What I love most about this city are the parks and green spaces. When you have a little free time, there's always an open space, urban park, or secret garden nearby where you can go to relax. One really interesting project, the High Line, is a 2.3 km. long park built on an elevated section of a former railway line. It's a wonderful pedestrian area and has fabulous views of the Hudson River, Manhattan, and the New York City skyline.

**Kiyomi**

The nightlife here is amazing. There are plenty of places to go and things to do in the evening, with thousands of cafés, restaurants, and nightclubs. But what I like best about Tokyo are the unusual places to eat out. Last week, I had dinner at the seafood restaurant Zauo, where the tables are on a boat and you catch your own fish from the aquarium, which the chefs then cook for you. It was lots of fun!

**Klaus**

In most big cities, there aren't enough roads that are safe for bicycling. But here in Copenhagen, there are over 400 km. of bike paths, so you can ride everywhere with no danger, avoiding traffic jams and staying in shape at the same time. There aren't many people who regularly use a car here – in fact, most people go to work or school by bike or on foot. Some use the Cycle Snake, an elevated bike path over the harbor. It was built especially for bicyclists, and the views from it are spectacular!

**Lola**

New Orleans sure has rhythm! You hear live music on almost every street: there's always a jazz band playing, or a few musicians jamming together in a café or on a street corner. My favorite time of year is Mardi Gras – the famous carnival celebration with music and colorful parades. Some people complain that there are too many tourists here at Mardi Gras, but I think everyone should be able to see the greatest free show on Earth!

**3** Match the words in each box to make compound nouns. Check your answers in the text.

| bike   traffic   pedestrian   night | area   life   jam   path |

**Go to Vocabulary practice:** compound nouns, page 140

**4** Read the text again. Are the sentences true (T) or false (F)? Correct the false sentences.
1. There aren't many green spaces in New York. ___
2. There are trains on the High Line. ___
3. It's not dangerous to ride a bike in Copenhagen. ___
4. Cars aren't allowed on the Cycle Snake. ___
5. In Tokyo, the restaurants are all pretty similar. ___
6. At Zauo, customers catch the fish and cook it. ___
7. There's live music everywhere in New Orleans. ___
8. A lot of tourists visit New Orleans for Mardi Gras. ___

**5** Which city sounds like the best one to live in? Why? Discuss your answers in pairs.

quantifiers ■ compound nouns    LANGUAGE  4A

**6** Look at the highlighted words in the text. Put them in the correct category. Then read the Grammar box.
1 small quantities: not much, _____ , _____ , _____
2 large quantities: a lot of, _____ , _____
3 zero quantity: not any, _____
4 more or less than necessary: too much, _____ , _____

> **Grammar  quantifiers**
>
> Small quantities:
> There's **not**/There **isn't much** time, hurry up!
> There are**n't many** people on this beach.
> Can I have **a little** cake and **a few** cookies, please?
>
> Zero quantity:
> There's **no** bread/There is**n't any** bread.
>
> Large quantities:
> We have **a lot of/lots of** work today.
> There are **plenty of** bananas if you're hungry.
>
> More or less than necessary:
> There's **too much** traffic. There are **too many** cars.
> There's **not**/There is**n't enough** ice cream for everyone.

Go to Grammar practice: quantifiers, page 118

**7 A** ▶ 4.3 **Pronunciation: sentence stress** Listen to the sentences. Which syllables are stressed?
1 I've been to a lot of museums.
2 I don't go to many concerts.
3 I know a few nice restaurants.
4 There are plenty of stores in my area.
5 My friends don't have enough free time.
6 There's no live music in my town.
7 It's too noisy where I live.
8 There's too much stress in my life.

**B** ▶ 4.3 Listen again and repeat the sentences.

**8** Change the sentences in exercise 7A so they are true for you. Compare your sentences in pairs.

**9** ▶ 4.4 Choose the correct quantifiers to complete the text. Listen and check.

> not enough   a few   a little   plenty of   too   too many

## Melbourne number 1, again!

Melbourne has come first again in the list of the best places to live. Only ¹_____ cities like Zurich and Vancouver have come first more than once, but Melbourne has won it for the fifth consecutive year! It's such an interesting and vibrant city, with ²_____ things to do. The climate is great – it's never ³_____ hot or cold, which makes it perfect for strolling around the harbor or the pedestrian areas downtown and admiring the colorful street art. If you like ⁴_____ culture, spend a day exploring the city's museums, art galleries, and the Arts Centre, which looks like the Eiffel Tower! Getting around is easy, too, but with more than a million people driving into the city every day, there are ⁵_____ traffic jams and ⁶_____ parking spaces. Taking the streetcar is easy and convenient, though.

Go to Communication practice: Student A page 159, Student B page 168

**10** Discuss what you think of the following things in your city in pairs.

> downtown   public transportation   pedestrian areas   nightlife   art galleries   parking lots
> bike paths   department stores   shopping malls   nightclubs   traffic jams   sports centers

A *In my opinion, there aren't enough pedestrian areas here.*
B *You're right. There's too much traffic, so we need more pedestrian areas.*

**Personal Best**  Write five sentences about what an ideal city would be like. Use a quantifier in each sentence.

31

# 4 SKILLS
LISTENING understanding key points ■ linking consonant sounds ■ common verb phrases

## 4B City or country?

**1** In pairs, make a list of advantages and disadvantages of living in the city and living in the country.

**2** Complete the sentences with the verbs in the box. Which sentences are about living in the city? Which sentences are about living in the country?

> have (x2)  catch  meet (x2)  miss (x2)  take

1 It's easy to _____ a friend and _____ coffee or a snack.
2 It's difficult to _____ new people.
3 I _____ the peace and quiet and being surrounded by nature.
4 Public transportation isn't great. If you _____ a bus, you have to wait ages to _____ the next one, or ask someone to _____ you by car.
5 The nightlife's great. It's easy to go out and _____ a good time.

**3** Which sentences in exercise 2 are true for where you live?

Go to Vocabulary practice: common verb phrases, page 141

### Skill  understanding key points

**When people speak, listen for the key points of the ideas they talk about.**
- People often emphasize the key points and can use expressions such as *most importantly, the main thing is*.
- They often repeat the key points using different words.
- They often give examples, reasons, and more information to support the key points.

**4 A** ▶ 4.6  Read the Skill box. Watch or listen to the first part of *Learning Curve*. Kate talks about studies on city and country life. Check (✓) the three key points.

1 People who live in the country live longer. ☐
2 People who live in the city are more stressed out. ☐
3 Country life is better when you work in the city. ☐
4 Young adults prefer to live in the city. ☐
5 Retired people prefer to live in the country. ☐

**B** ▶ 4.6  Compare your answers in pairs. Watch or listen again and check.

understanding key points ■ linking consonant sounds ■ common verb phrases  **LISTENING**   **SKILLS**   **4B**

**5** ▶ 4.7  Watch or listen to the second part of the show. Where do Tracy, Carlos, and Sing live and work? Check (✓) the correct options in the chart.

Tracy

Carlos

Sing

|  | lives in the ... |  | works in the ... |  |
| --- | --- | --- | --- | --- |
|  | city | country | city | country |
| Tracy |  |  |  |  |
| Carlos |  |  |  |  |
| Sing |  |  |  |  |

**6 A** ▶ 4.7  Watch or listen again. Are the sentences true or false? Correct the incorrect sentences.

1  Tracy loves where she lives because it's quiet.  _____
2  She likes knowing all her neighbors.  _____
3  She doesn't like commuting to work.  _____
4  Carlos thinks city life is very convenient.  _____
5  He misses the country.  _____
6  He enjoys having a lot of options for going out.  _____
7  Sing's a chef.  _____
8  He grows vegetables on the roof of a large building.  _____

**B** Who do you think has the best quality of life, Tracy, Carlos, or Sing?

---

**Listening builder** | **linking similar consonant sounds**

When a word ends in a consonant sound and the next word starts with the same consonant sound, we only pronounce the sound once, not twice. The linked sounds are not always the same letter.

It's similar.    Ethan knows.    We go to a sports center.

---

**7** ▶ 4.8  Read the Listening builder. Look at the sentences and mark where the consonant links are. Listen and check. Then practice saying the sentences.

1  It's an old house, so it took three years to modernize it.
2  It's easy to keep in touch with them.
3  We get together every weekend.
4  I just took a photo of it.
5  See you next time.

**8 A** Discuss these questions with a partner.

1  Would you prefer to live and work in the city or the country? Why?
2  How far would you be happy to travel to work or school every day? Why?
3  Where would you prefer to spend a weekend away, in a city or in the country? Why?

**B** Change partners. Discuss the key points of your conversation in 8A with your new partner.

**Personal Best**   Imagine you've moved to the country. Write a paragraph about what you like about country life and what you miss about the city.

# 4 LANGUAGE
comparatives and superlatives, as … as ■ describing homes

## 4C A place to stay in NYC

**1 A** What kinds of accommodations is the website advertising? What are the advantages and disadvantages of using a website like this?

**B** Look at three places to stay in New York. Which one do you prefer? Why?

### ▶ reservedirect.com – find your perfect vacation home
Reserve directly with homeowners and hosts around the world. Stay in someone's home and really experience local life.

**Studio apartment near Central Park**
==Modern==, ==stylish== studio apartment, 30 sq. m, with double bed, bathroom, and kitchen. TV, WiFi, and air conditioning.
**Good location:** a short distance from the Museum of Modern Art and Times Square. $175 per night

**Houseboat for rent**
==Cozy== houseboat with sofa bed. Kitchen with fridge and microwave. Shower room. Amazing views of the Empire State Building and Manhattan skyscrapers.
**Location:** New Jersey; short walk to Manhattan ferry. $95 per night

**Artist's house in Harlem**
Two comfortable, ==bright== and ==spacious== double rooms in our beautiful Victorian house. Full breakfast provided. Eat with other guests and your friendly hosts. Fashionable neighborhood. Close to subway station. $140 per night

**2** Match the definitions with the highlighted words in the text.
1 very light _____   3 not old _____   5 big _____
2 fashionable _____   4 warm and comfortable _____

**Go to Vocabulary practice:** describing homes, page 142

**3** How would you describe your home on *reservedirect.com*? Tell your partner what kind of home it is, where it is, and what it's like.

**4 A** ▶ 4.12 Listen to Jon and Louise deciding where to stay in New York. Choose the correct advantage and disadvantage they mention for each place.

| accommodation | advantages | disadvantages |
|---|---|---|
| studio apartment | ¹modern / convenient | ²too expensive / too small |
| houseboat | ³cheap / cozy | ⁴uncomfortable bed / basic |
| artist's house | ⁵fashionable area / convenient | ⁶expensive / shared bathroom |

**B** Which place do they choose?

**5 A** ▶ 4.13 In pairs, complete the sentences from the conversation with the adjectives in the box. Listen and check.

expensive   big   fashionable   convenient   comfortable   cheaper

1 It's *by far* the most _____ .
2 Well, it's as _____ as our old apartment.
3 It's *far* _____ than the other two places.
4 We don't need to stay in one of the most _____ areas in New York.
5 A sofa bed isn't as _____ as a normal bed, is it?
6 It's *slightly* less _____ than the studio apartment.

**B** Look at the sentences in 5A and answer the questions. Then read the Grammar box.
1 Which sentences are comparatives? Which are superlatives?
2 Which comparative form means that two things are the same?
3 Which word and phrase in *italics* mean "a lot"? Which word means "a little"?

comparatives and superlatives, *as … as* ■ describing homes  **LANGUAGE 4C**

### Grammar: comparatives and superlatives, *as … as*

**Comparatives (two things):**
That apartment is **slightly bigger than** ours.
Our new sofa is **far more comfortable**.
Jack's apartment is **less spacious than** our house.
Your kitchen is **as big as** Robert's.

**Look!** We can use **slightly** for a small difference and **far** for a big difference.

**Superlatives (three or more things):**
This is **the nicest** present I've **ever** received.
It's one of **the most expensive** cities **in the world**.
This is **by far the least fashionable** part of town.

**Look!** We can use **by far** to emphasize a superlative.

Go to Grammar practice: comparatives and superlatives, *as … as*, page 119

**6 A** ▶ 4.15 **Pronunciation:** /ə/ sound Listen to the sentences. Notice the /ə/ sound in the underlined parts of the words.

1 It's cheap<u>er</u> th<u>a</u>n my old house.
2 Apartments aren't <u>a</u>s expensive <u>a</u>s houses.
3 It's th<u>e</u> biggest apartment I've ev<u>er</u> seen!
4 Is there a nic<u>er</u> hotel th<u>a</u>n this one?

**B** ▶ 4.15 Listen again and repeat the sentences.

**7** Complete the sentences with the correct form of the adjectives in parentheses, and any other words needed.

1 Sit on the sofa! It's much _____ the floor. (comfortable)
2 The team that wins the World Cup is _____ team _____ the world. (good)
3 I'm going to be late! This is by far _____ bus I've _____ taken! (slow)
4 It's 75 sq. m. – It's slightly _____ my apartment, which is 70 sq. m. (spacious)
5 Villages aren't _____ towns. (big)
6 The song "Happy" is one of Pharrell Williams' _____ songs. (famous)

**8** Complete the sentences with comparatives. Use the adjectives in the box or your own ideas. Compare your sentences in pairs.

| enjoyable  exciting  boring  cheap  expensive |
| relaxing  stressful  difficult  easy  comfortable |
| convenient  tasty  spicy |

*Italian food isn't as tasty as Mexican food.*
1 Italian food _____ Mexican food.
2 English _____ Chinese.
3 Soccer _____ tennis.
4 Being a teacher _____ being a student.
5 Being married _____ being single.
6 Living in a small town _____ living in a city.

Go to Communication practice: Student A page 159, Student B page 169

**9** In pairs, ask and answer questions with the words in the chart.

| Who<br>What<br>Which | is/are<br>was/were | the best<br>the most beautiful<br>the funniest<br>the most exciting<br>the tastiest<br>the most stressful<br>the most expensive<br>the scariest<br>the most interesting | meal<br>city<br>movie<br>shoes<br>person<br>country<br>vacation<br>day<br>book<br>team | in the world?<br><br>you've ever | been on?<br>met?<br>visited?<br>eaten?<br>had?<br>read?<br>bought?<br>seen?<br>known? |

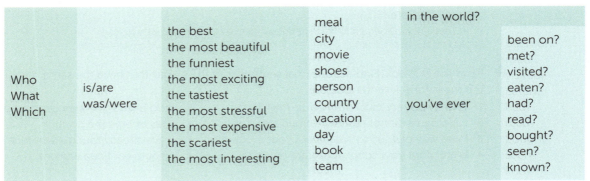

Choose two famous people and write four sentences to compare them.

35

# 4 SKILLS  WRITING  writing an informal e-mail ■ informal discourse markers

## 4D Hope to hear from you soon!

**1** Look at the picture. What is happening? Read the e-mail and check.

---

**Subject: News**

Hey Pete,

1   Great to hear from you! Sorry for not writing sooner, but I've been really busy.

2   That's fantastic news about your master's. You're so lucky! Raleigh is such a beautiful city, and the university's great. I'm sure you'll do really well – you've always been hardworking. Don't forget to have some fun though! So, when do classes start? Have you found a place to live yet?

3   Anyway, I have some great news, too. Did I tell you I applied for a job in San Francisco a few months ago? Well, I got the job! I'm an assistant website designer. It's much more interesting than my old marketing job, and San Francisco's an amazing place. I only got here last week, but I've already found a really cool apartment to rent (see photo). It's not as big as my old place, but it's very bright and modern. I can get downtown, where I work, in under ten minutes. Convenient!

4   Why don't you come to San Francisco for vacation this summer? I'd love to see you, and we could explore the city and enjoy the nightlife!

5   By the way, do you remember Ruth Taylor from high school? Well, she works here, too! I couldn't believe it when I saw her on my first day in the office. She's just as funny as she was when we were in high school. It's so nice to have someone at work I already know.

6   Speaking of work, I'd better get back to it because I have a report to finish by tomorrow. It's only my first week, and I'm already pretty busy here.

Hope to hear from you soon!

Lots of love,

Yasmin

---

**2** Read the e-mail again and answer the questions.
  1 What is Pete going to do in Raleigh?
  2 Why has Yasmin moved to San Francisco?

**3** Match paragraphs 1–6 with e-mail functions a–f.
  a inviting ____        c a reason to end the e-mail ____   e responding to news ____
  b giving news ____    d opening comments ____             f giving more news ____

> **Skill** writing an informal e-mail
>
> We write informal e-mails to people we know well, such as friends, family members, and colleagues.
> • Use contractions like *it's* and *can't*.
> • Use incomplete sentences like *Great to hear from you, Sorry for not writing sooner, Can't wait to see you!*
> • Use informal greetings and endings like *Hey/Hi, How are things? Lots of love, See you soon, All the best,* and *Take care*.
> • Start a new paragraph for each new topic to make your e-mail easy to read.

**4** Read the Skill box. Find the informal sentences in the e-mail that have the same meaning as the more formal sentences 1–8.
  1 Thank you very much for your e-mail.
  2 I apologize for not replying immediately.
  3 I was very pleased to hear about your program.
  4 When does your school program begin?
  5 I also have some very good news.
  6 I was offered the position.
  7 I have already found a very nice apartment.
  8 I should continue working.

36

writing an informal e-mail ■ informal discourse markers  **WRITING**  **SKILLS**  **4D**

**5** Read Pete's reply to Yasmin's e-mail. Order sentences a–g.

Subject: **News**

Hi Yas,

**a** ☐ Anyway, I have to go, I have a meeting with my advisor in 20 minutes. Speak soon! Don't forget to let me know about July.

**b** ☐ **Anyway**, I have some great news. Do you remember my British cousin, Mo?

**c** ☑ *1* Great to hear from you! Really happy you're enjoying your new job in San Francisco.

**d** ☐ **So**, have you made any new friends there yet?

**e** ☐ **Speaking of** invitations, I'd love to visit you in San Francisco. How about the first two weeks of July? Can't wait to see you!

**f** ☐ **By the way**, why don't we get together with Ruth Taylor for coffee when I come? I haven't seen her in ages.

**g** ☐ Well, he's getting married in Brighton in March, and he's invited me to the wedding. I'm really looking forward to it. I already have a new suit (see photo). What do you think?

Take care,

Pete

**6** Pete wrote his e-mail in four paragraphs. Which lines of the e-mail (a–g) do you think he included in each paragraph?

Paragraph 1 _____     Paragraph 3 _____
Paragraph 2 _____     Paragraph 4 _____

**7** Look at the words in **bold** in exercise 5. Which two have a similar meaning?

> **Text builder** | **informal discourse markers**
>
> We use informal discourse markers to link ideas and help the reader understand the organization of our ideas. We can also use these in informal spoken English.
>
> **To change the subject:**
> *Anyway, I have some great news, too.*    **So**, *when do classes start?*
>
> **To introduce a less important subject:**
> *By the way, do you remember Ruth Taylor from high school?*
>
> **To return to a subject:**
> *It's so nice to have someone at work I already know.* **Speaking of** *work, I'd better get back to it ...*

**8** Read the Text builder. Complete the sentences with discourse markers. Compare your answers in pairs.

1 There's a new department store near my apartment. _____ shopping, have you heard about that new online store?

2 Important news! Jamie just moved to Boston because he got a new job with the Boston Globe! _____ , he's started playing soccer.

3 I'm not really enjoying my job at the moment ... _____ , how did your exam go?

4 I'm hoping to get a job soon, so I can share an apartment with some friends. _____ housing, have you moved yet?

**9** **A** **PREPARE** Think of a friend or family member who recently gave you some news. Plan how to respond to the news, decide what news you'd like to give, and invite him/her to do something.

**B** **PRACTICE** Write your e-mail. Use the ideas in the Skill box and the Text builder to help you.

**C** **PERSONAL BEST** Exchange your e-mail with a partner. Read his/her e-mail. Do the paragraphs and discourse markers help you understand the organization of ideas?

**Personal Best**  Write a reply to your partner's e-mail. Respond to his/her news and give more news of your own.   37

# 3 and 4 REVIEW and PRACTICE

## Grammar

**1** Cross (**X**) the sentence that is NOT correct.

1. a  I'm taking my driving test at 3:30 this afternoon.
   b  I'm going to take my driving test next year.
   c  I'll take my driving test at 3:30 this afternoon.
2. a  He's the man whose brother is a pop singer.
   b  He's the man which went out with Jenny.
   c  He's the man Jenny used to go out with.
3. a  There aren't no tickets left for the concert.
   b  There aren't any tickets left for the concert.
   c  There are no tickets left for the concert.
4. a  I think it's the funniest movie I've ever seen.
   b  I think it's the most funny movie I've ever seen.
   c  I think it's funnier than the last movie we saw.
5. a  It's after midnight. Should I call you a cab?
   b  It's after midnight. Do I call you a cab?
   c  It's after midnight. I'll call you a cab.
6. a  Uncle Jack, who works as an accountant, lives in Sydney.
   b  Jack is my uncle who works as an accountant in Sydney.
   c  Uncle Jack, that works as an accountant, lives in Sydney.
7. a  His new apartment isn't big enough for four people.
   b  His new apartment isn't enough big for four people.
   c  His new apartment is too small for four people.
8. a  It's one of the expensivest restaurants in my city.
   b  It's one of the most expensive restaurants in my city.
   c  It's much more expensive than the other restaurants in my city.

**2** Use the words in parentheses to complete the sentences so they mean the same as the first sentence.

1. I plan to spend three weeks in Mexico next year.
   I _____ three weeks in Mexico next year. (going to)
2. She's the woman. She lives on the second floor.
   She's the woman _____ on the second floor. (who)
3. There were only a few people at the party.
   There _____ at the party. (many)
4. Sam is more helpful than Tom.
   Tom _____ Sam. (as ... as)
5. Would you like a cup of coffee?
   _____ make you a cup of coffee? (I)
6. That's my sister's new car. She bought it from my cousin.
   That's my sister's new car, _____ from my cousin. (which)
7. Nicholas is too young to drive a car.
   Nicholas _____ to drive a car. (old)
8. My brother is more generous than my sister.
   My sister is _____ my brother. (less)

**3** Choose the correct options to complete the text.

The place ¹*that / where* Maria Simonetti lives is very unusual. It is a little village in the south of Italy ²*which / who* has over 300 centenarians – people ³*which / who* are 100 years old or more. So although Maria ⁴*is celebrating / should celebrate* her 100th birthday next month, she's not ⁵*by far / one of* the oldest people in her village, as over 50 of the inhabitants of the village are over 110. Maria's seven grandchildren, ⁶*who / that* are all in their sixties, are organizing a big party to celebrate, and ⁷*they're going to / they will* invite her relatives and friends from all over Italy. Her ⁸*most young / youngest* grandson, Filippo, is a chef, and ⁹*he'll / he's going to* bake her a special cake with ten candles on it, one for each decade of her life. So, what's her secret? Well, everyone says Maria's a very sociable and positive person. She still has a ¹⁰*few / little* friends and relatives in the village, and someone visits her every day. Also, Maria has a very healthy diet. She eats ¹¹*much / lots of* fish, vegetables, and fruit, and she doesn't eat ¹²*much / many* sugar or salt.

## Vocabulary

**1** Circle the word or phrase that is different. Explain your answer.

1. modern            tiny
   comfortable       impatient
2. friendly          next-door neighbor
   close friend      classmate
3. bike path         art gallery
   shopping mall     sports center
4. easygoing         polite
   unreliable        helpful
5. confident         huge
   sensitive         kind
6. town              country
   balcony           suburbs
7. stay in shape     keep in touch
   get along         make up
8. roof terrace      pedestrian area
   basement          first floor

38

## REVIEW and PRACTICE 3 and 4

**2** Match the words in the box with definitions 1–8.

> unsociable  traffic jam  get along well  anxious
> department store  basement  cozy  parents

1  a part of a building that is below the ground  _____
2  comfortable and warm  _____
3  a large store with different sections  _____
4  does not enjoy being with other people  _____
5  a person's mother and father  _____
6  worried and afraid  _____
7  have a friendly relationship  _____
8  a line of cars that is not moving  _____

**3** Choose the correct options to complete the sentences.

1  Can you _____ me to your cousin, Sarah?
   a  meet          b  get to know    c  introduce
2  I _____ my girlfriend at a party.
   a  knew          b  met            c  kept
3  I enjoy working here as my _____ are friendly.
   a  colleagues    b  classmates     c  couples
4  My team played very badly, and _____ the game 4–0.
   a  won           b  lost           c  missed
5  I've invited all my _____ to my wedding.
   a  parents       b  relationships  c  relatives
6  I usually _____ my friends on the weekend.
   a  get together with  b  get to know   c  get along well with
7  He was late for work as he _____ his train.
   a  caught        b  lost           c  missed
8  My apartment is on the top _____ .
   a  balcony       b  floor          c  terrace

**4** Complete the e-mail with the words in the box.

> basement  helpful  first floor  parking lot  spacious
> convenient  next-door neighbor  apartment building

Hi Adam,

I have the keys to my new place! It's on the [1]_____ of a large [2]_____ . It has two bedrooms, so it's pretty [3]_____ . There's a [4]_____ in the [5]_____ of the building where I can leave my car. It's really [6]_____ . My [7]_____ seems nice and really [8]_____ – he's offered to carry my heavy boxes on moving day!  Can you help, too?

Love,
Mel

## Personal Best

**Lesson 3A**
Name five personality adjectives that describe your relatives.

**Lesson 4A**
Name five things in your city using compound nouns.

**Lesson 3A**
Write two sentences for future plans, and one for a promise.

**Lesson 4A**
Write four sentences about your classroom using quantifiers.

**Lesson 3B**
Write four sentences using these linkers: *as*, *since*, *that's why*, and *so*.

**Lesson 4B**
Name four verb phrases using *have*, *take*, *catch*, and *keep*.

**Lesson 3C**
Name five relationship verbs.

**Lesson 4C**
Describe an apartment or house you've visited using five adjectives for describing homes.

**Lesson 3C**
Write four sentences about someone you know using relative clauses: two defining and two non-defining.

**Lesson 4C**
Write five sentences to describe your city using comparative and superlative adjectives.

**Lesson 3D**
Give two expressions you can use to give news and two to respond to news.

**Lesson 4D**
Write four sentences to a friend using *anyway*, *so*, *by the way*, and *speaking of*.

39

# UNIT 5 Money and shopping

**LANGUAGE**  zero and first conditional; future time clauses ■ money

## 5A Spend, spend, spend

**1** In pairs, do the quiz. Is your partner a spender or a saver?

**1** If I see something I really like on sale,
  a I usually buy it (whether I need it or not).
  b I ask for it for my birthday.
  c I don't buy it. My savings are for important things!

**2** If I feel a bit down,
  a I go shopping – it's called "retail therapy"!
  b I go for ice cream.
  c I check my savings account – the numbers there always make me feel happy.

**3** If I see something in a store this weekend that I really want, but can't afford,
  a I'll buy it with my credit card.
  b I'll borrow money from a friend or relative.
  c I'll save up until I can afford it.

**4** When my phone stops working,
  a I'll replace it with the latest model, probably the most expensive!
  b I'll replace it with a new model, but nothing too expensive.
  c I'll get a free one with the cheapest contract.

Go to Vocabulary practice: money, page 143

**2** Work in pairs. Answer the questions.
  1 Have you ever wasted money on something you've never used?
  2 Would you prefer to be broke and happy, or wealthy and unhappy?
  3 When you lend someone money, how long do you give him or her to pay you back?
  4 If you need to borrow money from someone, who do you ask? Why?
  5 When do you take money out and pay with cash? When do you prefer to pay with a card?
  6 What would you like to spend your savings on?

**3** ▶ 5.3 Listen to two friends, James and Sarah, doing the first two questions of the quiz. Are they spenders or savers?

**4 A** ▶ 5.4 Complete the sentences from the conversation. Listen and check.
  1 If I see something I like _____ _____ , I usually get it.
  2 If you spend all your money, you won't be able to _____ _____ for a motorcycle.
  3 As soon as I _____ _____ , I'll call you.

**B** Look at the sentences in 4A. Underline the present tenses. (Circle) the future forms.

**5 A** Match the sentences in exercise 4A with structures a–c and functions d–f. When do we use a present tense to talk about the future?
  a *if* + simple present, future with *will* _____
  b *if* + simple present, simple present _____
  c future time word + simple present, future with *will* _____
  d a situation or routine that is generally true _____
  e two connected future events _____
  f a possible future event and its result _____

40

zero and first conditional; future time clauses ■ money    LANGUAGE   5A

**B** Look at the quiz questions again. Which of the structures and functions in 5A are they? Then read the Grammar box.

> **Grammar** zero and first conditional; future time clauses
>
> Zero conditional (routines or situations that are generally true):
> If it **rains**, I **take** an umbrella.
>
> First conditional (possible future events and their results):
> If it **doesn't rain**, I**'ll go** to the beach tomorrow.
>
> **Look!** In conditional sentences, we can use **unless** (if ... not):
> Unless it rains, I'll go to the beach.
>
> Future time clauses (two connected future events):
> As soon as I **get** paid, I**'ll pay** you back.    We **won't eat** until you **get** home tonight.
>
> **Look!** In a future time clause, we use the simple present not will:
> I'll do my homework when the movie ends. NOT ~~when the movie will end~~.

Go to Grammar practice: zero and first conditional; future time clauses, page 120

**6 A** ▶ 5.6 **Pronunciation:** intonation Listen to the conditional sentences. Notice the falling intonation.
1 Plants die if they don't get enough water.
2 If my husband has a cold, I usually catch it.
3 Unless Jo lends me $15, I won't be able to go.
4 I won't go shopping if the meeting finishes late.

**B** ▶ 5.6 Listen again and repeat the sentences with the same intonation.

**7 A** Choose the correct options to complete the text.

## Save money without even trying

As soon as you ¹*start / will start* following these weekly tips from our money expert, Marta Benz, you'll save money without even trying!

### Make your own coffee

²*If / Unless* I get up early, I never have time to make coffee before leaving for work, so it's tempting to buy some on the way to the office. Buying coffee every day might save time, but it doesn't save money. If you ³*make / 'll make* coffee at home next week, you ⁴*save / 'll save* at least $25. That's an annual saving of $1,250!

### Pay with cash

I always ⁵*pay / will pay* by credit card when I ⁶*go / 'll go* shopping. It's much easier than finding an ATM. However, I ⁷*'ll / won't* take my card with me when I ⁸*go / will go* shopping next. Why? Because research shows that if people ⁹*pay / will pay* by credit card, they ¹⁰*don't / won't* realize how much they're spending. Paying with hard-earned cash is more "painful," so we spend less.

**B** In pairs, discuss which tip is the most helpful. Can you think of any other money-saving tips?

Go to Communication practice: Student A page 159, Student B page 169

**8** Complete the sentences so they are true for you. Then compare your sentences in pairs.
1 If the weather's nice tomorrow, I _____ .
2 I'll probably _____ next week unless _____ .
3 I _____ next summer if I can afford it.
4 I _____ if I go shopping this weekend.
5 If I save enough money in the next six months, I _____ .
6 I usually _____ if I feel stressed out.
7 I'll keep studying English until _____ .
8 I _____ as soon as I get home tonight.

**A** *What will you do if the weather's nice tomorrow?*
**B** *If the weather's nice tomorrow, I'll probably go jogging. And you?*

Write six sentences with future time clauses, using words from the Vocabulary practice.

# 5 SKILLS — READING identifying opinions ■ *even, just*

## 5B Black Friday

**1** Look at the title of the text and the pictures on page 43. Discuss the questions in pairs.

1 Describe the pictures. What do you think is happening?
2 Have you bought any bargains recently? What were they? Where did you buy them?

**2** What do you know about "Black Friday"? Choose the sentence that you think is correct. Then read the first paragraph and check.

1 Black Friday takes place just after Christmas.
2 On Black Friday, stores offer a lot of bargains.
3 It's called "Black Friday" because stores lose a lot of money on that day.

> **Skill** identifying opinions
>
> **When you read a text that contains opinions, look for:**
> - phrases that introduce opinions: *it seems to me that, as far as I'm concerned, if you ask me.*
> - adjectives that express opinions: *amazing, disappointing, successful, disgusting, awful*
> - opinions expressed indirectly and comparisons with *like*: *People aren't that polite* = People are impolite. *It's like watching paint dry* = It's boring.

**3 A** Read the Skill box and skim the text. Who has a negative opinion about Black Friday? Who enjoys it? Who dislikes it, but always goes?

**B** Read the second paragraph again and find:

1 three phrases which introduce opinions.       3 an opinion expressed as a comparison with *like*.
2 three adjectives which express opinions.

**4** Read the text again. Are the sentences true (T) or false (F)? Correct the false sentences.

1 For Andy, the most important thing about Black Friday is the low prices. _____
2 Andy thinks it's normal for shoppers to behave badly on Black Friday. _____
3 Jen thinks that some people lose control on Black Friday. _____
4 Jen doesn't mind if shoppers are aggressive on Black Friday. _____
5 Chris thinks people save money to buy things they need on Black Friday. _____
6 Chris believes that stores offer fantastic special offers on Black Friday. _____

**5** Complete the sentences with *even* or *just*. Scan the text and check.

1 Stores offer huge discounts and special offers for _____ one day.
2 This year was _____ more successful than last year.
3 I got _____ what I wanted.
4 People yell at each other, and there are _____ fights!
5 It seems to me they _____ go crazy when they see a bargain.
6 I'm not _____ sure if the bargains are actually real.

> **Text builder** *even, just*
>
> We use *even* to emphasize surprising information, comparisons, and negatives.
> surprise: *I speak French, English, and **even** Chinese.*
> comparisons: *His new car is **even** faster than his old one.*
> negatives: *He's never **even** heard of my favorite singer!*
>
> We use *just* to mean *only, exactly,* or *simply.*
> only: *There's **just** one store on my street.*
> exactly: *This shirt is **just** my size.*
> simply: *I **just** called to say I love you.*

**6** Read the Text builder. What do *even* and *just* mean in the sentences in exercise 5?

**7** Do you think big shopping events like Black Friday are a good idea? Why/Why not?

identifying opinions ■ *even, just* READING  SKILLS  5B

# Going crazy for a bargain

Black Friday takes place in the U.S. right after Thanksgiving, on the last Friday in November, when stores offer huge discounts and special offers for just one day. It marks the start of the holiday shopping season and takes its name from the fact that this is the first day of the year that stores traditionally start making a profit, going from "in the red" to "in the black." However, the event is now international and more famous for the aggressive behavior of people hunting for low-priced TVs, tablets, and designer clothes. I went to a department store to talk to shoppers about their views on all aspects of the Black Friday phenomenon.

Outside I met Andy, a retired salesclerk, who had lined up all night outside the store to get in first. "Obviously, you can find some amazing discounts," he said, "but if you ask me, the best thing is the experience itself. It's so exciting – camping outside the night before, getting your hands on the latest widescreen TV, reduced from $600 to $249. Personally, I think this year was even more successful than last year – I got just what I wanted," he said, trying to fit two TVs, five different games consoles, and a vacuum cleaner into his car. I asked Andy about his views on Black Friday's bad reputation. "It doesn't worry me too much. People yell at each other, and there are even fights! But as far as I'm concerned, it's part of the event. If you don't like it, don't come."

Inside the store, Jen, a nurse, was waiting to pay at the checkout. "Every year, I say I'm not going to come, but here I am again," she said with a tired smile. What doesn't she like about it? "People aren't that polite on Black Friday. It seems to me they just go crazy when they see a bargain. And what do we buy? More coffee makers, tablets, stuff we already have, so why are we buying more? I couldn't resist this hairdryer and smartphone today, though, so I suppose I'm part of the problem." She is not a fan of the behavior of some shoppers, however. "It can be chaos, with people kicking and pushing each other out of the way. Sometimes you even see people fighting in front of their kids, and I saw one woman break her wrist as she fell trying to defend her new microwave. To be honest, I find it pretty disgusting."

Finally, I spoke to Chris, a student who had only come into the store to buy a charger for his phone. "I'd forgotten it was Black Friday. I can't believe how many people are here." But aside from that, how does he feel about the day? "From my point of view, it's a terrible idea as it encourages people to be materialistic and spend money on items they can't afford. They pay by credit card and get into debt … it's sad and unnecessary." Chris went on to make the most interesting point I'd heard all day. "I'm not even sure if the bargains are actually real. Some stores seem to increase prices before Black Friday and then lower them, so people think there are huge discounts!" And yet, all over the world, people go crazy for those Black Friday bargains, year after year.

**Personal Best** — Imagine you were at this department store on Black Friday. Write a short paragraph describing your opinion of it.

# 5 LANGUAGE
predictions: *will, be going to, may/might* ■ shopping

## 5C Tomorrow's world of shopping

**1 A** Read two people's comments about shopping. Complete the comments with words from the box.

order   in-store   products   delivery   item   salesclerk

I prefer ¹_____ shopping. It's important to see an ²_____ before buying it, and to be able to ask a ³_____ for help or advice.

It's so quick to ⁴_____ things online, and home ⁵_____ is really convenient. In the future, I think most companies will only sell their ⁶_____ online.

**B** Discuss the questions in pairs.
1  Do you prefer online or in-store shopping? Why?
2  What have you bought in a store recently?
3  What have you bought online recently?
4  How do you think we will shop in the future?

Go to Vocabulary practice: shopping, page 143

**2**  Read the title of the text. In pairs, discuss what you think is happening in the pictures.

## THE FUTURE OF SHOPPING

We look at some of the exciting changes that we might see in the not-so-distant future, both in stores and online, but also beyond!

### In-store technology
Like in the movie *Minority Report*, face-recognition systems will greet customers by name when they arrive, record what they buy and which parts of the store they spend most time in, and collect information about product preferences by measuring facial expressions. They'll then use all this information to send personalized recommendations and special offers to shoppers' phones while they shop.

### Try before you buy – virtually!
Many clothing stores already have interactive mirrors in the store, which let you try on different clothes virtually at the swipe of a hand. The mirrors use augmented reality to show how the clothes will fit. Similar "magic mirror" app technology is being developed to browse online stores and virtually try on clothes at home, too. We predict that this might be the most popular new technology!

### The changing face of stores
Judging by their popularity at present, there are probably going to be more "pop-up" stores – small, temporary stores in places like train stations, parks, or anywhere where there are a lot of people. Meanwhile, many stores may simply stop selling things and become showrooms for companies to display their products. In this way, people will browse in a store and will be able to see and touch the different products, but they will have to order them online.

### Neither in-store nor online
As our lives get busier, companies will definitely install more large touch screens in public spaces, where people can browse and order what they want without going to a store. Virtual supermarkets are already available in the subway system in Seoul, South Korea. Passengers order groceries while waiting for their train, and they are delivered to their home the same day.

**3 A** Read the text. Match 1–5 with a–e to make predictions.
1  In-store technology, such as facial recognition, will
2  Pop-up stores are probably going to
3  People will browse in a store, but buy online and many stores will
4  The writers predict that interactive mirror apps might
5  As our lives get busier, we will definitely

a  collect information about our shopping habits and preferences.
b  be the most successful new technology.
c  see more touch screens in public places.
d  appear in more places because they are very popular at the moment.
e  stop selling things and become showrooms.

44

predictions: *will, be going to, may/might* ■ shopping    LANGUAGE  **5C**

**B** Which of the shopping predictions do you think are a good idea? Why?

**4** Look at the predictions in exercise 3A again. Choose the correct options to complete the rules. Then read the Grammar box.
1 We use *going to* for predictions based on *someone's opinion / present evidence*.
2 We use *will* for predictions based on *someone's opinion / present evidence*.
3 We use *might* and *may* for predictions we are *sure / not sure* about.
4 We use *will definitely* to say that the prediction is more *certain / uncertain*.

> **Grammar** predictions: *will, be going to, may/might*
>
> **General predictions:**
> I don't think Robert **will** arrive on time.
> Robots **probably won't** replace humans.
>
> **Predictions based on present evidence:**
> She looks like she**'s going to** have her baby very soon!
> Look at those clouds! It**'s definitely going to** rain.
>
> **Less certain predictions with modal verbs:**
> It **may** be cold later. The weather forecast said it's possible.
> Jill **might** come to dinner. She hasn't confirmed.
>
> **Look!** With *will* and *going to*, we can use **probably** to make a prediction less certain and **definitely** to make it more certain.

Go to Grammar practice: predictions: *will, be going to, may/might*, page 121

**5 A** ▶ 5.10 **Pronunciation:** word stress Listen to the sentences and look at the words in **bold**. How many syllables do they have in fast speech? Which syllable is stressed?
1 He'll **probably** be late.
2 I **probably** won't stay awake.
3 It's **definitely** going to be sunny.
4 It's **definitely** not going to snow.
5 She's **probably** going to leave.
6 I'll **definitely** call you.

**B** ▶ 5.10 Listen again and repeat.

Go to Communication practice: Students A and B page 160

**6** Choose the correct options to complete the text.

### Experts predict the future – what will the world be like in 2050?

"I think we'll ¹*definitely be / be definitely* able to buy emotions online, upload them to our brains, and we ²*may be / maybe* able to share them online on social media. If a friend posts a photo of her wedding day, we ³*will probable / will probably* be able to experience exactly what she was feeling."

"Robots ⁴*probably won't / won't probably* only help us with the housework, but they'll also take care of children, and – this is crazy, but possible – they ⁵*might / will* even become our closest friends. In the future, this technology ⁶*is going to / won't* be much more advanced, and robots and gadgets will sense how we feel and adapt to our emotions."

"In 2050, all kitchens ⁷*might not / might* have 3D printers that will be able to make dinner. 3D printed pizza, anyone? NASA is already experimenting with 3D printed food for trips to Mars and beyond. If it's successful, technology like this ⁸*may / might definitely* help solve the problem of world hunger."

**7** In pairs, make predictions about the future. Use some of the ideas below or your own ideas.

( work ) ( pollution ) ( robots ) ( wearable technology ) ( my life ) ( housing )
( space travel ) ( computers ) ( social networks ) ( transportation ) ( food )

*I don't think we'll work in offices in the future. We won't need to talk face-to-face with our colleagues as we'll be able to communicate online. What do you think?*

**Personal Best** Complete the following sentences with a prediction: *Next week ..., Next year ..., In five years ... .*

**5 SKILLS  SPEAKING**  explaining what's wrong ■ taking something back to a store

## 5D It's not working

**1** In pairs, ask and answer the questions.
1 Have you bought anything that you've had to take or send back to the store?
2 What was the problem?
3 Was there a solution? What happened?

**2** Look at the picture. What do you think the object in the picture is? What might be the problem with it?

**3** ▶ 5.11 Watch or listen to the first part of *Learning Curve*. What is the customer's problem? Choose the correct option.
a He bought the item by mistake.
b The 3D visor he bought isn't working.
c There's something wrong with the video game he bought.

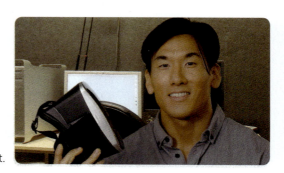

### Conversation builder   explaining what's wrong

**Problems with electrical items**
I can't get it to work/turn on.
It's not working. / It doesn't work. / It won't work.
It keeps crashing.
There's something missing.
There's something wrong with the …

**Problems with clothes and other items**
It's too big/small/tight/baggy.
It doesn't fit.
It's broken/scratched/torn.
It's the wrong size/model/color.
I've changed my mind. I don't want it any more.

**4** ▶ 5.12 Read the Conversation builder. Complete the customer's description of the problem with the visor. Listen and check.

**Customer**  I bought this visor at a reduced price to use with my video games, and I can't get it to ¹_____ . I'd like to return it.
**Marc**  So what seems to be the problem with it?
**Customer**  It won't, you know, work with the video game. I put it on, and it keeps ²_____ . You know, it just stops ³_____ right away. I think there might be something ⁴_____ in the program or it's just ⁵_____ .

**5** In pairs, practice explaining what is wrong with something. Talk about three things each.

explaining what's wrong ■ taking something back to a store  **SPEAKING**  **SKILLS**  **5D**

**6** ▶ 5.13 Watch or listen to the second part of the show. Choose the correct option to answer the questions.

1 At first, what does the customer want Marc to do?
   a exchange the item for the same model
   b exchange the item for a different model
   c give him a refund
2 What happens in the end?
   a Marc fixes the item, and the customer is satisfied.
   b Marc agrees to give the customer a refund, but he can't find his receipt.
   c The customer exchanges the item for a new model.

> **Skill** taking something back to a store
>
> When you take something back to a store, explain clearly, but politely, what you want.
> - Use *I'd like* and *Could I* to sound polite, e.g., *I'd like to exchange it. Could I return it, please?*
> - Add phrases like *I think*, *just*, and *if that's possible* to make your request sound less direct. *I'd just like one in a smaller size. I think I'd like a refund, if that's possible*.
> - If you're not happy with the proposed solution, explain what you want frankly and firmly, using phrases like *to be honest* and *actually*. *To be honest, I'd just like a refund. Actually, I think I'd prefer a refund.*

**7** Read the Skill box. Did the customer explain what he wanted clearly and politely?

**8** Order the words to make sentences from the conversation. Who said each sentence, Marc (M) or the customer (C)?

1 to / be / seems / the / what / problem / it / with ?   ____
2 return / I'd / to / it / like   ____
3 look / take / could / a / I / it / at ?   ____
4 honest / I'd / to / be / think / I / like / it / exchange / to   ____
5 refund / get / a / please / could / I ?   ____
6 I'd / think / I / refund / like / a   ____
7 absolutely / need / just / I / see / receipt / to / your   ____
8 speak / can / to / manager / your / I / please ?   ____

**9** Order sentences a–g to make another conversation in a store.

a ☐ **Salesclerk:** Of course. Can I have a look at it?
b ☐ **Customer:** Actually, I'd prefer a refund.
c ☐1☐ **Salesclerk:** Good morning. Can I help you?
d ☐ **Customer:** Yes, sure. Here you are.
e ☐ **Salesclerk:** You're right. There's something wrong with the switch. Would you like to exchange it?
f ☐ **Salesclerk:** No problem. Could I have your receipt and credit card?
g ☐ **Customer:** Hi. I bought this hairdryer yesterday, but it isn't working. Could I return it, please?

**Go to Communication practice:** Students A and B page 160

**10 A PREPARE** In pairs, prepare a conversation in a store. Decide on:
- the item
- the problem
- what the customer wants
- what solutions are possible

**B PRACTICE** In pairs, practice the conversation. Take turns being the customer.

**C PERSONAL BEST** Listen to another pair's conversation. Does the customer explain clearly what's wrong? Are both people polite? Can you use something from this conversation in your own? Practice your conversation again.

**Personal Best** Think of five new products and make a list of possible problems with them.

# UNIT 6

# Work and education

**LANGUAGE** present perfect and simple past, *already*, *yet*, *recently* ■ work and careers (1)

## 6A  Career change

1 In pairs, put phrases a–f in order from 1–6.
   a ☐ get a job          c ☐ apply for a job    e ☐ attend an interview
   b ☐ get a promotion    d ☐ retire             f ☐ get a degree

   **Go to Vocabulary practice:** work and careers (1), page 144

2 In pairs, discuss your career so far or your hopes for your future career.

3 Read the text quickly. Which two careers has Fabrice Muamba had?

### RISING STAR'S CAREER CHANGE

Fabrice Muamba has had an extraordinary life so far. He has lived on two continents and has had two successful careers. He also nearly died on the soccer field in front of a live TV audience of millions. We take a look at his life and his new career.

Fabrice lived in the Democratic Republic of Congo when he was a child, but he has lived in the UK since he was eleven. His career as a soccer player began with a training program at Arsenal Football Club when he was fourteen. Three years later, he finished school and became a full-time professional soccer player. "It was hard, and I had to train every day, but that's how my career really started," he says.

As a professional soccer player, Fabrice was a rising star who scored many goals, signed multimillion dollar contracts, and was frequently named Player of the Season. However, during an important quarter-final game, Muamba's heart stopped, and he collapsed. It was over an hour before his heart started again, and he was in the hospital for a month. Surprisingly, he made an excellent recovery, but he had to change careers for medical reasons. "I've had to go back to the beginning again with my career, and learn completely new skills," he says, but his new career as a journalist is going well. He has recently completed a degree in sports journalism with a job placement at the BBC, and has already written articles for a national newspaper.

Fabrice has learned a lot from changing careers, and he has become an ambassador for a program called Life Skills, which helps young people prepare for the world of work. So, what advice does he give young people? "I'm really grateful for having so many opportunities and that I've been able to try different things. So that's my main advice: you have to be open to trying lots of new things in order to succeed."

Adapted from theguardian.com

4 **A** Read the text again. Are the sentences true (T) or false (F)? Correct the false sentences.
   1 He **has had** a normal life. _____
   2 Fabrice **lived** in the UK when he was a child. _____
   3 He **has lived** in the U.S. since he was eleven. _____
   4 He **became** a professional soccer player after he finished school. _____
   5 He **had** to change careers because of a health problem. _____
   6 He **has** recently **completed** a degree in sports journalism. _____
   7 He **has** already **written** articles for the BBC. _____
   8 In his life, he **has had** a lot of opportunities. _____

   **B** Which verbs in **bold** in 4A are present perfect? Which are simple past?

48

present perfect and simple past, *already, yet, recently* ■ work and careers (1)    LANGUAGE   6A

**5** Match the verbs in **bold** in exercise 4A with functions a–e. Then read the Grammar box.
  a finished past actions ____ ____ ____
  b recently finished past actions ____
  c past actions with *already* ____
  d life experiences ____ ____
  e unfinished past actions
     that continue in the present ____

> **Grammar** present perfect and simple past, *already, yet, recently*
>
> **Present perfect for past experiences in your life:**
> I**'ve visited** over 20 countries.
> He**'s** never **been** to the U.S.
>
> **Present perfect with *already* and *yet*:**
> She**'s already bought** her ticket.
> **Have** you **read** my e-mail **yet**?
>
> **Simple past for finished actions in the past:**
> I **got** my first job in 2015.   She **lived** here for 10 years.
>
> **Present perfect for recent past actions:**
> I**'ve been** tired lately.
> We **haven't seen** Harry recently.
>
> **Actions that start in the past and continue in the present:**
> I**'ve studied** English <u>since</u> I was eight years old.
> I**'ve known** him <u>for</u> years.
>
> **Look!** We use *since* with a point in time and *for* with a period of time.

Go to Grammar practice: present perfect and simple past, *already, yet, recently*, page 122

**6 A** ▶ 6.3 **Pronunciation:** present perfect and simple past Listen to the sentences. Notice the difference between the present perfect and simple past.
  1 a I've lived here for five years.   b I lived here for five years.
  2 a He's met her before.   b He met her before.

**B** ▶ 6.4 Listen and complete the sentences. Which are present perfect? Which are simple past?
  1 I _____ him a few times.
  2 We _____ our vacation.
  3 He _____ a good job.
  4 They _____ to take the course.
  5 She _____ the company.

**7 A** ▶ 6.5 Choose the correct options to complete the conversation. Listen and check.

> A How long ¹*has Karen been / was Karen* in her current job?
> B She ²*'s been / was* there for a month. She's a project manager in a construction company.
> A Was she looking for a job for a long time or ³*has she gotten / did she get* a job quickly?
> B A long time. She ⁴*'s been / was* unemployed for two years.
> A ⁵*Has she done / Did she do* an internship with that company before she got the job?
> B No, she didn't. When she ⁶*'s applied / applied* for the job, she didn't know the company.
> A ⁷*Has she ever gotten / Did she ever get* a promotion?
> B She got a promotion in her last job, but she ⁸*hasn't gotten / didn't get* one on this job yet.
> A ⁹*Has she taken / Did she take* any training courses recently?
> B She ¹⁰*'s taken / took* a project management course when she was unemployed.

**B** Work in pairs. Ask your partner about a friend or relative who has a job. Use the questions in 7A and your own ideas.

Go to Communication practice: Student A page 160, Student B page 169

**8** In pairs, use the prompts to ask and answer the first questions in the present perfect. Then ask for more details in the simple past.
  1 how long / live in your house or apartment?   why / move there?   where / live before?
  2 see / any good movies recently?   which movie / see?   you / enjoy it?
  3 go / on vacation this year?   where / go?   have / a good time?
  4 how long / know your newest friend?   how / meet?   where / meet?

Personal Best   Write four sentences about your life. Use the present perfect and the simple past.   49

# 6 SKILLS LISTENING
understanding specific information ■ sentence stress ■ work and careers (2)

## 6B Dream job

**1** Answer the questions in pairs.
1 Do you know anyone who is doing their dream job?
2 What kind of work do they do? What does it involve?
3 Why do they enjoy it?
4 What would your dream job be?

**2** What's the difference between the pairs of words? Discuss in pairs.
1 job / career
2 employer / employee
3 part-time / full-time
4 CV / application form

**Go to Vocabulary practice:** work and careers (2), page 144

**3** In pairs, make a list of the five most important things you need for job satisfaction.

 **Skill** understanding specific information

It's often important to understand specific information and specific words.
- Read the questions carefully and identify what kind of information you need.
- Think about the possible words you may hear.
- Important words are usually stressed in a sentence. *My **friend**, who's a **chef**, was **laid off**, so she **started** her own **business** making **wedding cakes**.*
- Try not to confuse similar-sounding words. *He's employed. He's unemployed. She's fourteen. She's forty.*

**4** ▶ 6.7 Read the Skill box. Watch or listen to the first part of *Learning Curve*. Make a note of some stressed words you hear for topics 1–4.

| 1 Penny's current job | |
| --- | --- |
| 2 Penny's previous job | |
| 3 the study about job satisfaction | |
| 4 temporary job agencies | |

**5** ▶ 6.7 Watch or listen again. Write one word in each blank to complete the sentences.
1 Penny finds her current job _____ .
2 She used to be a _____ assistant.
3 She found her previous job _____ .
4 The working conditions in her previous job were _____ .
5 One study shows that only _____ % of people like their jobs.
6 Even if they have well-paid jobs, other people feel _____ at work.
7 Working conditions have changed, and some people don't want a _____ job.
8 The _____ largest employer in the U.S. is a temp agency.

**6** Discuss the questions in pairs.
1 What are the advantages of having a permanent job? And a temporary job?
2 Which would you like at this stage in your life? And in the future?

understanding specific information ■ sentence stress ■ work and careers (2)   LISTENING   SKILLS   6B

**7** ▶ 6.8 Watch or listen to the second part of the show and answer the questions.
1 What's Ira's job?
2 Does he enjoy it?
3 Which job has Kelly applied for?
4 Does she have any experience in that profession?
5 What's Janet's job?
6 Is it a full-time job?

Ira

**8** ▶ 6.8 Watch or listen again. Complete the notes about Ira, Kelly, and Janet with a word or phrase that you hear.

> Ira's responsible for making the store ¹_____ . When he started working there, it was a ²_____ job. He took over as the manager when his uncle ³_____ .

Kelly

> Kelly has sent her ⁴_____ , a ⁵_____ , and a salary request to the TV company. She's also sent them an ⁶_____ , and has called them ⁷_____ times. Simon recommends asking if she can do an ⁸_____ at the company, instead.

Janet

> Janet used to work with monkeys, but she got a ⁹_____ , and now she works with gorillas. She's always wanted to be a ¹⁰_____ .

**Listening builder    sentence stress**

English speakers stress the most important words in a sentence. These are usually words that carry meaning: nouns, adjectives, and verbs. "Grammar" words, such as auxiliaries, prepositions, and pronouns, are often unstressed. There can be one or more unstressed words between the stressed words. The more unstressed words there are between two stressed words, the more quickly they are pronounced.
I'd **like** to **ask** you about **work**. Do you **have** a **job**?

**9 A** Read the Listening builder. Look at the stressed words in sentences 1–5. How many unstressed words do you think there are in each blank?
1 _____ hard _____ find _____ dream job.
2 Working conditions nowadays _____ different _____ were _____ past.
3 _____ always known _____ kind _____ job _____ wanted _____ do _____ adult.
4 _____ times _____ call _____ company _____ job interview?
5 _____ more important _____ have _____ well-paid job _____ rewarding job?

**B** ▶ 6.9 Listen and write the unstressed words in the blanks. Then practice saying the sentences.

**10** In pairs, talk about three of the work-related topics below.

stressful jobs    writing your résumé    job interviews    salaries
working conditions    rewarding jobs    employers

**Personal Best**   What advice would you give to someone younger than you who doesn't know what job or career he or she wants to have?

51

# 6 LANGUAGE   present perfect continuous and present perfect ■ education

## 6C School days

**1** In pairs, decide if the words and phrases in the box are positive or negative.

> get into trouble   pass a test   cheat   behave   fail an exam   get good grades

**Go to Vocabulary practice:** education, page 145

**2** Discuss the questions in pairs.

1 Which schools have you been to?
2 Who was your favorite teacher/professor? Why?
3 Did you get into trouble in school? What for?
4 What are your best and worst school memories?

**3** Look at the title of the TV show in the preview. In pairs, discuss what you think the show is about. Read the preview and check your ideas.

### Are our kids tough enough?
# Chinese School

According to the latest research, Chinese children are better than UK children at subjects like math and science. Is this because of the way Chinese students learn? In a fascinating experiment, five teachers come from China to teach a group of teenagers in a UK school for four weeks, using traditional Chinese teaching techniques. At the end of the month, students take exams and compare their grades with the rest of their school year. Which teaching system will get the best grades? Last episode of this three-part series tonight.

**4 A** ▶ 6.13 Listen to an extract from a radio show about the TV show, *Chinese School*. Complete the notes in the table.

|  | UK school system | Chinese school system |
| --- | --- | --- |
| class size | 1_____ students | 2_____ students |
| schedule | from 3_____ a.m. to 4_____ p.m. | from 5_____ a.m. to 6_____ p.m. |
| method | Students usually ask 7_____, discuss their 8_____, and do a lot of 9_____ tasks. | Students listen to the 10_____ and take 11_____. Very 12_____ teachers. |

**B** Which school system is more similar to your country? Which do you think will get the best grades at the end of the show?

**5 A** ▶ 6.14 Complete the sentences from the radio show with the words in the box. Then listen and check.

> using   teaching   been   watching   starting   liked

1 Have you been _____ the show over the past few weeks?
2 For the past month, teachers from China have been _____ at a UK school.
3 They've been _____ Chinese teaching techniques.
4 They've been _____ school at 7 a.m.
5 The students haven't _____ this different style of teaching very much."
6 The teachers have _____ very strict.

**B** Look at the sentences in 5A and answer the questions.

1 Are they finished or unfinished states and actions? (Has the TV show finished?)
2 Which sentences contain action verbs? Which sentences contain state verbs?
3 Look at the action verb sentences. Are they single actions or longer, repeated actions?
4 Do we use *have + been + -ing* with action verbs or state verbs?

present perfect continuous and present perfect ■ education  **LANGUAGE 6C**

**6** Read the Grammar box. Which sentences in exercise 5A are in the present perfect continuous and which are in the present perfect?

> **Grammar** present perfect continuous and present perfect
>
> **Present perfect continuous:**
> To emphasize a longer or repeated action over a period of time.
> I**'ve been waiting** for you since 3 o'clock!   He**'s been coming** to this English class for three years.
>
> To talk about a recent past action that has a result in the present:
> I'm tired because I**'ve been studying** all day.
>
> **Present perfect:**
> We don't use the present perfect continuous with state verbs – we use the present perfect.
> I**'ve known** Laura since we were in elementary school. NOT I've been knowing
>
> **Look!** We often use the present perfect continuous to ask and answer questions using *how long*, *for*, and *since*.
> **How long** have you been studying English?   I've been studying English **for** ten years/**since** I was twelve.

Go to Grammar practice: present perfect continuous and present perfect, page 123

**7** Match sentences 1–5 with replies a–e. Then complete the replies with the present perfect continuous or present perfect form of the verbs in the box.

| learn   wait   play   not be   not study |

1 Did you know there are no buses today?
2 Have you passed your driving test yet?
3 Why is Jon so tired?
4 Your French isn't very good, is it?
5 What's wrong with Rob?

a No, it isn't. I _____ it for very long.
b Because he _____ basketball all day.
c No, I didn't. I _____ here at the bus stop for ages!
d No, I haven't. I _____ to drive for three years now.
e I'm not sure, but he _____ happy since he failed that exam.

**8 A** ▶ 6.16 **Pronunciation: weak form of *been*** Listen to replies a–e from exercise 7. Is the word *been* stressed? Does it have a long or short vowel sound?

**B** ▶ 6.16 Listen, check, and repeat. Then practice questions 1–5 and answers a–e in pairs.

Go to Communication practice: Student A page 160, Student B page 170

**9 A** When did these things happen in your life? Write something for each category.

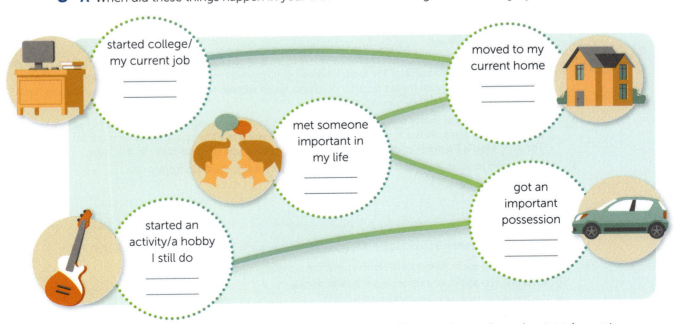

started college/my current job
moved to my current home
met someone important in my life
got an important possession
started an activity/a hobby I still do

**B** Work in pairs. Look at your partner's notes in exercise 9A and ask questions about each event. Include a "How long" question for each event.

**Personal Best**  Write five sentences with the present perfect or present perfect continuous about your day today.

# 6 SKILLS  WRITING — writing a cover letter ■ prepositions after verbs, nouns, and adjectives

## 6D I am writing to apply …

**1** Look at the job ad. Would you like to do a job like this? Why/Why not? What skills, qualifications, and experience is the employer looking for?

### Internship at The L.A. Media Factory

We are looking for an intern to work in our international media center in Los Angeles. The job involves writing articles about the entertainment industry for media organizations around the world. We are particularly interested in recent graduates with some experience in writing.

**Candidates should:**
- have some experience in digital journalism
- have excellent writing skills
- be highly organized
- have good attention to detail
- work well on a team
- speak English and Spanish fluently.

To apply, please send your CV to Linda Sayer, explaining why you are interested in the position, and providing details of your qualifications, skills, and any relevant experience.

**2** Read the cover letter. Does Pablo respond to all the information in the job ad? Is he a good candidate for the job? Why/Why not?

---

**Subject:** Job application – internship position

**Attachment:** CV Pablo Alonso.pdf

Dear Ms. Sayer:

1 I am writing to apply for the internship position at The L.A. Media Factory, as advertised on internships.com. Please find attached my CV.

2 As you can see from my CV, I have recently completed a degree in Journalism and Media Studies at the University of San Antonio. I believe the skills, experience, and qualities I have developed make me an ideal candidate for the internship position.

3 I am extremely interested in the position because I am passionate about writing and digital media, and I would like to have a career in digital journalism. As part of my degree, I studied areas such as TV and Film Studies, and Digital Journalism. I also completed a six-week job placement, writing short articles for a local newspaper.

4 In addition to my studies, I am currently working as a writer. I am responsible for producing social media posts for a local film society. My work involves writing short movie reviews and guides to increase the film society's social media presence. These tasks require skills such as good organization, time management, and attention to detail.

5 I am a responsible, hardworking person who works well alone and as part of a team. I speak fluent English, and I am a native Spanish speaker. I would welcome the opportunity to work for The L.A. Media Factory, and I am confident I would be a valuable addition to the team.

6 Thank you for considering my application. I look forward to hearing from you.

Sincerely yours,

Pablo Alonso

---

**3** Read the cover letter again. Match sections 1–6 with the information they contain (a–f).

a relevant experience and skills (with specific examples) _____
b relevant academic or professional qualifications _____
c saying which job you're applying for _____
d saying thanks and asking for a response _____
e personal qualities and any additional relevant skills _____
f more relevant experience and skills _____

writing a cover letter ■ prepositions after verbs, nouns, and adjectives   **WRITING**   **SKILLS**   **6D**

> **Skill** writing a cover letter
>
> We write cover letters to introduce ourselves when we apply for a job. We usually send one with our résumé.
> - Respond to the information in the job ad. What skills, experience, and qualifications are they looking for?
> - Organize your letter so it is brief, easy to read, and makes the employer want to find out more about you.
> - Use formal language (*I have been* NOT ~~*I've been*~~, *I would like* NOT ~~*I want*~~; *a great deal of* NOT ~~*lots of*~~).
> - Use a formal greeting and ending (*Dear Sir/Madam:* … *Yours truly,* or *Dear Mr. Smith:* … *Sincerely yours,*).

**4** Read the Skill box. Read sentences 1–8 and underline their formal equivalents in the cover letter.

1  I'm writing because I want the intern job.
2  I think I'm perfect for the job.
3  I really like the job because I like writing.
4  Right now, I work as a writer, too.
5  In this job, I have to write short movie reviews.
6  I need skills like good organization for this job.
7  I really want to work for you. I'd be fantastic!
8  Thanks for your time. Talk soon!

**5** Complete the sentences with a preposition. Then check your answers in the cover letter.

1  I am writing to apply _____ the internship position.
2  I have recently completed a degree _____ journalism.
3  I am extremely interested _____ the position.
4  I am responsible _____ producing social media posts.
5  Thank you _____ considering my application.

> **Text builder** prepositions after verbs, nouns, and adjectives
>
> Some verbs, nouns, and adjectives are followed by a preposition.
> **Verbs:**
> apply **for**, work **as**, look forward **to**, thank (you) **for**
>
> **Nouns:**
> a career **in**, a degree **in**, a certificate **in**
>
> **Adjectives:**
> ideal **for**, interested **in**, passionate **about**, responsible **for**
>
> **Look!** A noun or a verb + *-ing* usually follow these prepositions:
> Thank you for **your e-mail**.   I am looking forward to **hearing** from you.   I'm interested in **taking** a course.

**6 A** Read the Text builder. Complete the sentences with a preposition and information that is true for you.

1  I would like to apply _____ .
2  Eventually, I would like to work _____ .
3  I would like a career _____ .
4  I am passionate _____ .

**B** Compare your answers in pairs.

**7 A** **PREPARE** Choose one of the job ads below. Make notes about the skills, qualifications, and relevant experience to include in your cover letter. Plan how to organize the information.

### SUMMER SCHOOL WELCOME STAFF

We are looking for welcome staff to receive and support our summer school students (aged 14 – 18) and do administration tasks in our summer school office. You should have excellent communication skills, work well on a team, and be able to use Word, Excel, and Powerpoint. Experience in working with teenagers a plus.

### FASHION BLOGGER

Do you have a passion for fashion? Are you good at photography? City-based blogger wanted to write ten blog posts a week for an international lifestyle website. No professional qualifications required, but we are looking for someone with good organization and time-management skills who has experience in writing a blog.

**B** **PRACTICE** Write your cover letter. Use formal language and phrases with prepositions.

**C** **PERSONAL BEST** Exchange letters with a partner. Which job did he/she apply for? Does he/she respond to everything in the job ad? What do you like best about his/her letter?

**Personal Best**  Imagine you are ten years older. Write two paragraphs about your qualifications, skills, and experience.

# 5 and 6 REVIEW and PRACTICE

## Grammar

**1** Choose the correct options to complete the sentences.

1. If the bus _____ soon, we'll take a cab.
   a won't arrive   b doesn't arrive   c didn't arrive
2. Look at all this traffic! We _____ be late for our flight.
   a 're going to   b 're going   c won't
3. I _____ in Auckland for five years, from 2008 to 2013.
   a 've lived   b lived   c live
4. I _____ to call her this morning, but there was no answer.
   a 've tried   b tried   c 've been trying
5. We'll go to the park when the rain _____.
   a is going to stop   b will stop   c stops
6. Tom _____ go to the party. He often doesn't go out because he works a lot.
   a will   b 's going to   c might not
7. I _____ to the supermarket today, so you don't need to go shopping.
   a 've already been   b 've been already   c already gone
8. _____ your best friend since you were in school together?
   a Have you been knowing   b Have you known   c Did you know

**2** Use the words in parentheses to complete the sentences so they mean the same as the first sentence.

1. You'll be late for work if you don't get up now.
   You _____ up now. (won't)
2. It's possible that she'll go to college next year.
   She _____ next year. (may)
3. Julia traveled to Mexico ten days ago, and she's still there.
   Julia _____ ten days. (been)
4. James started that game at two o'clock, and he's still playing it.
   James has _____ two o'clock. (since)
5. I won't go to bed until this movie ends.
   I _____ this movie ends. (as soon as)
6. I'm sure that my team won't lose the game.
   My team _____ the game. (win/definitely)
7. My brother still hasn't learned to drive.
   My brother _____. (yet)
8. When did you start taking piano lessons?
   _____ taking piano lessons? (how long)

**3** Choose the correct options to complete the text.

Companies such as Google and Nissan ¹*conducted / have been conducting* tests on driverless cars for the last ten years. They ²*have been using / used* powerful computers, which control the speed and direction of the driverless cars automatically. If the tests ³*will be / are* successful, we ⁴*might / won't* see driverless cars on our roads in the next five years. Our technology expert, Dan Jones, gave his opinion of driverless cars: "I think there ⁵*won't / will* be far fewer traffic accidents in the future. Unlike humans, computers don't usually make mistakes!"

Dan thinks that driverless cars ⁶*won't / will* make driving safer and ⁷*can / might* help to reduce traffic congestion. However, if they ⁸*will start / start* selling driverless cars in five years, ⁹*do / will* drivers want to buy them? Driver Joe Dawson told us what he thinks: "I don't need a driverless car. I ¹⁰*have passed / passed* my driving test in 1992, so ¹¹*I've been driving / I drive* for over 25 years, and in all that time, ¹²*I never have / I've never had* an accident."

## Vocabulary

**1** Circle the word that is different. Explain your answer.

1. manager / employee — working conditions / employer
2. delivery / career — checkout / cart
3. get good grades / do an internship — look for a job / take a training course
4. graduate / salesclerk — principal / professor
5. cash / coin — product / bill
6. permanent / wealthy — rewarding / part-time
7. CV / application form — salary / cover letter
8. full-time / term — nursery school / boarding school

## REVIEW and PRACTICE 5 and 6

**2** Match the words in the box with definitions 1–8.

> browse   professor   reasonable
> waste money on something   be broke
> strict   unemployed   get fired

1   not too expensive     _____
2   spend money on something unnecessary     _____
3   not have any money     _____
4   college or university teacher     _____
5   demanding good behavior     _____
6   without a job     _____
7   look at things you may decide to buy     _____
8   do something bad and lose your job     _____

**3** Choose the correct options to complete the sentences.

1   My bank gave me a $9,000 _____ for a new car.
    **a** bill        **b** loan        **c** borrow

2   When I went to the store, the jeans I wanted were _____ so I couldn't get any.
    **a** sold out        **b** paid for        **c** ordered

3   Gloria _____ her exams because she didn't study.
    **a** cheated        **b** failed        **c** passed

4   When the factory closed, 500 workers _____ .
    **a** got jobs        **b** retired        **c** were laid off

5   I put $75 _____ my savings account every month.
    **a** by        **b** into        **c** for

6   I have to borrow some money _____ my parents to pay for my vacation.
    **a** from        **b** for        **c** of

7   If you do well at work, you might get a _____ .
    **a** qualification        **b** good grade        **c** promotion

8   Sometimes I have to work twelve hours a day, plus weekends! Now I'm looking for a less _____ job.
    **a** stressful        **b** rewarding        **c** varied

**4** Put the words in the box under the correct headings.

> return something   do an internship   mortgage
> schedule   employee   taxes   order something online
> take a training course   college   in stock
> special offer   get a degree   ATM   get experience
> savings account   study for

| money | shopping |
|---|---|
|  |  |

| work and careers | education |
|---|---|
|  |  |

## Personal Best

**Lesson 5A**
Describe five things you have done with money this week.

**Lesson 6A**
Describe five things one of your relatives has done in his/her career.

**Lesson 5A**
Write three sentences: one zero conditional, one first conditional, and one with a future time clause.

**Lesson 6A**
Write three sentences about your day using the present perfect and *never, lately,* and *yet.*

**Lesson 5B**
Write one sentence with *even* and one with *recently.*

**Lesson 6B**
Think of three adjectives for a job you would like.

**Lesson 5C**
Describe three things that happened the last time you went shopping.

**Lesson 6C**
Name five types of schools.

**Lesson 5C**
Write three predictions: one with *will,* one with *going to,* and one with *might.*

**Lesson 6C**
Write three sentences using the present perfect continuous.

**Lesson 5D**
Give three expressions you can use to explain what's wrong.

**Lesson 6D**
Name a verb, a noun, and an adjective that are followed by a preposition.

# UNIT 7 Entertainment

**LANGUAGE** the passive ■ movies

## 7A Lights, camera, action!

**1 A** Match the types of movies in the box with pictures a–d.

> animation   action movie
> horror movie   romantic comedy

**B** Have you seen any of these types of movies recently? Which movies did you see?

Go to Vocabulary practice: movies, page 146

**2** Look at the picture in the text. What type of movie is *The Martian*? Would you like to see it?

### THE MARTIAN

**Plot**

The year is 2035. A team of astronauts is sent on a mission to Mars, but a storm forces them to abandon their mission and fly back to Earth. As they are preparing to leave, astronaut Mark Watney, played by Matt Damon, disappears. The team thinks he has been killed, so they leave without him. When NASA realizes he has survived, they organize a dangerous mission to save him before his supply of food, water, and oxygen runs out. Will he be rescued before it's too late?

**NASA's involvement**

Scientists at NASA worked closely with the director of *The Martian*, giving advice about the science behind space travel and the technology needed to survive on Mars. Jessica Chastain, who plays the commander of the Mars mission in the movie, spent time with astronaut Tracy Caldwell Dyson to learn more about life in space. Real missions to Mars are being planned for the 2040s, so NASA's advice was based on the latest research.

**Interesting facts**

- *The Martian* was directed by Ridley Scott, who has made other science-fiction movies, including *Alien* and *Blade Runner*.
- It was shot in Jordan because the desert is similar to the color of Mars.
- A few days before the movie was released, scientists discovered water on Mars.

**3** Read the text. Are the sentences true (T) or false (F)?

1. In the movie, Watney survives the storm and NASA tries to rescue him. _____
2. Jessica Chastain plays the astronaut Tracy Caldwell Dyson. _____
3. NASA is planning to send astronauts to Mars in our lifetime. _____
4. The director of *The Martian* was Matt Damon. _____
5. In the movie, the astronauts find water on Mars. _____

**4 A** What tenses and forms are the **bold** verbs in column A?

| Column A | | Column B |
|---|---|---|
| NASA **sends** a team of astronauts to Mars. | → | A team of astronauts ¹_____ to Mars. |
| NASA **is planning** real missions to Mars. | → | Real missions to Mars ²_____ . |
| The team thinks the storm **has killed** Watney. | → | The team thinks Watney ³_____ . |
| Ridley Scott **directed** *The Martian*. | → | *The Martian* ⁴_____ by Ridley Scott. |
| **Will** NASA **rescue** Watney before it's too late? | → | ⁵_____ Watney _____ before it's too late? |

58

the passive ■ movies   **LANGUAGE   7A**

**B** Complete the sentences in column B so they have the same meaning as the sentences in column A. Check your answers in the text.

**5 A** Look at the pairs of sentences in exercise 4A. Answer the questions.
1 Which sentences use the active form of the verbs? Which use the passive?
2 In column A, do we know who/what did the action of the verbs in **bold**? And in column B?

**B** Complete the rules and answer the questions about the passive. Then read the Grammar box.
1 We make the passive with the verb _____ and the _____ form of the main verb.
2 We change the tense of the passive by changing the tense of _____ .
3 What is more important: the action, or the person who did the action? _____
4 If we want to say who/what did the action, which word do we use? _____

### Grammar   the passive

Simple present:
English **is spoken** here.

Simple past:
The bridge **was built** in 2010.

Present continuous:
That new movie **is being shown**.

Present perfect:
My bag **has been stolen**!

Future with *will*:
My laptop **will be fixed** next week.

Go to Grammar practice: the passive, page 124

**6** ▶ 7.5 **Pronunciation:** past participles Look at the past participles. Say how the vowel sounds are pronounced: /oʊ/, /ʌ/ or /ɔ/. Listen, check, and repeat.

shown   chosen   won   lost   spoken   known   dubbed   done

**7 A** Complete the text with verbs in the passive using the past participles in exercise 6.

# Did you know …?

• When a movie ¹_____ , voice actors usually provide the dialogue in different languages, but sometimes the dubbing ²_____ by the original actors, for example, Jodie Foster (French) and Viggo Mortensen (Spanish).

• *The Martian* ³_____ on a screen in space shortly after it was released. Astronauts watched it on the International Space Station. Maybe one day, it will be watched on Mars!

• The name "Oscars" ⁴_____ by accident – an executive director of the Film Academy said the statues looked like her Uncle Oscar, and the name stuck! Since the awards began, about 3,000 Oscar awards ⁵_____ .

• It's surprising how many statues ⁶_____ ! Angelina Jolie hid hers and doesn't know where it is, and Matt Damon can't find his. Marlon Brando, who ⁷_____ best _____ for his role in *The Godfather*, lost both of his statues.

• Na'vi, the language created for the 2009 movie *Avatar*, ⁸_____ still _____ today! Fans learn new words and talk to other Na'vi speakers on learnnavi.org.

**B** ▶ 7.6 Listen and check. Practice saying the passive sentences with the correct pronunciation of the past participles.

Go to Communication practice: Student A page 161, Student B page 170

**8** In pairs, talk about your favorite movie. Use the questions to help you.

• What type of movie is it?
• Who was it directed by?
• Who stars in the movie?
• What is the plot of the movie?
• Where and when is it set?
• Is it based on a true story or a novel?
• Does it have good special effects and a good soundtrack?
• Was the movie shown with subtitles or was it dubbed?

**Personal Best**   Write five sentences with the passive about your favorite movie star.

59

# 7 | SKILLS | READING guessing the meaning of words from context ■ referencing: *this* and *that*

## 7B Action man

**1 A** Who's your favorite actor or action hero? Why?

**B** Look at the picture in the text on page 61. What job does the man on the left do? Read the text quickly and check. What's his name?

> **Skill** guessing the meaning of words from context
>
> You can sometimes guess what a word means by looking for clues in the word and in the sentence.
> • Look at the sentence and identify what type of word it is (verb, noun, adjective, etc.).
> • Identify any parts of the word that you already understand.
> • Look at the immediate context of the word in the clause and sentence, and look at the wider context of the word in the surrounding sentences.
> • After guessing the meaning, read the sentences again to see if your guess makes sense in context.

**2 A** Read the Skill box. Look at the **bold** words 1–6 in the text. What types of word are they?

**B** Choose the correct definition for the **bold** words. Underline the parts of the text that helped you guess the meaning from context.

| | | |
|---|---|---|
| 1 **a** a dangerous car | **b** a movie director | **c** a dangerous action |
| 2 **a** a camera | **b** where a movie is shot | **c** a screen |
| 3 **a** body parts | **b** damage to your body | **c** responsibilities |
| 4 **a** boring | **b** crazy | **c** fascinating |
| 5 **a** amazing | **b** climbing | **c** jumping |
| 6 **a** exciting | **b** falling | **c** dangerous |

**3** Read the text again and answer the questions.

1 Did the stunt in the first paragraph go well? Why was Vic worried?
2 Has Vic had a successful career? How do you know?
3 Who wrote a book about Vic?
4 How often does Vic get hurt in his job?
5 What do Vic's wife and children do?
6 When they were young, what kind of games did Vic play with his children?
7 Which movies does Vic have great memories of? Why?
8 What comparison is made between special effects and stunts?

**4** Underline four other words in the text that you don't know. Can you guess their meaning from the surrounding context?

> **Text builder** referencing: *this* and *that*
>
> We can use *this* and *that* to refer back to ideas that have already appeared in the text. The ideas can be nouns or whole phrases:
> Vic has broken **his legs, an arm, his ribs, and his nose. This** is only the start of a long list of injuries.
> **Vic jumped from a running horse onto a moving tank. That** even amazed director Steven Spielberg.

**5** Read the Text builder. Look at the fourth paragraph of the text. Find one example of *this* and one of *that*. Do they refer back to nouns or phrases?

**6** Discuss the questions in pairs.

1 Which movies have amazing special effects or stunts? Why are they amazing?
2 Would you like to be a stunt performer? Why/Why not?
3 What other jobs are there in the movie industry? Would you like to do any of them?

guessing the meaning of words from context ■ referencing: *this* and *that*   READING   SKILLS   7B

# World's greatest stunt performer

The car raced forward. It was already on fire, but the driver never stopped. The vehicle went up a ramp, into the sky, and then crashed into a bus. Finally, the driver got out and walked away, happy with the ¹**stunt**. Although it had gone smoothly, it had been hard to watch for Vic Armstrong, the stunt director on the ²**movie set**. The driver was his son, Scott, who was following in his father's footsteps in the most dangerous way possible.

Even though the general public has probably not heard of Vic Armstrong, everyone has certainly seen him in action because Vic is the world's greatest stunt performer. In his career, he has been the stunt double for almost every major Hollywood star, including Tom Cruise and Arnold Schwarzenegger, and he can play almost anyone as long as there's danger involved.

It's a life that has taken him all around the world. Armstrong has now written about his life in his autobiography, *The True Adventures of the World's Greatest Stuntman*, and it's a bone-crunching tale. In his career, Vic has broken his legs, an arm, his ribs, and his nose. This is only the start of a long list of ³**injuries** – bumps and bruises are an everyday occurrence in his working day. There's never a ⁴**dull** moment in his life of excitement, even if he himself admits that some of his stunts are a little risky, such as ⁵**leaping** out of a moving helicopter onto the side of a mountain.

Fortunately, Vic doesn't work alone. His company, Armstrong Action, is a family affair. Vic met his wife, Wendy, when they were both stunt performers on *Superman 2*. At the time, she was substituting the superhero's girlfriend, Lois Lane. Vic, of course, was Superman. His son Scott and their other three children eventually went into the business, too. That's hardly surprising because they were encouraged to face danger from an early age. When Vic's kids were just five years old, he put a special airbag in their garden for the children. This was for a game which involved jumping out of the upstairs window!

Their childhood wasn't all play, however. Vic's daughter Georgina first appeared on screen at the age of four, and was working with Steven Spielberg on the *Indiana Jones* movies before her seventh birthday. The *Indiana Jones* movies remain a career highlight for Vic, too, and not just because he was the stunt double for megastar Harrison Ford (pictured above with Vic). In one stunt, which is probably one of his most famous ones, Vic jumped from a running horse onto a moving tank. That even amazed director Steven Spielberg.

No special effects or computer-generated images can truly recreate how ⁶**thrilling** it is to see stunt performers jump off a building or set themselves on fire. Indeed, it is the work of people like Vic, Wendy, and their children that helps make these movies so exciting and realistic. Without people like the Armstrongs, there would be lights, camera … but no action!

Personal Best   Write a paragraph about what being a stunt performer involves.

# 7 LANGUAGE — modals of ability and possibility ■ TV and music

## 7C Got talent

**1** Complete the TV guide below with the types of programs in the box.

talent show   the news   game show   documentary

| Tuesday | What's on … |
|---|---|
| 18.30 | **Make a Fortune!** The ¹_____ where contestants win $1,000 for each correct answer. |
| 19.00 | **Natural Focus** This week's nature ²_____ looks at the marine life in Antarctica. |
| 20.00 | ³_____ **at 8** The latest stories from our reporters around the world. |
| 21.00 | **Sing! Sang! Sung!** It's the final of the popular ⁴_____ . Who will win the top prize? |

Go to Vocabulary practice: TV and music, page 147

**2** Answer the questions in pairs.
1 What types of shows do you like? What's your favorite TV series?
2 Who is your favorite singer or band? Have you ever seen them live?

**3 A** Look at the title of the text and the pictures. What type of show is it?

**B** Read the text. What talent do these two people have? What's unusual about their stories?

# WHO'S GOT TALENT?

*Got Talent* has been shown in over 60 countries and is now the most popular talent show in the world.
Here are two unusual stories from two different countries.

### Shaheen Jafargholi

Shaheen was 12 years old when he sang *Who's Lovin' You* by Michael Jackson on *Britain's Got Talent* and amazed the judges. He later received an invitation from the singer to perform during his "This Is It" tour. Tragically, Jackson died soon after, so Shaheen wasn't able to sing with his hero, but his family asked Shaheen to sing at Jackson's memorial concert in front of a TV audience of a billion people! He can act, too, having appeared in the soap opera *EastEnders*, and he'd like to be able to continue with his acting career in the future.

### Jennifer Grout

The audience laughed when 23-year-old Jennifer Grout couldn't understand the question, "What's your name?" the first time she appeared on *Arabs Got Talent*. Jennifer couldn't speak Arabic, but she was able to sing a perfect version of *Baeed Annak* by the Egyptian singer, Umm Kulthum. One judge commented, "You can't speak a word of Arabic, but you can sing better than some Arab singers!" Jennifer was one of the three finalists, and she hopes that in the future, she'll be able to make an album of traditional Moroccan music.

**4 A** Match the two parts to make complete sentences. Check your answers in the text.

1 Jackson died before the tour, so Shaheen **wasn't able to**
2 Shaheen **can**
3 He'd like **to be able to**
4 The audience laughed when Jennifer **couldn't**
5 Jennifer couldn't speak Arabic, but she **was able to**
6 She hopes that in the future, she**'ll be able to**

a continue with his acting career.
b act, too.
c sing with his hero.
d sing a perfect version of *Baeed Annak*.
e understand the question, "What's your name?"
f make an album of traditional Moroccan music.

modals of ability and possibility ■ TV and music     **LANGUAGE**     **7C**

**B** Look at the sentences in 4A again and answer the questions. Then read the Grammar box.

**1** Which tense or form are the words in **bold**? Match them with the forms below.

simple present _____     simple past     _____ , _____ , _____

future with *will* _____     infinitive form _____

**2** Complete the rules with *can, could, be able to,* or *was able to.*

We use _____ for present ability and possibility.

We use _____ or _____ for past ability and possibility.

For other tenses and forms, we use _____ .

> **Grammar**     **modals of ability and possibility**
>
> **Ability:**
> *She **can** play the piano really well.*
> *I **couldn't** swim when I was young.*
> *I**'ll be able to** speak French one day.*
> *Sam would like **to be able to** sing.*
>
> **Possibility:**
> *He **can't** come tonight because he's sick.*
> *I **couldn't** wait because I was in a hurry.*
> *I**'ll be able to** go skiing in the U.S.*
> *I **haven't been able to** visit him yet.*
>
> **Look!**  We usually use **can** for the simple present and **could** for the simple past and conditional forms.
> We use **be able to** for other tenses and forms when it's not possible to use a form of *can:*
>
> *After my exams, I**'ll be able to** relax.* NOT ~~I will can relax~~.

**Personal Best**

**Go to Grammar practice:** modals of ability and possibility, page 125

**5 A** ▶ 7.11  **Pronunciation:** /ey/ and /ʊ/ sounds Listen to the six sentences. Pay attention to the pronunciation of *able* and *could.*

**1** I haven't been able to exercise today.

**2** I've been able to drive since I was 17.

**3** I won't be able to go out tonight.

**4** I couldn't sleep late last weekend.

**5** When I was young, I could play an instrument.

**6** I couldn't understand the teacher earlier.

**B** ▶ 7.11  Listen again and repeat. Are the sentences true for you?

**6** ▶ 7.12  Complete the text with the verbs in the box and the correct form of *can/could* where possible, or *be able to.* Then listen and check.

play   not believe   live   paint (x2)   travel   walk

Aelita Andre was once described as the youngest professional artist in the world. She **1**_____ since she was nine months old. In fact, she **2**_____ before she **3**_____ or talk. When she was two, an art gallery director saw her paintings and decided to exhibit them. When he found out how old she was, he **4**_____ it.

Aelita's paintings have sold for thousands of dollars, and she **5**_____ to see them in prestigious art galleries all over the world.

She usually leads a pretty normal life. She **6**_____ the violin, is learning the drums, and would like to **7**_____ forever!

**Go to Communication practice:** Student A page 161, Student B page 170

**7 A** Complete each sentence with two pieces of information about yourself.

**1** I've never been able to _____ .

**2** I hope I'll be able to _____ in ten years.

**3** I'd love to be able to _____ in the future.

**4** I was able to _____ when I was younger.

**B** In pairs, ask and answer questions about the sentences in 7A. Give more information.

**A** *What have you never been able to do?*

**B** *Well, I've never been able to sing very well. I love singing, but I sound awful!*

**Personal Best**     Make excuses for missing a class yesterday, a party today, and a doctor's appointment tomorrow.     63

# 7 SKILLS SPEAKING  giving directions ■ asking for information

## 7D Could you tell me where it is?

**1** What do you prefer to do when you need directions to get somewhere? Why?
- use a folded map or street guide
- use a GPS or online map
- ask someone for directions

**2** ▶ 7.13 Watch or listen to the first part of *Learning Curve* and answer the questions.
1. Where is Taylor going?
2. What is she going to do there?
3. How does she try to get directions there?

**3** ▶ 7.13 Watch or listen again. Are the sentences true (T) or false (F)? Correct the false sentences.
1. Taylor is near a park. _____
2. She's on 23rd Street. _____
3. Ethan tells her to take 23rd Avenue and keep going straight past the park. _____
4. Penny tells her the movie theater is near the department store. _____

### Conversation builder | giving directions

**Describing the location**
The ... is on the other side of the ...
It's on the left/right.
It's across from/next to/near a ...
It's on Queen's Street.
It's ten minutes away on foot.

**Saying how to get there**
Take/Go up 23rd Street. / Follow this road.
Go straight ahead. / Keep going straight (until you get to/come to ...)
Take a right / Turn right (at the traffic circle).
Take the first right (after the traffic light).
Go down/up/along/around/through/past the ...

**4** Look at the map. Which icons represent the following places?

parking lot   restaurant   tourist information
cell-phone store   your house
hospital   gas station

**5** Give your partner directions to one of the places on the map. Don't say which place it is. Your partner will follow your directions and tell you which place the directions were for.

giving directions ■ asking for information **SPEAKING** **SKILLS** **7D**

**6** ▶ 7.14 Watch or listen to the second part of the show. Answer the questions.
1 How many movie theaters are there in the neighborhood? _____
2 What are they called? _____
3 Which theater does Taylor want? _____
4 Which road is it on? _____

**7** ▶ 7.14 How did Taylor ask the couple for directions? Complete the sentence. Watch or listen again and check.

> Excuse me. _____ to bother you, but do you know _____ the movie theater _____ ?

### Skill  asking for information

When we ask for information, we try to sound polite. We can also politely ask for clarification or confirmation of the information.
- Begin with a polite phrase. *Excuse me. / Sorry to bother you, but …*
- Use indirect questions, which sound more polite than direct ones.
  *Do you know where the theater is?* NOT ~~Do you know where is the theater?~~
  *Could you tell me where the movie theater is?* NOT ~~Could you tell me where is the movie theater?~~
- Use intonation to sound polite.
- Ask the person to clarify or confirm the information. *Sorry, did you say take a right? So, it's straight ahead and the first building on the left?*

**8** ▶ 7.15 Read the Skill box. Listen to five people asking for information. Check (✓) the things that each speaker does and complete the chart.

| speaker | begins with a polite phrase | uses an indirect question | uses polite intonation |
|---|---|---|---|
| 1 | | | |
| 2 | | | |
| 3 | | | |
| 4 | | | |
| 5 | | | |

**9 A** ▶ 7.16 Make indirect questions. Listen, check, and repeat.
1 Where's the park?
  Could you tell me where _____ ?
2 Does this bus stop near the movie theater?
  Do you know if _____ ?
3 Is the movie theater downtown?
  Do you know if _____ ?
4 What's the name of this area?
  Could you tell me what _____ ?
5 Are there any vegetarian restaurants in this town?
  Do you know if _____ ?

**B** In pairs, ask and answer the indirect questions. Add a polite phrase to begin.

Go to Communication practice: Student A page 161, Student B page 165

**10 A** **PREPARE** In pairs, choose a place in your town or city. Imagine you are there. Choose two other places and think about how to get there from your starting point.

**B** **PRACTICE** Take turns asking for and giving directions to the places. Be polite when you ask for the information, and ask for clarification or confirmation if necessary.

**C** **PERSONAL BEST** When you asked for information, did you sound polite? When you gave directions, were you clear? Can you make any improvements? Find another partner and ask and answer again.

**Personal Best** Write directions from your local bus or train station to your place of work or study.

# UNIT 8 Sports and health

**LANGUAGE** tag questions ■ sports, places, and equipment

## 8A On the field, in the pool

**1** ▶ 8.1 Listen to six sports commentators. Match the six sports places they mention with pictures a–f.

1 pool _____
2 circuit _____
3 court _____
4 field _____
5 track _____
6 rink _____

Go to Vocabulary practice: sports, places, and equipment, page 148

**2 A** ▶ 8.5 Listen to a radio program about the unusual sports in the pictures. Complete the notes in the chart below.

| sport | three-sided soccer | underwater hockey | bossaball |
|---|---|---|---|
| Where is it played? What equipment is used? | On a hexagonal [1]_____ with three goals and a ball. | In a swimming pool, using a [3]_____ to push a "puck." | On a [5]_____ filled with air, with trampolines on each side of a [6]_____ . |
| How do you win? | By letting in fewer goals than the other [2]_____ . | The team with the most [4]_____ wins. | You [7]_____ points by hitting or kicking the ball over the net. |

**B** Which of these sports would you like to try? Why?

**3** ▶ 8.6 Complete the host's questions with the tag questions in the box. Listen and check.

isn't it   have you   can you   aren't you   didn't you   don't you

1 You're going to tell us about some unusual sports, _____?
2 It's pretty much like normal soccer, _____?
3 You actually played in a game this weekend, _____?
4 You can't swim very well, _____?
5 You have one last sport to talk about, _____?
6 You haven't played bossaball yet, _____?

tag questions ■ sports, places, and equipment **LANGUAGE** **8A**

**4 A** Look at the sentences in exercise 3 again. When do we use tag questions? Choose a or b.
   a when we don't know the answer to the question
   b when we already know the answer, but we're just checking

   **B** Choose the best option to complete the rules. Then read the Grammar box.
   1 When the statement is affirmative, the tag question is *affirmative / negative*.
   2 When the statement is negative, the tag question is *affirmative / negative*.
   3 We form tag questions with *an auxiliary + pronoun / a pronoun + auxiliary*.

   > **Grammar** tag questions
   >
   > **Checking information:**
   > She **plays** volleyball, **doesn't she**?
   > We **saw** that movie last year, **didn't we**?
   > Tom **doesn't eat** meat, **does he**?
   >
   > **Starting a conversation:**
   > The bus **is** pretty late, **isn't it**?
   > You **worked** in the bank, **didn't you**?
   > The weather **isn't** very nice today, **is it**?

   Go to Grammar practice: tag questions, page 126

**5 A** ▶ 8.8 **Pronunciation:** intonation Listen to the sentences. Does the intonation in the tag question go up (↗) or down (↘)?
   1 We've been to this restaurant before, haven't we?
   2 You can't come to the party tonight, can you?
   3 Her last name's Henderson, isn't it?
   4 Your sister doesn't have a car, does she?
   5 You went to the gym this morning, didn't you?
   6 They won't stay at her house all week, will they?

   **B** ▶ 8.8 Listen again and repeat.

**6 A** Complete the sentences with a tag question.
   1 It's about eight thirty now, _____ ?
   2 The weather was awful yesterday, _____ ?
   3 You didn't come to class last week, _____ ?
   4 You aren't Canadian, _____ ?
   5 It'll be a nice day tomorrow, _____ ?
   6 You've done your homework, _____ ?

   **B** In pairs, ask and answer the questions in 6A. If necessary, change the information in the sentences so you're checking information you already know.
   A *It's about 7:15 now, isn't it?*   B *Yes, it is.*

   Go to Communication practice: Student A page 162, Student B page 171

**7 A** Ask and answer the questions in pairs. Try to remember your partner's answers, but don't write anything.

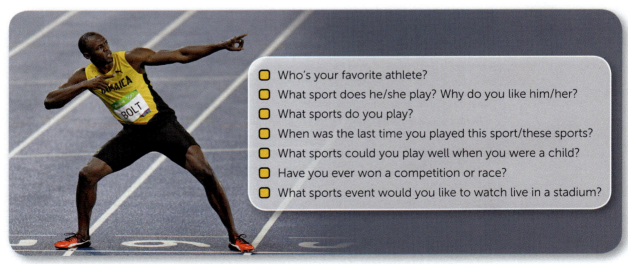

- Who's your favorite athlete?
- What sport does he/she play? Why do you like him/her?
- What sports do you play?
- When was the last time you played this sport/these sports?
- What sports could you play well when you were a child?
- Have you ever won a competition or race?
- What sports event would you like to watch live in a stadium?

   **B** Look at the questions again. In pairs, check the answers using tag questions.
   A *Your favorite athlete is Usain Bolt, isn't it?*
   B *Yes, it is. You're right. / No, it isn't. It's Cristiano Ronaldo.*

**Personal Best** Write six statements with tag questions to start a conversation with someone.

# 8 SKILLS LISTENING understanding facts and figures ■ intonation ■ health and fitness

## 8B So many ways to get in shape

**1 A** Are the health and fitness facts and figures below true or false? Discuss your answers in pairs.

### Health and fitness facts and figures

1. In a lot of countries, people spend millions on **healthy lifestyle** choices (gyms, fitness clubs, healthy food). They spend more than double the amount on fast food.
2. 37% of people who pay for gym memberships to **get in shape** never use them.
3. About two thirds of adults are **overweight** or need to lose weight.
4. For a healthy, **balanced diet**, men need 2,000 calories a day, and women need 2,500.

**B** What do the words in **bold** mean? Compare your ideas in pairs.

**Go to Vocabulary practice:** health and fitness verb phrases, page 149

**2** Answer the questions in pairs.
1. Do any of the facts in exercise 1A surprise you?
2. Do you have a healthy lifestyle?
3. What do you think the objects in the picture to the right are?
4. How do you think they help people get in shape?

**3**  8.10 Watch or listen to the first part of *Learning Curve*. Check (✓) the facts which are mentioned.
a Ethan's app counts how many steps he takes every day. ☐
b The word *pedometer* means "foot measurer." ☐
c Pedometers were invented in Greece. ☐
d One in three people doesn't get any exercise at all. ☐
e People who work out with a partner are more motivated to get exercise. ☐
f The average cost of a gym is $700 a year. ☐

### 🔧 Skill  understanding facts and figures

When listening for detailed information, we often need to understand facts and figures accurately.
- Before you listen, find out what type of information you need to listen for. For example, is it a number, a person, a time, a place, etc?
- Use the general context to predict when you'll hear numbers, e.g., when talking about times, dates, distances, prices, and percentages.
- Recognize words that often follow numbers: currencies ($, £, €), percent, decimal points, and ways of describing statistics: *one in four people, one fifth of the population, the average, three times as many*.

**4** ▶ 8.10 Read the Skill box. Watch or listen again and answer the questions.
1. How many extra steps do pedometer users take every day? _____
2. What percentage of people in the U.S. get enough physical activity? _____
3. How many miles do people walk if they take 10,000 steps a day? _____
4. What percentage of couples who exercise separately quit? _____
5. What percentage of couples who exercise together quit? _____

understanding facts and figures ■ intonation ■ health and fitness   **LISTENING**   **SKILLS**   **8B**

**5** Discuss the questions in pairs. Give reasons for your answers.
1 Do you enjoy walking as a way to keep active?
2 Have you ever used a pedometer, or would you like to try one?
3 Is exercising with a friend or partner a good idea?

**6** ▶ 8.11 Watch or listen to the second part of the show. Are the sentences true or false? Correct the false sentences.
1 Bindi does weightlifting once a week. _____
2 Taylor's client is training for the Ironman triathlon. _____
3 Ironman athletes swim 2.4 miles, cycle 112 miles and run 26 miles. _____
4 Half a marathon is 30 miles. _____
5 Joe has always been in good shape and healthy. _____
6 Joe and his wife took up ballroom dancing. _____
7 Neither Joe nor Louis go to the gym. _____
8 Louis doesn't get a lot of exercise. _____

**7** Would you like to take up triathlon training, weightlifting, or ballroom dancing? Why / Why not? Discuss in pairs.

> **Listening builder** intonation
>
> When listening to fast English, listen for phrases which help you follow units of meaning. In a phrase, the intonation usually falls towards the end.
> *There are so many ways to get in shape.*
> *Some people play sports, while others eat a balanced diet and stay active.*

**8 A** ▶ 8.12 Read the Listening builder. Listen to these sentences. How many phrases does the speaker use?
1 She's trained with me for three months and works very hard.
2 We take classes twice a week and go out dancing every Saturday night.
3 One study looked at married people who joined a gym together.
4 At the end of the day, people feel good when they meet their goals.

**B** ▶ 8.12 Listen again and pay attention to the intonation. Then practice saying the sentences.

**9** In groups, discuss the following statement:

> *Our generation is a lot healthier than our parents and grandparents were at our age.*

You could talk about the following things:

amount of exercise   diet   amount of stress   sleep   good or bad habits

**Personal Best**   Describe a healthy day you've had recently and an unhealthy one.

69

# 8 LANGUAGE  modals of obligation and advice

## 8C Is there an app for that?

**1 A** What apps do you have on your phone? What are they for? How often do you use them?

**B** Look at the three apps. What do you think each app does? How can they help you improve your health?

**2 A** Read the posts by Sophie, Tom, and Kate below. They ask their friend Rob, a fitness expert, for advice. What problems do they have? Choose the correct options.

1 Sophie *can't sleep at night / isn't sure how much sleep she needs*.
2 Tom *feels out of shape / wants to lose weight*.
3 Kate *is looking for a new job / is stressed out*.

**B** Which app do you think Rob recommends for each person? Read his replies and check.

**Sophie**
I have to get up at 5 a.m. every day as I start work at 7. I don't go to bed till after midnight, so I'm only getting 5 hours of sleep a night. When I drive to work, I'm so sleepy! How do I know if I'm getting enough sleep? @RobDanes, you have a lot of health apps – can you recommend one for me?

**Rob**
Check out *Sleep Friend*. It tells you when you should go to bed and get up. It also monitors sleep cycles, so it knows when you're in a light sleep or a deep sleep, and its alarm goes off when you're sleeping lightly. You should get more than 6 hours of sleep a night, though, and you can't drive when you're very tired!

**Tom**
Rob, I didn't know you were such an expert! Got any suggestions for me? This morning I had to run for the bus, and I felt awful. I'm so out of shape. I really have to get more exercise, but I just don't have time to go to the gym or take fitness classes.

**Rob**
Hi Tom! You don't have to go to the gym to get in shape. Try the *Workout for 7* app. It's really worked for me. You exercise really hard for 7 minutes, and it has the same effect as going running or working out at the gym. The app shows you exactly what to do.

**Kate**
While you're giving everyone advice, Rob, can you give me some? I really need to chill out. I'm so anxious about my new job that I can't relax, and it's really worrying me. I've heard that meditation can help. Is there an app for that?

**Rob**
Hey Kate! You shouldn't worry about it – we all get stressed. Just learn some meditation techniques that you can do at home regularly. Get the *iRelax* app. It shows you what to do, creates a meditation schedule, and reminds you when to do it. Good luck and let's get together soon.

**3 A** Are the sentences true (T) or false (F)? Correct the false sentences.

1 *Sleep Friend* wakes you up when you're in a deep sleep. _____
2 *Workout for 7* isn't as good as going running. _____
3 *iRelax* tells you when to meditate. _____

modals of obligation and advice   LANGUAGE  8C

**B** Complete the sentences with the words in the box. Who said each sentence? Check your answers in the text.

can't   have to (x2)   should   don't have to   shouldn't

1 I _____ get up at 5 a.m. every day.
2 You _____ get more than six hours of sleep.
3 You _____ drive when you're very tired!
4 I really _____ do more exercise.
5 You _____ go to the gym to get in shape.
6 You _____ worry about it.

**4** Match the sentences in exercise 3B with functions a–f. Then read the Grammar box.

a It isn't necessary to do this. There isn't any obligation. _____
b I think it's a good idea to do this. _____
c It's prohibited or against the law to do this. _____
d I don't think it's a good idea to do this. _____
e It's necessary to do this. It's an external obligation. _____
f It's necessary to do this. It's a personal obligation. _____

### Grammar   modals of obligation and advice

**Obligation:**
We **have to** be at the airport at 2 p.m.
She **has to** remember to get Jo a birthday present.

**Prohibition:**
You **can't** take photos in the museum.

**No obligation:**
I **don't have to** get up early. It's Sunday.

**Advice:**
You **should** go to bed earlier.
You **shouldn't** swim after eating.

Go to Grammar practice: modals of obligation and advice, page 127

**5 A** ▶ 8.14 **Pronunciation: sentence stress** Listen to the sentences. <u>Underline</u> the stressed words or syllables.

1 She has to leave now.
2 You don't have to pay to enter.
3 I have to remember my keys this time!
4 You can't speak during the test.
5 They should get a cab.
6 You shouldn't eat so much cheese.

**B** ▶ 8.14 Listen again and repeat the sentences.

**6 A** ▶ 8.15 Listen to a radio program about rules and laws in different countries. Complete the sentences with the missing information and the correct form of have to, can, or should.

1 In some places in India, people studying to be teachers _____ take _____ classes, and soon police officers will _____ do the same.
2 In some Indian states, you _____ use your _____ while driving, even if it's a hands-free device.
3 In the U.S., you _____ talk too loudly on your cell phone. It can be considered _____ .
4 In Canada, you _____ wear a _____ when riding a motorcycle and a normal bicycle.
5 On the Internet, it says that in California you _____ ride your bike in a _____ !
6 In France, children _____ go to school on _____ , but they _____ go on Wednesday afternoons, or wear a uniform.

**B** Is it the same or different in your country? Discuss in pairs.

Go to Communication practice: Student A page 162, Student B page 171

**7** In pairs, talk about …
- something you've had to get up really early for.
- something important you have to remember to do this month.
- something you'll have to do next year.
- something a relative or teacher often says you should or shouldn't do.
- something you can't do in high school/in college/at work.
- something you often had to do when you were younger.

**Personal Best**   Write a message asking Rob for advice. Then write Rob's reply.

71

# 8 SKILLS  WRITING  writing a report ■ adding information

## 8D Sports in my country

**1** Read the webpage and look at the pictures. Have you tried any of these sports, seen them live, or watched them on TV? Discuss in pairs.

### International *SPORTS* Organization

Which sports are popular in your country? Which sports activities would you recommend to a visitor to your country? Write a report for ISO members about sports in your country, and we will post it on this webpage.

Jude, U.S.

baseball  football  basketball

POSTED: 12 May

SEE *MORE* ...

David, Argentina

soccer  surfing  volleyball

POSTED: 18 May

SEE *MORE* ...

Maarit, Finland

ice-swimming  hockey  pesäpallo

POSTED: 25 May

SEE *MORE* ...

**2 A** Read the first paragraph of a report from the website. Who wrote the report: Jude, David, or Maarit?

### Sports in my country

1 _____
Sports are a very popular leisure activity in my country, and there are fantastic facilities in most towns and cities. Finland has a very cold climate, though, and in winter, parts of the country are covered with snow for six months. This means that people enjoy doing different sports activities in different seasons.

2 _____
Cross-country skiing is an extremely popular sport here. As there are very few mountains in Finland, people ski on flat land through the country's forests. It is a great way to stay in shape and enjoy the country's natural beauty. Ice skating and hockey are popular as well as skiing. Moreover, hockey, ski jumping, and snowboarding are popular spectator sports.

3 _____
A lot of Finns enjoy swimming in indoor and outdoor pools, in the sea, or in the country's lakes. In addition to this, thousands of people regularly go ice-swimming.

They go to frozen lakes where they cut holes in the ice and jump in the water. I would recommend going ice-swimming after a visit to a hot sauna, which is another national tradition.

4 _____
It is easy to play any of the world's most popular sports here. There are tennis courts and soccer fields everywhere, and basketball has recently become very popular. In addition, if you are interested in discovering Finnish sports, I suggest trying pesäpallo. This is a fast-moving bat-and-ball sport that is similar to baseball and is usually played in the warmer summer months.

5 _____
Sports are a big part of life in Finland. This is one reason why the country produces many world champions, like Formula One auto-racing driver Mika Häkkinen. It is possible to practice any major sport here, but while you are visiting us, remember to try out our local sports and traditional activities as well.

**B** Read the whole report. Do you think it's interesting and easy to follow? Discuss in pairs.

writing a report ■ adding information **WRITING** | **SKILLS** | **8D**

---

🔧 **Skill**  writing a report

**Make your report interesting and easy for the reader to follow.**
- Organize the content of your report into sections with one main topic in each section. A section can contain one or more paragraphs.
- Use headings for each section of your report.
- Include relevant factual information, and make some suggestions or recommendations for the reader, e.g. *I suggest + -ing, I would recommend + -ing, remember to + base form.*
- Reports are usually fairly formal, so avoid using informal language.

---

**3 A** Read the Skill box. Match headings a–e with sections 1–5 in the report.

a Our success at sports _____
b National and international sports _____
c Sports and climate in my country _____
d Winter sports _____
e Water sports _____

**B** What recommendations does the writer make? Match sentence parts 1–3 with a–c to make complete sentences. Then check your answers in the text.

1 I would recommend
2 If you are interested in discovering Finnish sports, I suggest
3 While you are visiting us, remember

a trying pesäpallo.
b to try out our local sports and traditional activities.
c going ice-swimming.

---

🧩 **Text builder**  adding information

**We can use these phrases to add information to a sentence or paragraph:**

| | |
|---|---|
| **as well** | There is a national tournament every year, and there are several regional competitions, **as well**. |
| **as well as** | Swimming, bicycling, and walking are all popular with adults, **as well as** children. |
| **In addition (to this)** | **In addition to** road cycling, track cycling is popular as a spectator sport. |
| | We have had great international success in soccer in recent years. **In addition**, our national basketball team has won the World Championship twice. |

**Look!** We can use *moreover* instead of *in addition* in more formal writing:
*Sports keep you in shape.* **Moreover**, *they are a good way to meet people.*

---

**4** Read the Text builder. Look at the report again and answer the questions.

1 Find one example of each *as well* phrase in Maarit's report.
2 What does *this* refer to in the *In addition to this* phrase?

**5** Write complete sentences with the prompts and the phrases in **bold**.

1 many parks / public tennis courts / table tennis tables
**as well as**
2 Formula One / a popular spectator sport / motorcycle racing / becoming more popular
**in addition**
3 our beaches / perfect for inexperienced surfers / advanced surfers
**as well**
4 this traditional game / great fun / it / a great way to stay in shape
**moreover**
5 our soccer team / won the World Cup / our baseball team / very successful
**in addition to this**

**6 A** PREPARE Think about which sports are popular in your country and what recommendations you would make for a visitor. Plan four or five section headings.

**B** PRACTICE Use the Skill box to help you write a report on sports in your country. Include relevant information under each section heading.

**C** PERSONAL BEST Choose two or three sections from your report. Read them aloud to your partner, but don't read the section heading. Can your partner guess the headings for each section?

---

**Personal Best** Think of a sports activity in your local area that people can do for free. Add an extra section to your report.

# 7 and 8 REVIEW and PRACTICE

## Grammar

**1** Choose the correct options to complete the sentences.
1. The play *Romeo and Juliet* _____ by Shakespeare.
   a wrote   b was written   c be written
2. I would like to _____ play the guitar like you.
   a can   b could   c be able to
3. Stephen's been working there for years, _____ ?
   a is he   b isn't he   c hasn't he
4. You _____ take a taxi to the airport. I can drive you.
   a don't have to   b have to   c couldn't
5. The new James Bond movie _____ in Mexico.
   a is going to filmed   b is going to be filmed
   c is going to be film
6. _____ speak to Mike or Alan this week?
   a Have you able to   b Have you been able to
   c Have you could
7. It won't rain this afternoon, _____ ?
   a won't it   b it won't   c will it
8. You _____ use your cell phone while you're driving. It's against the law.
   a can't   b don't have to   c have to

**2** Use the structures in parentheses to complete the sentences so they mean the same as the first sentence.
1. I think you passed the test. Am I right? (tag question)
   You passed the test, _____ ?
2. I hope I can go up the Empire State Building when I visit New York. (modal of possibility)
   I hope I'll _____ up the Empire State Building when I visit New York.
3. George Lucas directed the first *Star Wars* movie. (passive)
   The first *Star Wars* movie _____ George Lucas.
4. It's not necessary to pay to use expressway in the UK. (modal of obligation)
   You _____ to use expressways in the UK.
5. The new factory will make over 500,000 cars a year. (passive)
   Over 500,000 cars a year _____ at the new factory.
6. I couldn't drive until I was 22 years old. (modal of ability)
   I wasn't _____ until I was 22 years old.
7. I don't think you'll be able to come to my wedding. Is that true? (tag question)
   You won't be able to come to my wedding, _____ ?
8. It's not a good idea to go swimming just after lunch. (modal of advice)
   You _____ just after lunch.

**3** Choose the correct options to complete the text.

## Could you be a mentor?

Developing your new career or business ¹*can / can't* be easier with a mentor – someone with experience in the same industry who can help and encourage you. One famous mentor was Steve Jobs, who ²*was guided by / guided* Mark Zuckerberg in the early days of Facebook. We talk to Laura and Rob about their experience of mentoring.

Laura, what does the role of mentor involve?

My role is to encourage Rob and give him advice, like "You ³*should / can* do some more market research."

But you can't make decisions for him, ⁴*can / can't* you?

No. Rob ⁵*has / doesn't have* to make his own decisions. A good mentor ⁶*can / has to* believe in the person's ability to develop.

Rob, you had a difficult time before you met Laura, ⁷*hadn't / didn't* you?

Yes. I had a lot of knowledge about the industry, but no experience. Laura's given me a lot of practical advice, which has helped build my confidence. I got a promotion yesterday, and it's great to know I ⁸*could / 'll be able to* talk to her about any issues that come up in my new role.

## Vocabulary

**1** Circle the word that is different. Explain your answer.

| | | |
|---|---|---|
| 1 | documentary | thriller |
|   | director | action movie |
| 2 | pool | field |
|   | racket | court |
| 3 | track and field | diving |
|   | track | auto racing |
| 4 | game show | channel |
|   | sitcom | soap opera |
| 5 | tracks | playlist |
|   | hits | cast |
| 6 | have a balanced diet | get a good night's sleep |
|   | get exercise | have bad habits |
| 7 | net | bat |
|   | stick | rink |

**REVIEW and PRACTICE** **7** and **8**

**2** Match the words in the box with definitions 1–10.

> plot court be in shape sequel script soundtrack
> romantic comedy audience episode cartoon

1 have good physical health because of
exercise _____
2 the music that is played during a movie _____
3 the story of a movie or book _____
4 a funny movie about love _____
5 the place where you play ball games _____
6 a part of a TV series _____
7 a TV show with characters that are
drawn _____
8 a movie that continues the story of a previous
movie _____
9 the people who watch a TV show live in the
studio _____
10 the written form of a movie _____

**3** Complete the sentences with the words in the box.

> live set in scene hits get stressed
> horror musicals album

1 I don't usually enjoy _____ because I don't like it
when the story is told through songs.
2 Have you ever seen your favorite singer _____ in
concert?
3 The movie *Titanic* stars Leonardo DiCaprio and is
_____ 1912.
4 It's not healthy to _____ so often.
5 I think this is the band's best _____ . It has lots of their
biggest _____ on it.
6 That's the most terrifying _____ movie I've ever seen!
7 My favorite _____ in the movie is the car chase
through Moscow.

**4** Put the words in the box in the correct columns.

> series shot net playlist ice skating subtitles
> on tour ads ball talk show band the news
> animation circuit goal special effects

| movies | TV |
|---|---|
| | |
| **sports** | **music** |
| | |

# Personal Best

**Lesson 7A**
Name four movies you've seen and say what types of movies they are.

**Lesson 8A**
Name three sports places and three pieces of sports equipment.

**Lesson 7A**
Describe a movie in four sentences that use the passive.

**Lesson 8A**
Write three questions about your classmates using tag questions.

**Lesson 7B**
Write two sentences. In the second sentence, use *this* or *that* to refer to something in the first sentence.

**Lesson 8B**
Describe a healthy lifestyle using at least four verb phrases.

**Lesson 7C**
Name four TV shows you dislike and say what types of shows they are.

**Lesson 8C**
Write two sentences giving advice to a friend, using *should* and *shouldn't*.

**Lesson 7C**
Write three sentences about a friend using *be able to* in different forms.

**Lesson 8C**
Write three sentences about your English class using *have to*, *don't have to*, and *can't*.

**Lesson 7D**
Say three expressions you can use when you give directions.

**Lesson 8D**
Add some information to your sentence with *have to* (8C), using *as well as*.

75

# UNIT 9

# Food

**LANGUAGE** | uses of *like* ■ food and cooking

## 9A Chefs at home

**1** Look at the pictures. Find the words for each item of food in the text.

a _____  b _____  c _____  d _____  e _____  f _____  g _____

**2** Read the text. Would you like to try any of the dishes? Which one(s)?

## TOP CHEFS ... AT HOME

They're famous around the world for the delicious food in their restaurants. But what do the world's top chefs like to cook for themselves at the end of a long day or week at work?

**Mitsuharu Tsumura** (Lima)
Mitsuharu cooks sukiyaki for his family on Sunday. It's a meat dish, usually thinly sliced beef, which is slowly cooked at the table with vegetables, **soy sauce**, and sugar. The meat is then dipped in a small bowl of egg.

**Alain Allegretti** (New York)
Alain loves cooking pasta at the end of a long day when he wants something quick, easy, and delicious. He suggests having it with **garlic** and **olive oil**, or with tomatoes and herbs.

**Angela Hartnett** (London)
When Angela is in a hurry, she makes canned tuna on **toast** with mayonnaise. For a simple yet special treat, her favorite dish is scrambled eggs on toast, which she recommends cooking very slowly.

**Daniel Boulud** (New York)
Daniel makes *salade meridionale* at home when he wants to relax. It's a salad with **shellfish**, **avocado**, eggplant, olives, peppers, **zucchini**, and other vegetables, with pesto and lemon.

Go to Vocabulary practice: food and cooking, page 150

**3 A** ▶ 9.4 Listen to three people talking about a dish they like. Put the dishes in the order they are mentioned from 1–3.

a ☐  b ☐  c ☐

uses of *like* ■ food and cooking      LANGUAGE 9A

**B** ▶9.4 Match questions 1–3 with replies a–g. Listen again and check your answers.
1 What do you like to eat at the end of a long day? ____ ____ ____
2 What's it like? ____ ____ ____
3 Would you like to try it? ____

a It's like spaghetti, but thicker.
b It's delicious.
c Soup with meatballs.
d No, thanks. I've already eaten!
e This! It's called *poutine*.
f Really tasty.
g Udon noodles.

**4** Underline four phrases with *like* in exercise 3B. Match them with the meanings of *like* (a–d) below. Then read the Grammar box.
a asking about a preference _____
b saying that something is similar _____
c asking for a description of something _____
d making a polite offer _____

> **Grammar** uses of *like*
>
> Talking about preferences:
> What do you **like** doing on Sundays?
> I **like** going to the movies.
>
> Talking about similarity:
> He**'s like** his father – very lazy!
> She **looks like** her mother.
>
> Asking for a description:
> What**'s** the weather **like**?
> What **was** the party **like**?
>
> Making a polite offer or request:
> **Would** you **like** a cup of coffee?
> I**'d like** the chicken salad, please.
>
> **Look!** We also use **would like** for something you want to do or have:
> I**'d like** to go home now.   I**'d** really **like** a motorcycle.

**Personal Best**

Go to Grammar practice: uses of *like*, page 128

**5 A** ▶9.6 **Pronunciation:** /dʒ/ sound *Did you* and *would you* can be pronounced with a /dʒ/ sound (like *job*). Listen to the questions. When do you hear /dʒ/?
1 Would you like some tea?
2 What would you like for dinner?
3 Did you like the shellfish?
4 What did you eat for breakfast?

**B** ▶9.6 Listen again and repeat. In pairs, ask and answer the questions.

**6 A** Complete the conversation with the correct form of *like*.

A ¹_____ food from other countries?
B Yes, I do. I really ²_____ Thai and Japanese food. Actually, I make it for my roommates. The flavors are amazing.
A ³_____ the last dish you made?
B Yes, they did! I made sashimi. It ⁴_____ sushi, but without rice. I served it with soy sauce and wasabi.
A What ⁵_____ ?
B It was delicious – really fresh and tasty, and the wasabi was really hot.
A Mmmm, I ⁶_____ to try that! Tell me, ⁷_____ to work as a chef?
B Yes, I'd love to.

**B** In pairs, practice the conversation. Change the replies so they are true for you.

Go to Communication practice: Student A page 162, Student B page 171

**7** Discuss the questions in pairs.
1 What do you like to cook or eat at the end of a long day? And at the end of the week?
2 Are you a good cook? Which dishes would you like to learn to make?
3 What was the first meal you cooked? What did it taste like?
4 What's your favorite dish for a special occasion? What's it like?
5 Have you ever eaten an unusual food or dish? What was it like?

**Personal Best** Write a short conversation about food. Use *like* in at least four different ways.

77

# 9 SKILLS | READING — reading for detail ▪ substitution: *one, ones*

# 9B Chocolate – the world's favorite superfood

**1** What do you think a *superfood* is? Read the first paragraph of the text on page 79 and check your answer.

**2** Read the whole text quickly. Why is chocolate a superfood? Which five benefits are mentioned?

> ### 🔧 Skill — reading for detail
>
> **When answering multiple-choice questions, you often have to look for detailed information in a text.**
> - First, read the text quickly. Then read the questions and <u>underline</u> the key words.
> - Scan the text and find the part that contains the information you need. Read that part in detail.
> - If a word from the answer options appears in the text, it doesn't mean that option is the correct answer. Read the sentence carefully to make sure the meaning of the option is the same as in the text.

**3** Read the Skill box. Then read the text again and choose the correct answers.

1 The author says that superfoods
   a are exciting.  b are unexciting.  c are unexciting, except for chocolate.

2 Where does cacao come from?
   a Panama  b Central America  c Germany

3 Why did the Kuna people have low blood pressure?
   a They drank tea.  b They were healthy.  c They drank cacao.

4 Which kind of chocolate has the most health benefits?
   a dark chocolate  b milk chocolate  c white chocolate

5 Which benefit does the author say is the most unusual?
   a Chocolate protects us from illness.
   b Chocolate makes us feel like we're in love.
   c Chocolate increases our intelligence.

6 What does the author warn the reader about? Choose two answers.
   a Chocolate isn't as healthy nowadays as it used to be.
   b Food with a high fat content can cause heart disease.
   c It's important to know who paid for the studies about chocolate and health.

> ### 🧩 Text builder — substitution: *one, ones*
>
> To avoid repeating a noun from earlier in the sentence or in a previous sentence, we can substitute the word *one* (singular) or *ones* (plural):
> ***Foods** that have received this label have been unexciting **ones** like spinach, garlic, or salmon.*
> *This creates the same **feeling** as the **one** you get when you fall in love.*

**4** Read the Text builder. <u>Underline</u> the eight examples of *one* or *ones* in the text. Which four are used to avoid repeating a noun? Which nouns are they substituting?

**5** Read the sentences. <u>Underline</u> the words that *one* or *ones* replace.

1 My train was delayed when I got to the station. The next one was an hour later, so I had to wait.
2 I was offered two free apps when I bought my phone. The ones I chose were both games.
3 There are lots of great restaurants all over the city, but the best ones are down by the harbor.
4 Every student was given the same math problem, but I was the only one who could solve it.
5 We serve lots of dishes in my restaurant, but the most popular ones are red curry and lasagna.

**6** In pairs, discuss the questions.

1 Is there any food that is a "guilty pleasure" for you?
2 Have you heard of any other superfoods? Do you eat them?
3 Do you believe the reports about the health benefits of superfoods?

78

# Chocolate – the superfood!

It's official! Chocolate is good for you! A team of researchers at the German Institute of Human Nutrition have discovered that there are many health benefits of eating chocolate every day. In fact, it's so good for you that it's being labeled the latest "superfood." Up to now, foods that have received this label have been unexciting ones like spinach, garlic, or salmon. Thankfully, now that chocolate has joined that elite group, we can all relax. That chocolate bar in your desk at lunchtime is no longer a guilty pleasure – it's a superfood.

Like many natural products, people have known for centuries that chocolate was a good thing, especially in Central America where cacao originated. The Aztec emperor Montezuma was particularly partial to it, drinking an estimated 50 cups a day (as an emperor with the power of life and death over his people, clearly nobody was brave enough to tell him that he couldn't have another one). Among the Kuna people of Panama, cacao was drunk like tea, and consequently, they had very low blood pressure.

There are many health benefits to eating chocolate on a regular basis. It's packed with minerals, especially ones such as selenium and zinc, which help fight disease. Chocolate is also an excellent source of flavanols, chemicals that lower your blood pressure and help keep your brain healthy, although neither milk nor white chocolate contain as high a percentage of these beneficial properties as dark chocolate does.

In addition to improving your physical health, chocolate makes you feel better, too. Researchers have discovered that eating chocolate releases a chemical in the brain that makes your heart beat more quickly. This creates the same feeling as the one you get when you fall in love. Perhaps most surprising of all, though, is the discovery that chocolate makes you smarter. One study found that countries where people eat the most chocolate also have the most Nobel Prizes. One example is Switzerland, home to Albert Einstein, where people eat an average of 9.5 kilos of chocolate a year!

Despite the evidence, some health experts remain critical of our love for chocolate. Unlike the Aztecs, people today rarely consume chocolate in its pure form. Instead, modern chocolate is often combined with milk and sugar, increasing its fat content. This means that professionals advise that chocolate should be consumed in moderation and only as part of a healthy diet.

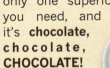

There is one further warning. Some critics have taken a critical look at the "chocolate is good" news stories. They point out that some of the research "proving" the health benefits of chocolate was funded by the chocolate industry, so I recommend that you keep this in mind. Despite these criticisms, there's no doubt that chocolate makes you feel good. So, forget spinach, blueberries, and all the others – there's only one superfood you need, and it's **chocolate, chocolate, CHOCOLATE!**

Write a paragraph about a healthy item of food.

# 9 LANGUAGE    -ing forms and infinitives ■ eating out

## 9C Eating out

**1** Look at the webpage below. What is unusual about Nadia's Place? Do you think a restaurant like this is a good idea?

**2** Complete blanks 1–4 in the menu with the words in the box.

Desserts   Main courses   Side dishes   Appetizers

**Go to Vocabulary practice:** eating out, page 151

**3** Discuss the questions in pairs.
1 Think about the last time you ate out. What was the food, atmosphere, and service like?
2 What food would you order at Nadia's Place?

**4** ▶ 9.9 Listen to an interview with Nadia. Order the topics she talks about from 1–5.
a ☐ future plans
b ☐ reactions to honesty payment
c ☐ how successful the business is
d ☐ the atmosphere
e ☐ reasons for opening Nadia's Place

**5 A** ▶ 9.10 Complete the sentences with the correct form of the verb in parentheses. Then listen and check.
1 Tell us why you decided _____ (open) a café-restaurant with no prices.
2 I opened this place _____ (do) something different.
3 _____ (eat) here is like having lunch at a friend's house.
4 It's a real community, and it's easy _____ (meet) new people.
5 I love _____ (come) to work each and every day!
6 In fact, we're thinking about _____ (open) a second café in an old theater.

**B** Match the sentences in 5A with rules a–f. Then read the Grammar box.

We use the -ing form:
a after some verbs, e.g., *like, love, enjoy, finish*. _____
b after prepositions. _____
c when a verb is the subject of the sentence. _____

We use the infinitive with *to*:
d after some verbs, e.g., *afford, decide, want*. _____
e after adjectives. _____
f to give a reason. _____

-ing forms and infinitives ■ eating out　　LANGUAGE　9C

### Grammar  -ing forms and infinitives

**-ing forms:**
- after some verbs:
As soon as he **finished eating**, he asked for the check.
- after prepositions:
I'm not very good **at remembering** people's names.
- when a verb is the subject of the sentence:
**Drinking** too much coffee is bad for you.

**Infinitives:**
- after some verbs:
We **decided to leave** a big tip as the service was excellent.
- after adjectives:
It's **nice to try** something different when you eat out.
- to give a reason:
I searched online **to find** a place that sells leather bags.

**Go to Grammar practice:** -ing forms and infinitives, page 129

**6 A** ▶9.12 **Pronunciation:** -ing  -ing is pronounced with an /ɪŋ/ sound (like *sing*), but in informal conversation, it is sometimes pronounced /ɪn/ (like *bin*). Listen to the sentences. When do you hear /ɪn/?
1  I'm not very good at doing the dishes.
2  Making birthday cakes is great fun.
3  I'm not very interested in reading books.
4  I don't mind driving if you're too tired.
5  He's interested in learning Arabic.
6  Choosing a dessert is always difficult!

**B** ▶9.12  Listen again and repeat the sentences.

**7** Choose the correct options to complete the text.

I'd heard about an interesting new café in town, so yesterday, a friend and I went there ¹*to try / trying* it. It's a really unusual place: the food and drink is free, but you pay for each minute you're there. Lots of people enjoy ²*to spend / spending* time in a café, but not everyone can afford ³*to buy / buying* lots of food and drink, so this café is a nice alternative.

Everyone has to make his or her own drinks and snacks and do the dishes, so it's a bit like ⁴*to be / being* at home. We made ourselves some toast and coffee. ⁵*To use / Using* the coffee machine was a bit challenging, but we managed it in the end!

At first, my friend found it hard ⁶*to relax / relaxing* completely as she was watching the clock and counting every minute, but the atmosphere was friendly, and ⁷*to have / having* the freedom to make our own drinks and snacks was great. We're definitely going back, and my friend has promised ⁸*to not / not to* worry about the clock next time!

**Go to Communication practice:** Student A page 163, Student B page 171

**8 A** Work in pairs. Complete the sentences with the correct form of the verbs in parentheses.
1  What kinds of restaurants do you like _____ to? Why? (go)
2  Is it easy _____ a table at your favorite restaurant on the weekend? (reserve)
3  Have you ever used an app _____ takeout for delivery? What was it like? (order)
4  Have you ever refused _____ something in a restaurant? Why? What happened? (eat)
5  _____ in a restaurants as a chef or waiter is very hard. Do you agree? (work)
6  Do you get excited about _____ new dishes, or do you prefer _____ ones you've had before? (try, eat)
7  Do you think it's important _____ about where the food we eat comes from? (think)
8  What's the next special occasion in your life? What will you do _____ it? (celebrate)

**B** Ask and answer the questions in 8A in pairs.

**Personal Best**  Write a paragraph about your favorite place to have lunch.

# 9 SKILLS  SPEAKING  making and responding to suggestions ■ making a group decision

## 9D  Why don't you try the curry?

**1 A** Look at the dictionary definition below. Then do the quiz.

> **foodie** *noun (informal)* a person with a particular interest in different types of good food and who enjoys new food experiences as a hobby.

### Are you a **foodie**?

1. When you eat out, you always want to discuss what you're eating.  YES  NO
2. You can identify the different ingredients in a new dish.  YES  NO
3. You always have an opinion about every dish that you order.  YES  NO
4. You always want to try a new restaurant to see what the chef does.  YES  NO
5. You want to try all kinds of national and international cooking.  YES  NO
6. You care about the quality of the ingredients in what you eat.  YES  NO

**B** In pairs, discuss your answers. Are you a foodie?

**2** ▶ 9.13  Watch or listen to the first part of *Learning Curve*. Check (✓) the things that are true about Jack.

1. He's an assistant chef. ☐
2. He's "Employee of the month." ☐
3. He writes a blog about food. ☐
4. He reviews restaurants for a magazine. ☐

**3** ▶ 9.13  Complete Simon and Jack's sentences with the words in the box. Watch or listen again and check.

> suggest  could  would  what  honest  about  rather  wondering

Simon:
- ¹_____ you like to try some?
- How ²_____ that one?
- To be ³_____, I'd ⁴_____ have the aubergine (eggplant).

Jack:
- So, ⁵_____ about the courgette (zucchini)?
- I ⁶_____ you try this chicken dish.
- I was ⁷_____ if we ⁸_____ have dessert now.

### Conversation builder — making and responding to suggestions

| Making suggestions | Responding positively to suggestions | Responding negatively to suggestions |
|---|---|---|
| Should we …? | Yes, let's. | Well, I'm not sure. I think I'd prefer … |
| Would you like to …? | | |
| I suggest you/we … | | |
| I was wondering if we could … | Of course. | To be honest, I'd rather …. |
| Why don't you/we …? | That sounds great. | I won't, if that's OK. |
| How/What about …? | Sure. | Can't we … instead? |
| Have you thought about/of …? | Great idea! | |

**4 A** Read the Conversation builder. In pairs, take turns reading sentences 1–5 and responding.

1. Should we go out for dinner tonight?
2. I was wondering if we could try the new Thai restaurant.
3. I suggest we get there at nine thirty.
4. Can't we get there a bit earlier, instead? How about eight thirty?
5. Why don't we ask some friends to join us?

**B** In pairs, make your own suggestions about eating out together and respond.

making and responding to suggestions ■ making a group decision  **SPEAKING**  **SKILLS** **9D**

**5** ▶ 9.14 Watch or listen to the second part of the show. Answer the questions.
1 Which two dishes do they rate?
2 Do they agree or disagree about their ratings?

**6** ▶ 9.14 Who says these sentences, Jack, Kate, or Simon? Watch or listen again and check.
1 What do you think of the courgette? _____
2 I love it. Delicious. _____
3 Only one star? Oh, come on, Simon. _____
4 It's delicious. Simon? _____
5 OK, then. Two stars! _____
6 I agree, but I say two stars because I thought it was very dry. _____
7 We'll have to agree to disagree! _____

> **Skill** making a group decision
>
> When we want to make a group decision, we can:
> - invite others to give their opinions and give our own.
> - try to persuade others to change their minds, or be persuaded to change our own mind!
> - accept that not everyone might agree in the end.

**7** Look at exercise 6 again. Put sentences 1–7 into the correct column in the chart.

| asking for and giving opinions | persuading others and changing your mind | agreeing or disagreeing |
|---|---|---|
|  |  |  |

**8 A** Order sentences a–f to make a conversation.
a ☐ **Ben** OK, then! They have some good dishes. But some of the others are boring.
b ☐ **Carl** Oh, come on! Their fish and seafood dishes are fantastic!
c ☐ **Alice** What do you think about the food at the Western Hotel?
d ☐ **Carl** I think we'll have to agree to disagree!
e ☐ **Ben** I think it's a bit boring.
f ☐ **Alice** I agree with Carl. I had some wonderful seafood there a couple of weeks ago.

**B** ▶ 9.15 Listen and check. Practice the conversation in groups of three.

**Go to Communication practice:** Student A page 163, Student B page 172

**9 A PREPARE** You are planning a special meal with some friends. In groups, think of suggestions for where to eat and what type of food to have. Use the ideas in the pictures or your own.

**B PRACTICE** In your groups, practice the conversation. Make suggestions, respond, and make a group decision if possible.

**C PERSONAL BEST** Identify one part of the conversation that you could improve and change it. Practice the conversation again. Do the other students in your group think it's improved?

**Personal Best** Make a list of three restaurants in your town or area. Give each one 1–5 stars and the reason for your opinion.

# UNIT 10 Right and wrong

**LANGUAGE** — reported speech ■ crime

## 10A Smooth criminals?

**1 A** Read the four headlines. Which are about a crime? Which are about a punishment?

1  Thief sent to **prison** for five years

2  Sixth **burglary** this week on Elm St.

3  $10,000 stolen in bank **robbery**

4  Man gets huge **fine** for driving too fast

**B** Match the words in **bold** in 1A with definitions a–d.
a  money you pay as punishment _____
b  stealing from a store or a bank _____
c  a place where criminals are sent _____
d  entering a home and stealing _____

Go to Vocabulary practice: crime, page 152

**2** Ask and answer the questions in pairs.
1  Is there a lot of crime where you live?
2  What crime stories have been in the news recently?

**3** Look at the picture in the text. What is on the men's faces? Read the text and check your answers.

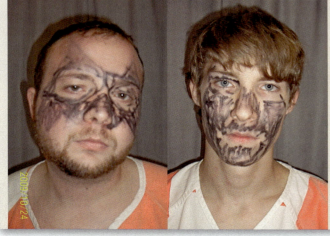

### Men attempt burglary with "worst disguise ever"

Two men have been arrested in Carroll, Iowa and charged with attempted burglary. Matthew McNelly, 23, and Joey Miller, 20, were caught after neighbors called 911 and said that two men were trying to break into an apartment. When police officers arrived at the apartment building, they asked witnesses what the men looked like. They said the men were wearing masks and black sweatshirts, and another witness told police they had driven away in a white car.

But when police spotted the white car shortly after and stopped it, they were amazed by what they saw. Instead of wearing real masks, the two burglars had drawn masks and beards on their faces with permanent black marker pen to hide their identities. One witness told reporters it was the worst disguise ever. It seems that, ironically, the "masks" were inspired by fictional crime-fighting superhero, Batman.

A legal expert said the pair would appear in court in a few weeks with their lawyers, and they would be charged with attempted burglary. Reporters asked the lawyers if they could comment on the case, but they did not respond.

**4 A** Who said these things? Write W (witness/es), P (police), R (reporters) or LE (legal expert).
1  "What **do** the men **look** like?" _____
2  "The men **are wearing** masks." _____
3  "They **drove** away." _____
4  "The pair **will appear** in court." _____
5  "**Can** you **comment**?" _____

**B** How are the sentences in 4A reported? Complete 1–5 below. Check your answers in the text.
1  They _____ witnesses _____ the men **looked** like.
2  They _____ the men **were wearing** masks.
3  Another witness _____ police they **had driven** away.
4  A legal expert _____ the pair **would appear** in court.
5  Reporters _____ the lawyers _____ they **could comment**.

reported speech ■ crime  **LANGUAGE**  **10A**

**5** Look at the sentences in exercises 4A and 4B and answer the questions. Then read the Grammar box.

1 How do the tenses and forms change from direct speech (4A) to reported speech (4B)?

1 simple present → _____
2 present continuous → _____
3 simple past → _____
4 future with *will* → _____
5 *can* → _____

2 Look again at exercise 4A. Which sentence is a *yes/no* question? Which is a *wh-* question? How do we report these two types of questions?

---

### Grammar  reported speech

**Direct statements:**
"*I'm feeling* tired." →
"*I can't* swim." →
"*It won't* rain." →

**Reported statements:**
She said (that) she **was feeling** tired.
Sam told us (that) he **couldn't** swim.
He said (that) it **wouldn't** rain.

**Direct questions:**
"**Do** you **like** sushi?" →
"**Where did** you **go**?" →

**Reported questions:**
She asked me **if** I **liked** sushi.
He asked me **where** I **had gone**.

**Look!** In reported questions, we don't use a question form:
She asked me **if I liked** sushi. NOT ~~She asked me if did I like~~

---

**Personal Best**

**Go to Grammar practice:** reported speech, page 130

**6 A** ▶ 10.5 **Pronunciation:** sentence stress  Listen to the sentences. Do we stress *if* and *that*? Do we stress *wh-* words?

1 They asked if I could help.
2 She asked if it would snow.
3 She told me that she'd passed!
4 I asked her why she'd left.
5 He asked me when I'd come.
6 I asked her where you'd gone.

**B** ▶ 10.5  Listen again and repeat.

**7 A** Who said these sentences and questions? Match 1–8 with the people in the box.

| salesclerk   weather forecaster   boss   teacher   dentist   neighbor   criminal   police officer |

1 "You'll have to work on the weekend."  _____
2 "I didn't do it!"  _____
3 "This won't hurt at all."  _____
4 "Why haven't you done the homework?"  _____
5 "Where were you at 9 p.m. on Friday?"  _____
6 "Do you want to pay by credit card?"  _____
7 "Can you turn the music down?"  _____
8 "There may be storms this weekend."  _____

**B** Change 1–8 in 7A into reported speech.

*My boss told me ...*

**Go to Communication practice:** Student A page 163, Student B page 172

**8 A** In pairs, ask and answer four of the questions.

1 What's your favorite English word?
2 Which ad on TV do you hate? Why do you hate this ad?
3 Are you going to go out on Friday night?
4 Have you ever paid a fine?
5 What did you do last night?
6 Can you touch your toes?
7 Will you move in the next two years?

**B** In different pairs, discuss which questions you were asked and what you replied.

*He asked me what my favorite English word was. I told him it was "enough."*

**Personal Best**  Write four things your teacher has said in class today using reported speech.

85

# 10 SKILLS   LISTENING   listening in detail ■ final /t/ and /d/ sounds ■ making nouns from verbs

## 10B Emergency!

**1** Discuss the questions below in pairs.
1. What different kinds of emergency services are there?
2. How do you contact the different emergency services in your country?
3. Do you know any emergency service numbers in other countries?
4. The police are there to protect, inform, and educate. Do you agree with this statement?

**2** Complete the rewritten statement from exercise 1.

*The police are there to provide _____, _____, and _____.*

**Go to Vocabulary practice:** making nouns from verbs, page 149

**3** ▶ 10.7   Watch or listen to the first part of *Learning Curve* and answer the questions.
1. Which two countries are mentioned?
2. What are the emergency phone numbers in these countries?
3. What nationality is Liz Francis?
4. Where did she go on vacation?

> **Skill** listening in detail
>
> It's often important to understand detailed information at a phrase and sentence level, and understand how the details relate to each other.
> - Read the questions and answer options carefully.
> - Identify the key words in the questions and answer options.
> - When listening, focus on the whole message, and not on individual words and phrases.
> - Don't choose an option based on hearing one word or phrase that appears in that option.

**4 A** ▶ 10.7   Read the Skill box and underline the key words in the questions and answer options below. Watch or listen again and choose the correct options to answer the questions.

1. What was the emergency situation?
   a. Liz needed an ambulance as she'd injured her foot.
   b. Liz needed help to escape a dangerous situation.
   c. Liz saw someone fall off a cliff into the ocean.

2. Who did Liz call?
   a. emergency services in the U.S.
   b. emergency services in the UK
   c. the police in the UK

**B** Discuss your answers in pairs. Can you explain why the incorrect options are wrong?

**5** What advice do you think Liz gives to tourists after her experience?

listening in detail ■ final /t/ and /d/ sounds ■ making nouns from verbs  **LISTENING**  **SKILLS**  **10B**

**6** ▶ 10.8 Watch or listen to the second part of the show. Which emergency service does each person talk about?

Renaldo

Ming

Lana

Fred

**7** ▶ 10.8 Watch or listen again and choose the correct options to complete the sentences.
1 Renaldo, a police officer from New York, worked
   a with a patrol officer who retired last year.
   b with a police dog who helped him arrest criminals.
   c as a police dog trainer with the K-9 unit.
2 Ming, a restaurant owner in London,
   a heard a smoke alarm and called 999.
   b called 999 when she saw a fire in her restaurant.
   c watched firefighters put out a fire in her restaurant.
3 The bicyclist that Lana talks about
   a hit another man who was crossing the street.
   b was riding his bike in a dangerous way.
   c was hit by a car.
4 Fred's bike was stolen and
   a he called the police to report the theft right away.
   b the police caught the thief thanks to witnesses.
   c Kate might know who the thief is.

**8** Have you heard any unusual stories about emergency services? Tell your partner.

> **Listening builder**  final /t/ and /d/ sounds
>
> English speakers don't pronounce the /t/ and /d/ sound fully at the end of a word when the next word begins with a consonant. If the next word begins with a vowel sound, the sounds are linked. *And* is often pronounced without the /d/ sound, even when the next word begins with a vowel sound.
>
> We're talking abou(t) the emergency services.   He call(ed) the police an(d) ask(ed) them to help.
> What abou(t) you? Have you heard any unusual stories about emergency services?

**9** ▶ 10.9 Read the Listening builder. Listen and complete the sentences.
1 In the U.S., when we see a fire, want _____ crime, or _____ medical help, we call 911.
2 An emergency services dispatcher quickly _____ police in the UK.
3 I _____ as a patrol officer. _____ I was on the _____ foot.
4 He _____ and _____ many burglars, thieves, _____ criminals.
5 I _____ say something _____ emergency workers in London.

**10** In pairs, discuss the questions.
1 Have you ever called or received help from an emergency service? What happened?
2 What characteristics do people need to work in the different emergency services?

**Personal Best**   Would you like to work for an emergency service? Write five sentences explaining why/why not.

# 10 LANGUAGE  second conditional, *would*, *could*, and *might*

## 10C Do the right thing

**1** In pairs, discuss the questions.
1. Have you ever lost something on the street? Did you get it back? How?
2. Have you ever found something that someone else had lost? What did you do?

**2** Read the text and choose the best option to complete the title.
a keeps it    b gives it back    c sells it online

### Teenager finds movie star's wallet and ____

**What would you do if you found a wallet that belonged to a famous Hollywood actor? Would you keep it, try to sell it on eBay, or return it to the owner?**

This was the choice 17-year-old Tristin Budzyn-Barker had when he found a wallet in a Los Angeles restaurant. To his surprise, when he looked inside, he realized it belonged to Australian actor Chris Hemsworth, who played Thor in the *Avengers* movies. The address of Hemsworth's agent was in the wallet, so Tristin was able to return it, along with all the contents of the wallet.

When the actor got the wallet back, he had expected to find it empty, so he was amazed that the money was still in it. He invited Tristin to appear with him on a popular U.S. talk show, where Hemsworth thanked him publicly by giving him a reward – all the money in the wallet. The talk show host, Ellen DeGeneres, made Tristin's day even better by giving him another $10,000 reward.

**3** ▶ 10.10 Listen to two friends talking about the story. Do they agree that Tristin did the right thing?

**4** ▶ 10.10 Choose the correct options to complete the sentences. Listen again and check your answers.
1. What *would / do* you do if you *would find / found* someone's wallet?
2. *I'll / I'd* do the right thing. *I'll / I'd* definitely give it back. What about you?
3. If *I found / I'd find* a famous person's wallet, *I kept / I'd keep* it and maybe sell it online.
4. If you *keep / kept* the wallet, it *would be / was* theft!
5. If you *will give / gave* it back, the owner *will / might* give you a reward.
6. What about if you *don't / didn't* know who it belonged to? *Would / Will* you keep it then?
7. *I'd take / I took* it to the police station. It *might / would* belong to someone who really needed the money.

**5** Look at the sentences in exercise 4 and answer the questions. Then read the Grammar box.
1. Are the sentences about real or hypothetical situations and their consequences?
2. Do they refer to present and future situations, or past situations?
3. Which form do we use in the *if*-clause? Which form do we use in the main clause?

second conditional, *would*, *could*, and *might*  **LANGUAGE**  **10C**

### Grammar: second conditional, *would*, *could*, and *might*

Unlikely or impossible situations and their consequences:
*If* I **won** the lottery, I **wouldn't work**.
What **would** you **do** *if* someone **stole** your phone?
I'**d drive** to work *if* I **had** a car.
*If* a stranger **invited** you to a party, **would** you **go**?

**Look!** We can use *could* or *might* instead of *would*:
*If* they **lived** in the country, they **might** be less stressed.

Go to Grammar practice: second conditional, *would*, *could*, and *might*, page 131

**6 A** ▶10.12 Complete the sentences with the correct forms of the verbs in parentheses. Listen to Ana and Pete continue their conversation and check your answers.

1 If a salesclerk in a small store _____ you too much change, what _____ ? (give, do)
2 If he _____ me too much change, I _____ him. (give, tell)
3 _____ the salesclerk in a supermarket if he or she _____ you too much change? (tell, give)
4 If a salesclerk _____ me too much change in a supermarket, I _____ it. (give, might keep)
5 What _____ if your bank _____ $1,500 into your account by mistake? (do, put)
6 I _____ them. They _____ the mistake sooner or later. (tell, discover)

**B** What would you do in the situations in 6A? Discuss in pairs.

**7** ▶10.13 **Pronunciation: conditionals** Listen to the two sentences. Notice the difference between the first conditional and the second conditional sentences.

1 If I need some help, I'll ask you.
2 If I needed some help, I'd ask you.

**8 A** ▶10.14 Listen to the sentences. Are they first or second conditional? Choose the sentence that you hear.

1 a I'll come if I have time.
2 a If he has some money, he'll come.
3 a If you fall, I'll catch you.
4 a She'll help if she has time.

b I'd come if I had time.
b If he had some money, he'd come.
b If you fell, I'd catch you.
b She'd help if she had time.

**B** In pairs, take turns saying one of the sentences in 8A. Your partner will identify which sentence it is.

Go to Communication practice: Student A page 164, Student B page 172

**9 A** Use first or second conditional forms to complete the sentences. More than one answer may be possible.

1 What's the first thing you _____ if you _____ the lottery? (might buy, win)
2 If you _____ do any job, which job _____ ? (can, choose)
3 What _____ if you _____ free time this weekend? (do, have)
4 If you _____ your favorite movie star, what _____ him/her? (meet, ask)
5 If you _____ live in any city in the world, where _____ ? (can, live)
6 If you _____ a lot of money left at the end of this month, what _____ ? (have, could do)
7 If you _____ give your 16-year-old self some advice, what _____ ? (can, say)
8 Who _____ if you _____ some help to write a job application? (ask, need)

**B** In pairs, ask and answer the questions in 9A.

Personal Best | Write three sentences about how your life could be better.

89

# 10 SKILLS WRITING — writing a for-and-against essay ■ useful phrases for topic sentences

## 10D For and against

**1 A** Look at pictures a–d. Which are the worst things to do? Number them 1–4 (1 = the worst).

a cheating on an exam
b traveling without a ticket
c using a false name online
d taking a sick day when you're not sick

**B** Look at the pictures again. Do you know anyone who has done any of these things? Did he/she get caught?

**2** Read the first paragraph of the essay quickly. What do you think the full title of the essay is? In pairs, discuss your answers.

---

**Everyone should _____ . Discuss.**

*Alban Duval*

A lot of people use different names on the Internet, and as a result, it is difficult to know if information online is reliable. Many social media or review websites, such as Facebook, make people use their real names so everyone can trust the information they read. However, there are some situations when people need to be anonymous.

On the one hand, if everyone used his or her real name online, the Internet might be a more reliable and pleasant place. Using a false name online allows people to be dishonest or mean. A lot of people who insult and attack other people on the Internet would never do it under their real names or in real life. Other people use a different name to write reviews of their own restaurants or stores, and criticize other businesses.

On the other hand, some people have valid reasons for not using their real names online. There are many reasons why someone would prefer to remain anonymous. Teachers, for example, often prefer not to use their real names on social media as they want to keep their personal and professional lives separate. Another example is victims of crime, who prefer to use false names so criminals are unable to contact them.

To sum up, there are valid reasons why people would choose to use false names online, and there are also dishonest reasons. I do not believe that everyone should always use his or her real name. I think people should be able to choose. In my view, the problem is not the name people use, but what they write.

writing a for-and-against essay ■ useful phrases for topic sentences  **WRITING**  **SKILLS** **10D**

**3** In pairs, think of one argument for and one argument against the essay topic. Then read the whole essay. Were your ideas the same?

>  **Skill** writing a for-and-against essay
>
> **We write for-and-against essays to discuss both sides of an argument.**
> - Organize your essay into paragraphs. Aim for a minimum of four paragraphs: introduction, arguments for, arguments against, and the conclusion.
> - Start each paragraph with a topic sentence (a sentence that clearly introduces the topic of the paragraph).
> - Include at least one main point in each paragraph and support your topic sentence with examples.
> - Use formal language and an impersonal style. However, you can put your personal opinion in the conclusion. Use phrases like *I believe that, in my opinion, in my view*.
> - Don't use contractions, such as *isn't, don't*. Use full forms instead.

**4** Read the Skill box. Then answer the questions about Alban's essay.
1 In which paragraph does Alban give his arguments for the topic?
2 In which paragraph does he give his arguments against the topic?
3 What are the main points in each for and against paragraph? What examples does he give to support them?
4 When does Alban give his personal opinion? What phrases does he use to do this?

**5** Read the essay titles below. In pairs, think of arguments for and against each title, and examples to support these arguments. Use the ideas in exercise 1A and your own ideas.
1 Are exams good for learning?
2 Public transportation should be free for everyone. Discuss.
3 People should only have to work four days a week. Discuss.

> **Text builder** useful phrases for topic sentences
>
> **On the one hand**, smartphones can be very useful in certain situations.
> **On the other hand**, people tend to talk to each other less.
> **The main advantage of** smartphones is that they can be very useful in certain situations.
> **However, one disadvantage** is that people tend to talk to each other less.
> **To sum up**, most people take their smartphones everywhere, which has both advantages and disadvantages.

**6** Read the Text builder. Which phrases does Alban use in his topic sentences?

**7** Look at the topic sentences. Which essay in exercise 5 does each sentence come from? Do the sentences introduce an argument for, an argument against, or a conclusion?
1 The main advantage is that there would be fewer cars on the road, and the air would be less polluted.
2 To sum up, not charging passengers would help people who do not have much money, but the government would have to invest a lot of money to do this.
3 On the one hand, review usually helps people understand a subject better.
4 On the other hand, limiting the number of work days per week would make it very difficult to start a new business.
5 However, one disadvantage is that they are very stressful.

**8 A** **PREPARE** Choose an essay title from exercise 5. Make notes of the arguments for and against.

**B** **PRACTICE** Use the Skill box to help you write your essay. Use topic sentences and linking phrases at the start of each paragraph.

**C** **PERSONAL BEST** Work in pairs. Read the topic sentences from each paragraph to your partner. Can your partner guess what the rest of the paragraph will say?

---

**Personal Best** Write an alternative conclusion to the essay "Everyone should use his or her real name online."

# 9 and 10 REVIEW and PRACTICE

## Grammar

**1** Cross (**X**) out the sentence that is NOT correct.

**1** a What was your vacation in the U.S. like? ☐
 b What was like your vacation in the U.S.? ☐
 c Did you like your vacation in the U.S.? ☐

**2** a I love going to the movies. ☐
 b I'd love to go to the movies tonight. ☐
 c I love to go to the movies tomorrow. ☐

**3** a Eva told that she wanted to go to a museum. ☐
 b Eva said that she wanted to go to a museum. ☐
 c Eva told me that she wanted to go to a museum. ☐

**4** a If someone stole my bag, I'd tell the police. ☐
 b I'd tell the police if someone stole my bag. ☐
 c If someone would steal my bag, I told the police. ☐

**5** a Jonathan doesn't look like his older brother. ☐
 b Jonathan doesn't like his older brother. ☐
 c Jonathan isn't looking like his older brother. ☐

**6** a He's worried about to miss the train. ☐
 b He's worried about missing the train. ☐
 c He wouldn't like to miss the train. ☐

**7** a They asked me if the flight was on time. ☐
 b They asked me when arrived the flight. ☐
 c They asked me when the flight arrived. ☐

**8** a If I had a car, I'll drive you home. ☐
 b I could drive you home if I had a car. ☐
 c If I had a car, I'd drive you home. ☐

**2** Use the words in parentheses to complete the sentences so they mean the same as the first sentence.

**1** When you sing, your voice is similar to mine.
When you sing, you _____ me. (sound)

**2** I can't wait to see the next episode!
I'm looking _____ the next episode. (forward)

**3** Tom asked, "Does your girlfriend live in Boston, Adam?"
Tom asked Adam _____ in Boston. (if)

**4** We can't rent a car because I can't drive.
If I _____, we _____ a car. (could)

**5** Can you tell me something about Adele's new album?
What's _____? (like)

**6** Joe couldn't go out because he didn't have enough money.
Joe couldn't _____ out. (afford)

**7** Jane said to me, "I'll meet you outside the theater."
Jane _____ outside the theater. (said)

**8** You should go to bed earlier.
If _____, I'd go to bed earlier. (were)

**3** Complete the text with the correct form of the verbs in parentheses.

# Going underground

There are two main reasons behind the current interest in underground homes. Some local governments have started ¹_____ (build) homes underground to create more space in crowded cities. ²_____ (live) underground can also offer an escape from extreme temperatures and can provide relief from noise pollution. I decided to visit South Australia to find out what it's like to live underground.

A hundred years ago in the small mining town of Coober Pedy, miners dug cave homes in the hills ³_____ (avoid) the intense summer heat. Today, ⁴_____ (visit) the town's underground homes is a fascinating experience, and I was pleasantly surprised ⁵_____ (find) there was plenty of natural light from openings in the ground above. In addition, it was like ⁶_____ (be) in an air-conditioned house even though the temperature outside was 40 degrees Celsius. If I lived in Coober Pedy, or somewhere else very hot, I ⁷_____ (want) to live in an underground home because it is so cool.

I met some other tourists who were staying in an underground hotel, and I asked them if they ⁸_____ (enjoy) the experience. Most said that they ⁹_____ (have) a wonderful night's sleep the previous night because it was so quiet. One woman told me she ¹⁰_____ (may) even build her own underground home since her apartment ¹¹_____ (be) in a noisy area, and she ¹²_____ (want) to live somewhere quiet.

It seems that life underground has its advantages, which more of us may experience in years to come.

## Vocabulary

**1** Circle the word that is different. Explain your answer.

| | | | |
|---|---|---|---|
| **1** boiled | fried | baked | sliced |
| **2** steal | theft | rob | mug |
| **3** dessert | plate | main course | appetizer |
| **4** thief | robber | arrest | murderer |
| **5** achievement | confusion | disappointment | government |
| **6** rare | homemade | well-done | medium |
| **7** lime | zucchini | garlic | asparagus |
| **8** fork | knife | napkin | spoon |

92

# REVIEW and PRACTICE 9 and 10

**2** Match the words in the box with definitions 1–10.

> argument   leave a tip   takeout   order something   burglary
> studying   lentils   fine   protection   get the check

1   food bought from a restaurant to eat at home _____
2   these are often used in soups _____
3   entering a building illegally and stealing from it _____
4   money paid as a punishment _____
5   keeping something safe _____
6   give some money to the waiter after a meal _____
7   ask the waiter to bring you food or drink _____
8   ask for the piece of paper showing how much your food cost _____
9   an angry disagreement _____
10   learning in preparation for an exam _____

**3** Choose the correct options to complete the sentences.

1   I usually have _____ with my cereal for breakfast.
  **a** olive oil    **b** yogurt    **c** soy sauce
2   I'm not going to leave a big tip because the _____ was awful. It took hours!
  **a** service    **b** check    **c** atmosphere
3   I'd like to _____ a table for four for 8 p.m., please.
  **a** order    **b** reserve    **c** get
4   Should I put _____ carrots in the salad or sliced carrots?
  **a** grated    **b** melted    **c** rare
5   The two men _____ the house and took two laptops and $150 in cash.
  **a** mugged    **b** stole    **c** broke into
6   He has a lot of _____, so he often has ideas for stories.
  **a** imaginary    **b** imagine    **c** imagination
7   She made an important _____ when she chose to get a job instead of going to college.
  **a** information  **b** decision  **c** education
8   I'm vegan, so can I have the _____ please?
  **a** steak    **b** shellfish    **c** chickpeas

**4** Complete the text with the words in the box.

> stolen   prison   mugging   victim   witness   arrested
> suspect   mugged   broken   burglary

Police **1**_____ a 22-year-old man outside a shopping center yesterday afternoon. A **2**_____ said that the man had **3**_____ a businessperson and had taken his wallet. Fortunately, the **4**_____ of the **5**_____ wasn't badly hurt. When the police took the **6**_____ to the police station, they realized that he had previously spent six months in **7**_____ for **8**_____ . He had **9**_____ into a house and had **10**_____ a TV and $400 in cash.

## Personal Best

**Lesson 9A**
Name four adjectives that describe ways of cooking food.

**Lesson 10A**
Name four types of criminals.

**Lesson 9A**
Write four sentences about your favorite dish, using *like* in different ways.

**Lesson 10A**
Report three sentences or questions that people have said today.

**Lesson 9B**
Write a sentence using *one* and a sentence using *ones*.

**Lesson 10B**
Name four nouns that end with *-sion*, *-ment*, *-ation* and *-ion*.

**Lesson 9C**
Describe three things you did (or didn't do) the last time you went to a restaurant.

**Lesson 10C**
Write three second conditional sentences.

**Lesson 9C**
Write two sentences with *-ing* forms and two with infinitives.

**Lesson 10D**
Write two sentences with *On the one hand* and *On the other hand*.

**Lesson 9D**
Give four expressions for making and responding to suggestions.

**Lesson 10D**
Write a sentence starting with *To sum up*.

93

# UNIT 11 The natural world

**LANGUAGE** articles ■ the natural world

## 11A Nature goes viral

1 Which of the natural features below does your country have? Have you visited these places?

> rainforest   mountain range   volcano   waterfall   ocean   coast   desert   jungle

**Personal Best**

Go to Vocabulary practice: the natural world, page 153

2 **A** Look at the pictures in the text. What can you see? Where do you think each picture was taken?

**B** Read the text and check your ideas. Which is your favorite picture? Why?

### Nature goes viral
Here are four of our favorite nature photos that have gone viral.

The first photo shows the beauty of nature. Eric Nguyen took this incredible picture of a tornado in Kansas. The sun is shining through a gap in the clouds and has formed a rainbow. Tornadoes are the most violent type of storm on Earth, and there are over 1,000 tornadoes a year around the world. Many of them take place in Tornado Alley in the U.S.

This isn't a science-fiction movie – the people in the photo aren't really tiny. This is the Salar de Uyuni, the largest "salt flat" in the world, located in the southwest of Bolivia. It's completely flat – there are no hills or trees to give you a sense of perspective, so people love taking photos like this one there.

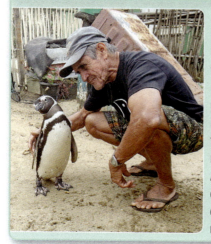

João Pereira de Souza is a bricklayer from Ilha Grande, a small island off the coast of Rio de Janeiro. One day, João found a penguin covered in oil in his backyard. He cleaned the penguin, fed him, and released him back into the Atlantic Ocean. The penguin comes back to visit João every year, and he has been named "Dindim."

This picture is a sensation on the Internet, especially among Batman fans. It's a photo of an iceberg in Newfoundland, Canada, which looks exactly like the crime-fighting superhero Batman. The photo was taken by Mike Parsons, a software engineer from Newfoundland.

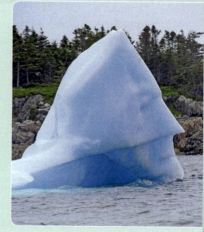

3 Complete the sentences. Check your answers in the text.

1 The _____ photo shows the beauty of nature.
2 The _____ is shining.
3 _____ are the most violent type of storm.
4 There are over 1,000 tornadoes a _____ .
5 Many take place in Tornado Alley in the _____ .
6 João Pereira de Souza is a _____ .
7 João released him back into the _____ .
8 It's the _____ salt flat in the world.
9 It's a _____ of an iceberg in Newfoundland.
10 The _____ was taken by Mike Parsons.

articles ■ the natural world  **LANGUAGE 11A**

**4** When do we use *a/an*, *the*, or no article? Match the sentences in exercise 3 with rules a–j. Then read the Grammar box.

a Use *a/an* when you mention something for the first time. ____
b Use *the* when there's only one of something. ____
c Use *the* with superlative adjectives. ____
d Use *a/an* to talk about frequency or speed. ____
e Use *the* with countries that include *united*, *republic*, and *kingdom*. ____
f Use *the* with the names of rivers, seas, and oceans. ____
g Use no article to talk about things in general. ____
h Use *the* with ordinal numbers (*first*, *second*, *third*, etc.). ____
i Use *the* to talk about something you've already mentioned. ____
j Use *a/an* to talk about somebody's job. ____

### Grammar articles

**Definite article (*the*):**
There's a car outside. **The** car's red.
You're **the** best person for the job.
Take **the** first street on the left.
He lives in **the** United States.

**Indefinite article (*a/an*):**
There was **a** very old man in the café.
I usually try to swim once **a** week.
The speed limit is 60 km. an hour.
He's studying to become **a** vet.

**No article:**
I love documentaries about nature.
Do you like coffee?
Spiders are horrible.
I'm going to work now.

Go to **Grammar practice:** articles, page 132

**5 A** ▶ 11.4 **Pronunciation:** *the* Listen to the sentences. Is *the* pronounced /ðə/ or /ðiː/ before a vowel sound?

1 **The** earthquake woke us up. _____
2 Is **the** volcano still active? _____
3 **The** Atlantic Ocean is huge. _____
4 Can you see **the** sea? _____

**B** ▶ 11.4 Listen again and repeat the sentences.

**6** Complete the text with *the*, *a/an*, or – (no article).

1_____ team of designers in Seoul, 2_____ South Korea, has been working on 3_____ project to make 4_____ rainy days more fun. 5_____ project is called *Project Monsoon*, and 6_____ team of designers plans to use 7_____ special type of paint that can only be seen when 8_____ ground is wet. So on 9_____ rainy days, people would see colorful pictures of 10_____ whales, turtles, and fish instead of the usual gray streets. 11_____ project was created to help 12_____ residents of Seoul look forward to 13_____ monsoon season, when most people normally stay at 14_____ home to avoid the rain.

Go to **Communication practice:** Student A page 164, Student B page 173

**7** Work in small groups. Discuss the statements.

1 Saturday is the best night of the week to go out.
2 Women are better than men at learning languages.
3 Classical music is more relaxing than pop music.
4 You should get exercise three times a week.
5 The best things in life are free.
6 Space travel is a waste of money.
7 The Internet is the most important invention ever.

**Personal Best** Write a paragraph describing a photo you have seen that has "gone viral."

**11** SKILLS     READING    understanding the writer's purpose ■ understanding noun phrases

# 11B  A disaster waiting to happen

**1** What happens during these natural disasters? Have any of these been in the news recently?

> earthquake   volcanic eruption   forest fire   flood   tsunami   hurricane

> ### Skill    understanding the writer's purpose
>
> When reading a text, look for clues that tell you the purpose of the whole text and parts of the text. The writer's purpose may be to:
> - give advice or a warning
> - give information, examples, facts, or opinions
> - describe a person, event, idea, or issue
> - make a comparison or contrast
> - explain a reason, cause, or result.

**2** Read the Skill box. Then read the text quickly. What is the general purpose of the text? Choose the best option.

   **a** to give travel advice to tourists in southern Italy
   **b** to describe everyday life and the reasons people live near a volcano
   **c** to warn people that volcanoes in Italy are dangerous

**3** Choose the correct option to answer the questions. Why does the writer …

   **1** … describe an earthquake in paragraph 1?
   **a** to explain why a volcano erupts
   **b** to compare an earthquake with a volcanic eruption
   **c** to describe how a volcanic eruption starts

   **2** … describe the AD 79 eruption of Vesuvius in paragraph 1?
   **a** to explain why he was worried about the earthquake
   **b** to explain how Pompeii and Herculaneum were destroyed
   **c** to give examples of places that were destroyed by volcanic eruptions

   **3** … include the quotation "Volcanoes will do whatever they feel like" in paragraph 2?
   **a** to explain that it is difficult to predict when Vesuvius will erupt
   **b** to give an example of how the local people aren't very worried
   **c** to warn visitors to be prepared for a volcanic eruption at any time

   **4** … mention *tomatoes* and *mud baths* in paragraph 4?
   **a** to give information about the geography of the area
   **b** to give examples of good things about volcanoes
   **c** to compare different tourist activities

   **5** … talk about canceled flights in paragraph 5?
   **a** to explain the only negative result of the most recent eruption on Etna
   **b** to explain how lives were put in danger by the eruption in 2007
   **c** to give people advice about traveling to this volcanic area

> ### Text builder    understanding noun phrases
>
> The subject of a sentence is not always a single noun. Sometimes the subject is a noun phrase which has several words.
>
> *Living near Vesuvius all their lives* has given them a feeling for the volcano's behavior.
> In Sicily, *25% of the island's population* lives on or around Mount Etna.

**4** **A** Read the Text builder. <u>Underline</u> the subjects of all the sentences in paragraph 6.

   **B** Which of the subjects that you underlined in paragraph 6 are noun phrases?

**5** In pairs, think of five questions you would ask people who live near a volcano.

understanding the writer's purpose ■ understanding noun phrases   READING   SKILLS   11B

# In the shadow of a volcano
*by Nick Daley*

1  When it starts, the floor begins to move. Cups and plates shake in kitchen cabinets. These are the signs that a volcanic eruption is coming, and it begins with an earthquake. When I felt one on my trip to Naples, in southern Italy, I felt panic, thinking that the "big one" was coming. I was terrified that the nearby volcano of Vesuvius would erupt just like it did in AD 79, destroying the towns of Pompeii and Herculaneum. Tragically, on that occasion thousands of people died.

2  This time, no eruption came. My hosts, a Neapolitan family, just smiled. Living near Vesuvius all their lives has given them a feeling for the volcano's behavior. From long experience, they know if something bad is happening. This is why nobody seems concerned. They are not alone in their relaxed attitude to the danger above their heads. "Volcanoes will do whatever they feel like," says another local resident, Ciro Russo, as he shrugs his shoulders and carries on with normal life.

3  It was my fascination with these people that drew me to Italy. Why do people choose to live under an active volcano despite knowing about the risks? Vesuvius is not even the only volcano in the country – in Sicily, 25% of the island's population lives on or around Mount Etna, another active volcano.

4  The most obvious answer to this question is that people have always lived in the area – these regions have been inhabited for thousands of years. In addition, living next to a volcano has some advantages. Chemicals in the volcanic ash create ideal conditions for agriculture, especially for tomatoes. Volcanoes also attract visitors, and that brings money. One popular tourist activity is bathing in hot mud baths on nearby volcanic islands.

5  Most important of all, the actual risk should be assessed. There hasn't been a big eruption on Mount Vesuvius since 1944. At that time, a few villages were evacuated, but older people in the area just remember roasting chestnuts on the hot magma in the streets. Etna has erupted more recently, but not enough to put lives in danger. The 2007 eruption simply caused a number of canceled flights because planes can crash if volcanic dust enters their engines (the dust is sharp, like glass).

6  People who live in the shadow of a volcano have a view of life that is different from the rest of us, and this provides an important lesson. As one elderly resident of the region says, "The volcano is part of our culture, it's part of life, and it's as beautiful as the sea." With danger so close to home, the people who live near these Italian volcanoes know how important it is to enjoy their day-to-day existence as much as possible, rather than worrying about the potential disaster that's waiting at the end of the road.

**Personal Best**  Write a paragraph about a natural feature that you have visited. Use some noun phrases.

97

# 11 LANGUAGE — third conditional ■ extreme adjectives

## 11C I will survive

**1** Have you ever gotten lost in the city or country? If so, what happened? Tell your partner.

**2** Read the text and answer the questions.
1 How did Ann get lost?  2 How did she survive?  3 How was she found?

### Grandmother survives nine days lost in the wild

A 72-year-old woman and her dog have been rescued after surviving for nine days alone in the White Mountains area of Arizona.

Ann Rodgers was driving to Phoenix to visit her grandchildren when her car ran out of gas on a deserted road. She couldn't use her phone because there was no signal, so she decided to leave her car and walk to higher ground. Instead, she got lost and spent the next nine days in danger of attack by bears and mountain lions. She survived by drinking river water, eating plants, and building fires to keep warm in **freezing** temperatures.

The search started four days after Ann disappeared, when her car was found by the road. Rescue teams searched the area on foot and with helicopters, but found nothing. Two days into the search, rescuers saw Ann's dog in a canyon. A helicopter searched the area and found a large "help" sign that Ann had made out of rocks and sticks. Ann had also left a note saying that she was **starving** because she hadn't eaten, and she was going to follow the river to find a farm.

The helicopter immediately flew into the canyon and found Ann. She was **filthy** and **exhausted**, but alive. Her rescuers hadn't expected to find her alive, and believe that if she hadn't made the "help" sign, they wouldn't have found her. However, they also think that leaving her car was a mistake – if she had stayed with her car, they would have found her more quickly.

Personal Best

**3** Look at the adjectives in **bold** in the text. Match them with definitions 1–4.
1 very dirty  2 very hungry  3 very cold  4 very tired

Go to Vocabulary practice: extreme adjectives, page 154

**4 A** Choose the correct option to complete the sentences about Ann's story.
1 Ann *stayed / didn't stay* with her car.
2 Rescuers *found / didn't find* her quickly.
3 If Ann *had / hadn't* stayed with her car, rescuers *would / wouldn't* have found her more quickly.

**B** Look at sentence 3 in 4A. Answer the questions.
1 Which clause is about a hypothetical situation in the past?
2 Which clause is about a possible consequence of the hypothetical situation?
3 Which clause contains a verb in the past perfect?
4 Which clause contains *would* + *have* + past participle?

**5 A** Complete the sentence. Check your answer in the last paragraph of the text.
If Ann _____ the "help" sign, rescuers _____ her.

**B** What really happened? Choose the correct options. Then read the Grammar box.
Ann *made / didn't make* the "help" sign. The rescuers *found / didn't find* her.

third conditional ■ extreme adjectives    **LANGUAGE 11C**

### Grammar: third conditional

Unreal past situations and their consequences:
*If you **had asked** me, I **would have helped**.* (You didn't ask me. I didn't help.)
*If I **hadn't called** you, I **wouldn't have heard** the news.* (I did call you. I heard the news.)

**Look!** We can put the *if* clause after the main clause. We don't use a comma:
*I wouldn't have heard the news **if I hadn't called you**.*

Go to Grammar practice: third conditional, page 133

**6** Match the clauses to make complete sentences.
1 If I'd studied harder,
2 If I hadn't gone to that party,
3 If I'd saved more money,
4 If I'd been good at sports,
5 If I hadn't been in such a hurry,
6 If I'd rested last weekend,

a I'd have been a professional soccer player.
b my cold would have got better.
c I wouldn't have forgotten to lock the door.
d I would have passed the exam.
e I'd have bought a car.
f I wouldn't have met my best friend.

**7 A** ▶ 11.7 **Pronunciation: weak form of *have*** Listen to the sentences and notice the pronunciation of *have* in *would have* and *wouldn't have*. Listen again and repeat the sentences.
1 If I'd studied harder, I would **have** passed the exam.
2 If I hadn't gone to that party, I wouldn't **have** met my best friend.
3 If I'd saved more money, I would **have** bought a car.

**B** Look at the sentences in 7A. Change them to make third conditional sentences that are true for you.
*If I hadn't studied last weekend, I would have failed the test.*

**8 A** ▶ 11.8 Listen to a survival expert talking about Ann's story. The expert also mentions another survival story. Why was it worse?

**B** ▶ 11.8 Complete the sentences about Ann and Victoria. Then listen again and check your answers.
1 Ann _____ if she _____ how to start a fire. (not survive, not know)
2 Victoria _____ if she _____ at night because it was so cold. (might die, sleep)
3 The rescue team _____ Victoria sooner if she _____ someone about her plans. (find, tell)
4 If Ann _____ enough gas in her car, she _____ a problem in the first place. (have, not have)
5 If they _____ a signal on their phones, both Ann and Victoria _____ for help. (have, can call)
6 If Victoria _____ some warmer clothes and food with her, she _____ so cold and hungry. (take, not be)
7 If she _____ a walking stick to her leg, she _____ her leg more. (not tie, might injure)
8 Ann _____ if she _____ near her car. (not get lost, stay)

Go to Communication practice: Student A page 164, Student B page 173

**9** Think about five important things that have happened in your life. Tell your partner what would have been different in your life if these things hadn't happened. Use these ideas or your own ideas.

- an exam you passed or failed
- a job you applied for
- a friend you met
- a new hobby you started
- a place you went to
- an important decision you made

*If I hadn't met my friend Lisa, I wouldn't have passed my English test. She's really good at English and helps me a lot.*

 Write four sentences about things that happened last week and what would have happened if they had been different.

# 11 SKILLS SPEAKING making recommendations ■ checking and clarifying information

## 11D The great outdoors

1  Think of two of your most memorable photos of activities, trips, or vacations in the great outdoors. Describe them to your partner. Talk about:
   - where the photos were taken
   - what the weather was like
   - who you were with
   - what you were doing
   - any natural features in the photos

2  ▶ 11.9  Watch or listen to the first part of *Learning Curve*. Choose the correct option to complete the sentence.

   Kate wants recommendations about …
   a  … where she should go on a trip to England.
   b  … where she should go for a week's vacation in the UK.
   c  … which mountain range in Scotland she should visit.
   d  … where she should go to escape the bad weather.

3  ▶ 11.9  Match the two parts to make complete sentences from Kate, Jack, and Simon's conversation. Watch or listen again and check.

   1  I made pasta with tomatoes and herbs. Tonight's special.
   2  I'd recommend
   3  I love Scotland. My grandmother lives in Glasgow.
   4  If I were you,
   5  You should
   6  Perhaps you

   a  You should go there.
   b  You really should try it.
   c  visit Scotland.
   d  could see the south coast of England.
   e  I wouldn't. It's too rainy!
   f  staying here in London and seeing places you've never seen.

### Conversation builder | making recommendations

**Asking for ideas**
What would you recommend?
What do you think I should do?
Do you have any ideas about … ?
Where would be the best place to …?

**Making recommendations**
I'd recommend Paris / I'd recommend going to Paris.
If I were you, I'd/I wouldn't …
Perhaps you could …
You (really) should …

4  Read the Conversation builder. Which recommendation phrase is the strongest?

5  In groups, ask for and make recommendations about three of the subjects.

   outdoor sports   places to relax   travel apps   saving money on transportation
   clothes to wear for traveling   staying warm/cool outdoors

making recommendations ■ checking and clarifying information  **SPEAKING**  **SKILLS**  **11D**

**6** ▶ 11.10 Watch or listen to the second part of the show. Are the sentences true (T) or false (F)? Correct the false sentences.
1 Simon recommends visiting the southeast of England. _____
2 Simon is from that part of England. _____
3 Kate makes her decision by tossing a coin. _____
4 Simon and Jack decide that "heads" means Dover and "tails" means Scotland. _____
5 Kate is going to drive to Glasgow. _____

> **Skill** checking and clarifying information
>
> We often need to check or clarify information, for example, facts, someone's feelings, or what someone means.
> • Use tag questions, e.g., *This is the train to Boston, isn't it?*
> • Say that you haven't understood, e.g., *I'm sorry, I'm not sure I understand what you mean.*
> • Summarize what the other person has said, e.g., *So what you're saying is …*

**7** ▶ 11.10 Read the Skill box. Watch or listen again. How does Kate check what Simon means when he talks about Dover?

**8 A** In pairs, order sentences a–i to make a conversation.
a ☐ Yes, I think so. And the days are still pretty long.
b ☐ I'm not sure I understand what you mean.
c ☐ That's right, and sometimes you get some really hot days.
d ☐ 1  I'm trying to plan a trip to England. When's a good time to go?
e ☐ I mean that the evenings are still pretty light.
f ☐ So what you're saying is that September's the best time.
g ☐ Great! I think September sounds perfect.
h ☐ Summer's a popular time, but it's very busy then. April and May can be pretty cold. September can be very nice, and kids are back in school by then. Winter's not a great time to go.
i ☐ Oh, I see. And it's usually pretty mild in September, isn't it?

**B** ▶ 11.11 Listen and check. Practice the conversation.

Go to Communication practice: Student A page 164, Student B page 173

**9 A PREPARE** In pairs, choose a beautiful region or national park in your country. One student is planning a trip there and will ask for recommendations. The other student will answer with his/her opinions. Think of what you could say.

**B PRACTICE** In pairs, practice your conversation. Take turns making recommendations. Check and clarify the information that you hear.

**C PERSONAL BEST** Could you improve the way you make recommendations or check information? Practice again with a new partner. Talk about a different place.

Personal Best   Write a list of recommendations for someone traveling in your country.   101

# UNIT 12 Getting away

**LANGUAGE** So/Neither do I ■ phrases with *go* and *get*

## 12A Dream destinations

**1** Read the dictionary definitions of *go away* and *get away* and answer the questions below.

> **go away (v)**
> leave your home to spend time in a different place, usually for a vacation or a business trip

> **get away (v)**
> go somewhere on vacation because you need to escape and have a rest

1 Are you going away anywhere soon?
2 When you need to get away, where do you go?

Go to Vocabulary practice: phrases with *go* and *get*, page 154

**2 A** Complete the blog post with the correct form of phrases with *go* and *get*.

### My dream destinations

I'm dreaming of ¹_____ away from it all, relaxing, and having some amazing experiences. Here's a list of my top five dream destinations and what I'd like to do there.

**1 Costa Rica: the rainforest**
I really want to ²_____ hiking in the rainforest in Costa Rica. I'd visit the Braulio Carrillo National Park and then hike alongside the crystal-clear waters of the Corinto River.

**2 Canada: the Northern Lights**
I'd love to travel to Canada to see the Aurora Borealis — the Northern Lights. Imagine seeing the nighttime sky full of color like that — amazing.

**3 The U.S.: a classic road trip**
I'd really like to ³_____ a road trip across the U.S. I'd rent a car in Chicago and drive along famous Route 66. It takes five days to ⁴_____ to California. You can't beat the freedom of the open road.

**4 The Galápagos Islands: swimming with sharks**
I've always wanted to ⁵_____ scuba diving around the Galápagos Islands. It would be amazing to see all the sea life there and swim with sharks!

**5 Florida: Shuttle Launch Experience**
I'd love to try the Shuttle Launch Experience at the Kennedy Space Center, and feel like I'm floating like an astronaut with the sensation of weightlessness.

**B** Would you like to go to any of these places or do these activities?

**3 A** ▶ 12.2 Listen to Paul and Lia talking about their friend Carl's blog post in exercise 2. Which two activities do Paul and Lia both want to do?

**B** ▶ 12.2 Listen again and match the statements with the replies.

1 I'm reading his blog right now.
2 I love hiking.
3 I've always wanted to see the Northern Lights.
4 I don't like the cold very much.
5 I don't really like long car rides.
6 I'd love to swim with sharks.
7 I wouldn't want to float like an astronaut.

a So have I.
b So do I.
c So am I.
d Neither do I.
e I wouldn't.
f Neither would I.
g I do.

102

So/Neither do I ■ phrases with *go* and *get*  **LANGUAGE 12A**

**4 A** Look at the replies in exercise 3B. Which ones ...
1 agree with an affirmative statement?
2 agree with a negative statement?
3 disagree with an affirmative statement?
4 disagree with a negative statement?

**B** Choose the correct options to complete the rules. Then read the Grammar box.
1 We use *so / neither* to agree with an affirmative statement.
2 We use *so / neither* to agree with a negative statement.
3 We use an *auxiliary / main* verb in the reply.

| Grammar | So/Neither do I |
|---|---|

Agreeing:
"I love studying English."   "So do I."
"I haven't finished yet."   "Neither have I."
"I was at home yesterday."   "So was I."
"I'm not going away this year."   "Neither am I."

Disagreeing:
"I didn't like the movie."   "I did."
"I'm really hungry."   "I'm not."
"I won't go there again."   "I will."
"I don't understand."   "I do."

Go to Grammar practice: *So/Neither do I*, page 134

**5 A** ▶ 12.4 **Pronunciation: auxiliary verbs and stress** Listen and underline the stressed words.
Do we stress the auxiliary verb?
1 Neither do I.
2 I will.
3 So do I.
4 Neither have I.
5 So did I.
6 I haven't.

**B** ▶ 12.4 Listen again and repeat.

Go to Communication practice: Student A page 165, Student B page 173

**6 A** Match statements 1–6 with replies a–f. Complete the replies with an auxiliary verb.
1 I've never been to the U.S.
2 I spent two weeks at the beach last year.
3 I won't go away with my family next year.
4 I wouldn't want to go on a road trip.
5 I don't like traveling by bus.
6 I really need to get away from it all.

a So _____ I. I've been so stressed out!
b I _____ ! I went to Miami last year.
c Neither _____ I. I prefer to drive.
d I _____ . I didn't get away at all.
e I _____ . We go on vacation together every year.
f Neither _____ I. I hate long car rides.

**B** In pairs, say the statements in 6A, changing them so they are true for you. Reply with a true answer.

A *I've never been to Europe.*   B *I have. I went to Spain last year.*

**7 A** Write one thing for each topic.

- an amazing place you've been to
- a place you haven't been to, but would like to visit
- something you don't like doing on vacation
- a future plan

**B** In pairs, discuss what you wrote in 7A. Agree or disagree and ask more questions.

A *I don't like playing sports when I'm on vacation.*   B *Neither do I – vacations are for relaxing! What do you like doing?*

 Write replies to the statements in exercise 3B. The replies should be true for you.

103

# 12 SKILLS    LISTENING  identifying agreement between speakers ■ air travel ■ linking: /w/ and /y/

## 12B Fly away

**1 A** Look at the e-ticket below and answer the questions.
1. What time does the flight **take off** from Los Angeles and **land** in New York?
2. What time do passengers have to **board** the plane? At which **gate**?
3. What's the passenger's seat number? Is it an **aisle seat** or a **window seat**?

**B** What do the words in **bold** in exercise 1A mean?

**Go to Vocabulary practice:** air travel, page 155

**2** Discuss the questions in pairs.
1. Do you like flying? Why/Why not?
2. What are the best and worst things about traveling by plane?

**3 A** ▶ 12.6  Watch or listen to the first part of *Learning Curve* and complete the summary.

> Today's show is about how people feel about flying. Penny and Ethan both get a little ¹_____ before a flight.
>
> Ethan mentions that ²_____ % of people are afraid of flying. Symptoms of this fear are feeling ³_____ and panicking. To help these people, there are courses at ⁴_____ where people can "practice" flying.
>
> Some people, however, simply don't want to travel by plane. They prefer to travel shorter distances by other means of transportation and stay longer in a place to explore the area. This is called "⁵_____ travel."

**B** ▶ 12.6  Compare your answers in pairs. Watch or listen again and check your answers.

**4** ▶ 12.7  How do we know that Ethan has the same opinion as Penny about flying? Listen and complete the conversation. Then read the Skill box.

> **Penny** I love flying. It's exciting. But I also get a little nervous when I'm about to fly.

> **Ethan** _____, Penny. And that's very common. Most people feel a bit nervous before they fly.

### Skill  identifying agreement between speakers

There are a number of ways English speakers show agreement with each other. Recognizing these will help you follow a conversation.
- Listen for what the first person's opinion is, and then listen carefully to how the second person responds.
- Listen for ways of agreeing: *So do I. Neither do I. Me too. I do, too. Me neither. It sure is. It certainly is. True. Exactly. Absolutely.*
- Sometimes the first person invites agreement: *You like flying, don't you? (No, I don't.)*

104

identifying agreement between speakers ■ air travel ■ linking: /w/ and /y/   LISTENING   SKILLS   **12B**

**5** ▶ 12.8 Watch or listen to the second part of the show. Penny talks to Hanna, Monroe, and Anoush. Which person ...

1 has arrived at his/her destination airport? _____
2 is going somewhere warmer? _____
3 wants to change his/her seat assignment? _____
4 had to change his/her travel plans due to bad weather? _____
5 works for an airline? _____
6 is going to work during the flight? _____

**6** ▶ 12.8 Watch or listen again. How do the speakers agree with Penny? Complete the responses.

That's a long flight!  →  Monroe: ¹Yeah, _____ _____ _____

That sounds a bit stressful!  →  Anoush: ² _____

They are very patient, aren't they?  →  Anoush: ³Yes, _____ _____ _____

**7** In pairs, say these phrases slowly, separating each word. Then say them quickly, linking each word. What happens between the words marked with a link?

1 So do I.   2 I do as well.   3 I agree.   4 No, he isn't.

---

### Listening builder — linking: /w/ and /y/

When a word ends in a vowel sound and the next word starts with a vowel sound, we usually link the words together by adding an extra sound.

When a word ends in /uː/, /ow/, or /aw/, we link it using /w/:

/w/ /w/ /w/
Who are you?   Go away.   How are you?

When a word ends in /ey/, /iy/, or /ay/, we link it using /y/:

/y/ /y/ /y/
Say it.   She agrees.   I understand.

---

**8 A** ▶ 12.9 Read the Listening builder. Listen to the phrases in exercise 7. Which sounds are used between the words marked with a link, /w/ or /y/?

**B** ▶ 12.9 Listen again and repeat the phrases.

**9** In pairs, discuss which of these things you prefer.

1 aisle seats or window seats
2 taking off or landing
3 setting off or arriving back home
4 traveling by plane or "slow travel"
5 traveling during the day or at night
6 being the passenger or being the driver/pilot

**Personal Best**  What advice would you give to someone who is afraid of flying?

105

# 12 LANGUAGE  modals of deduction

## 12C Around the world

**1** In pairs, answer the questions.
1 Do you ever watch TV game shows? Which ones?
2 Do you try to answer the questions? If so, do you often get them right?

**2** Read the instructions for the game show. Would you be a good contestant on the show? Why/Why not?

**9.00 p.m. Channel 7**

**What on Earth?**

In this popular game show, the teams see a photo of a famous place, building, or object from around the world. They get three clues, and guess where or what the photo is. They can ask for more clues if they can't guess, but the fewer clues they ask for, the more points they get!

**3 A** Look at the three pictures. Can you guess what each one shows and where they are?

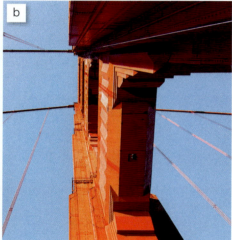

**B** ▶ 12.10  Listen to three pairs of contestants on the game show. Were any of your answers correct?

**4 A** Look at the sentences the contestants said. Which pictures were they talking about?

1 It must be the Golden Gate Bridge.
2 It must be some kind of statue.
3 It can't be the White House.
4 It can't be London.
5 It might be somewhere in Eastern Europe.
6 It might be the White House.

**B** Match the deductions in 4A with the information the contestants used to make the deductions.

a It's pretty.
b The clue was "it's not a capital city."
c It's not white!
d It's a bridge with a color in its name.
e It looks a bit like a head.
f It has a color in its name.

**5** Look at the deductions in exercise 4A again. What do *must*, *might*, and *can't* mean? Match deductions 1–6 with meanings a–c. Then read the Grammar box.

a I think this is possibly true. _____ _____
b I'm sure this is true. _____ _____
c I'm sure this isn't true. _____ _____

modals of deduction **LANGUAGE** **12C**

### 📖 Grammar  modals of deduction

**Something you think is true:**
You've been traveling since five o'clock this morning. You **must** be tired.

**Something you don't think is true:**
He **can't** be a doctor. He's much too young.

**Something you think is possibly true:**
Carla isn't here. She **might** be studying in the library since she has an exam tomorrow.

**Look!** We also use *may* or *could* for something that is possibly true:
James isn't here. He **may** be at home, or he **could** be at the gym.

**Go to Grammar practice:** modals of deduction, page 135

**6** Match sentences 1–6 with replies a–f.

1 I think Marta just arrived.
2 How old is Jack?
3 Do you think the neighbors are at home?
4 Ricardo is in such good shape!
5 Why didn't Helen eat any steak?
6 Tina's not answering her phone.

a I don't know. She **might be** a vegetarian.
b I know. He **must get** a lot of exercise.
c He's in college, so he **must be** at least eighteen.
d It **can't be** her. She said she wasn't coming.
e She **might be** swimming.
f They **can't be**. All the lights are off.

**7 A** ▶ 12.12 **Pronunciation: sentence stress** Listen to sentences a–f in exercise 6. Look at the words in **bold**. Which do we stress most, the modal verb or the main verb?

**B** In pairs, practice saying the sentences and answers in exercise 6.

**8** Complete the conversation in a restaurant with *might*, *must*, and *can't*.

A Oh look, there's the waiter, carrying a tray. There's nobody else in here, so that ¹_____ be our food.
B Didn't you order a pizza, though? That looks like pasta. It ²_____ be for us.
A Why is it taking so long? We're the only people here – the kitchen ³_____ be that busy!
B It hasn't been that long. There ⁴_____ be a problem, or the chef ⁵_____ be taking a coffee break. You didn't have any breakfast, did you? You ⁶_____ be starving!

**Go to Communication practice:** Student A page 165, Student B page 174

**9** Look at the two pictures. In pairs, use modals of deduction to talk about the pictures. Who are the people? Where are they? What is happening?

**Personal Best**  Work with a partner. Show each other photos on your cell phones and make deductions about the photos.  107

## 12 SKILLS | WRITING | writing an online review ■ adverbs of attitude

## 12D Five-star review

**1** Discuss the questions in pairs.
1. Have you ever had a very good or bad experience of a hotel, restaurant, or organized activity? What happened?
2. Have you ever read or written online reviews? What for?

**2** Read three online reviews quickly. How many stars (out of five) do you think each reviewer gave?

### The Sands Hotel, San Francisco

We stayed at The Sands Hotel to celebrate spring break in our final year of college. We were looking for a budget hotel downtown, and we couldn't be happier with our experience.

It's a two-star hotel, so we had expected the building to be pretty old with very small rooms, but, actually, all the rooms were bright and modern. It was pretty hot, though, and, unfortunately, they don't have air conditioning.

As this is a budget hotel, these are obviously not luxury accommodations, but it would be perfect for people who are looking for an affordable place to stay in a central location.

### La Gamba Tapas, Minnesota

My classmates and I went to La Gamba Tapas for our end-of-year meal last month. We were really looking forward to it, but I'm sorry to say that it wasn't a good experience.

They had told us that we wouldn't need a reservation, but, in fact, we had to wait forty minutes to get a table. The food wasn't bad, but we were told by our very rude waiter that they had run out of a lot of dishes. We had wanted to try their famous garlic shrimp – hopefully, next time they will have some. If we ever go back, that is!

All in all, the food at La Gamba Tapas is good, but I wouldn't recommend it to people who value good service.

### Horse & Holiday, Alberta, Canada

This summer, my boyfriend and I decided to go on a three-day horseback riding trip in the Rocky Mountains. The trip was great – it was well organized with helpful guides, and the views of the mountains were breathtaking.

According to the website, the trip is for riders of all abilities, but I had never ridden before, and I found it really difficult. Luckily, they were very sympathetic when I decided halfway through that I wanted to stop, and they arranged for a van to take me to the hostel.

People who ride well and really enjoy the great outdoors would have the trip of a lifetime, but it's definitely not for beginners.

writing an online review ■ adverbs of attitude  **WRITING**  **SKILLS** **12D**

> 🔧 **Skill** writing an online review
>
> We write a review to give our personal opinions about a product or service.
> - Describe your expectations before. Use phrases like *we had expected …, according to the website …* .
> - Describe what really happened. Use phrases like *in fact …, (but) actually …* .
> - Make a recommendation about who the product or service would be good for. Use phrases like *perfect for …, not really suitable for …* .

**3** Read the Skill box. Answer questions 1–3 for each of the three reviews.
  1 What were the reviewer's expectations?
  2 What actually happened?
  3 According to each reviewer, who would or wouldn't enjoy the experience?

**4** Find examples of positive and negative opinions in the three reviews.

| positive | negative |
|---|---|
|  |  |

> 🧩 **Text builder** adverbs of attitude
>
> We use adverbs of attitude to say what we think about something.
> *We had dinner at a famous steak restaurant. **Surprisingly**, they had vegetarian dishes.*
> *I had heard great things about the hotel, but, **unfortunately**, it had closed the previous month.*
> *The waiter was very rude. **Clearly**, he had more important things to do than serve us!*
>
> **Look!** Adverbs of attitude usually go at the beginning of a clause or sentence.

**5** Read the Text builder. Complete the sentences with adverbs. Then check your answers in the reviews.
  1 It was pretty hot, though, and, _____ , they don't have air conditioning.
  2 As this is a budget hotel, these are _____ not luxury accommodations.
  3 We had wanted to try their famous garlic shrimp – _____ , next time they will have some.
  4 _____ , they were very sympathetic when I decided halfway through that I wanted to stop.

**6** Match sentences 1–6 with a–f.
  1 According to the guidebook, White Shores was the best beach in the area.
  2 The restaurant looked old and dirty outside.
  3 The restaurant was the most famous one in town.
  4 I left my passport in the hotel.
  5 We had wanted to visit the castle in the Old Town.
  6 The bicycle tour lasts six hours.

  a Unfortunately, it closed at 4 p.m., and we got there at 5.
  b Obviously, it was also the most expensive.
  c Sadly, it was crowded, and the sea was polluted.
  d Clearly, you have to be in very good shape to go on it.
  e Luckily, the receptionist found it and gave it back.
  f Surprisingly, we had the best meal of our lives there.

**7 A** **PREPARE** Think about a hotel, restaurant, or service that you had a good or bad experience with. Make notes about why it was good or bad.

  **B** **PRACTICE** Use the Skill box to help you write an online review.

  **C** **PERSONAL BEST** Exchange reviews with your partner. Would you visit the place in your partner's review? Why/Why not?

**Personal Best** Imagine you are the manager of the company you reviewed. Write a post in response to the review.

# 11 and 12 REVIEW and PRACTICE

## Grammar

**1** Choose the correct options to complete the sentences.

1. **A** What does he do for a living? **B** He's _____ airline pilot.
   a the    b –    c an
2. If I _____ up late, I would have arrived in time for the meeting.
   a wouldn't have woken    b hadn't woken
   c didn't wake
3. **A** I can't play tennis very well. **B** Neither _____ .
   a can I.    b do I.    c can't I.
4. Only 10% of people pass their driving test the first time, so it _____ be difficult.
   a can    b must    c can't
5. _____ earthquakes are pretty common in Japan.
   a The    b An    c –
6. If she'd taken her umbrella to work, she _____ so wet.
   a wouldn't have gotten    b wouldn't get
   c hadn't gotten
7. **A** I wouldn't want to live in a large city. **B** Oh, I _____ .
   a like    b would    c wouldn't
8. Lucy _____ be a vegetarian. She had steak for dinner last night.
   a can't    b must    c can

**2** Use the structures in parentheses to complete the sentences so they mean the same as the first sentence.

1. He's an actor. I saw him on that talk show. (definite article)
   He's _____ I saw on that talk show.
2. I didn't know it was a secret so I told her. (third conditional)
   If I _____ it was a secret, I _____ her.
3. **A** I really enjoyed the movie. **B** I enjoyed it, too. (so)
   **A** I really enjoyed the movie. **B** _____ .
4. I'm sure this isn't Steve's car because his car's red. (modal of deduction)
   This _____ Steve's car because his car's red.
5. We go on vacation in April and September. (indefinite article)
   We go on vacation _____ year.
6. She worked 50 hours last week, so she was exhausted on the weekend. (third conditional)
   She _____ exhausted on the weekend if she _____ 50 hours last week.
7. **A** He hasn't seen the game yet. **B** I haven't seen it, either. (neither)
   **A** He hasn't seen the game yet. **B** _____ .
8. It's possible that David is at work. (modal of deduction)
   David _____ be at work.

**3** Choose the correct options to complete the text.

### Is that e-mail genuine?

We've all heard stories about ¹*the / –* people who trick others into giving them money or personal information. I wanted to learn how to protect myself online, so I asked for advice from Bill Young, ²*a / the* journalist for a consumer magazine.

Bill, how can we protect ourselves from ³*the / –* scammers?

Well, ⁴*the / –* first thing to do is to be aware that they exist. Don't reply to e-mails from people you don't know – they may not be genuine. I did once, and I began receiving twenty scam e-mails every day. If I hadn't replied, I wouldn't ⁵*had / have* ended up on the scammer's list of confirmed e-mail addresses. I didn't give the scammers my bank information, though, which is what they were asking for.

Yes, my elderly neighbor recently got ⁶*an / the* e-mail that looked like it was from her bank, asking for information about her account. She thought, "It ⁷*must / can't* be from the bank," so she sent the information, and a lot of money was stolen from her account. If she'd known more about scammers, she ⁸*must / might* not have believed that the e-mail was genuine. Now she wants to know all about them, and ⁹*so / neither* do I!

Good! If you get an unexpected e-mail, remember that it ¹⁰*can't / could* be fake. And, just as important, remember to change your passwords regularly, and always use different passwords for different accounts.

## Vocabulary

**1** (Circle) the word that is different. Explain your answer.

1. exhausted    miserable
   starving     gorgeous
2. rainbow      jungle
   forest       desert
3. departure board    gate
   take off     departure lounge
4. show your passport    check in
   pack         go through security
5. iceberg      hail
   tornado      hurricane
6. fantastic    filthy
   gorgeous     hilarious
7. earthquake   storm
   monsoon      flood
8. go to bed    go to school
   go home      go traveling

110

## REVIEW and PRACTICE 11 and 12

**2** Match the words in the box with definitions 1–8.

carry-on bag    hail    get somewhere    flight attendant
enormous    boarding pass    tiny    coast

1. arrive at a place _____
2. a person that looks after the passengers on a plane _____
3. very small _____
4. a bag you can bring with you on a plane _____
5. you show this when you get on a plane _____
6. the area of land next to the sea _____
7. small balls of ice that fall from the sky _____
8. extremely large _____

**3** Complete the sentences with the words in the box.

hurricane    canyon    away    furious
starving    hilarious    glacier    hill

1. We had a great view from the top of the _____ .
2. That romantic comedy is absolutely _____ .
3. I haven't been _____ this year. I need a vacation!
4. She was _____ when she saw that her neighbor had damaged her new car.
5. The _____ is 15 km. long, about 300 m. deep, and there's a river at the bottom.
6. I didn't have any lunch today, so I'm absolutely _____ . Let's have dinner now.
7. We were able to go inside the _____ and see the beautiful shapes of the ice.
8. The storms and strong winds during the _____ killed two people.

**4** Choose the correct options to complete the text.

### Marrakech, the Sahara, and the Atlas Mountains

I went ¹*for / on* vacation to Morocco last year with some friends. We spent the first day in Marrakech, where we went ²*on / to* a guided tour around the old town. On the second day, we decided to go ³*for / on* a trip to the ⁴*jungle / desert*, where we rode camels across the sand. It was fall, so although it was pretty hot during the day, it wasn't ⁵*boiling / freezing* like in the summer. The day after our visit to the Sahara, we ⁶*went on hiking / went hiking* in the Atlas Mountains. The view from the top of Mount Toubkal was ⁷*fantastic / hilarious*, but we ⁸*went / got* really cold, so we didn't stay there long. We didn't get back to Marrakech until after midnight, and I felt absolutely ⁹*gorgeous / exhausted*, so I went ¹⁰*to / in* bed and slept for twelve hours.

## Personal Best

**Lesson 11A** — Name three types of extreme weather.

**Lesson 11A** — Write three sentences about the natural world: one with *a/an*, one with *the*, and one with a noun with no article.

**Lesson 11B** — Write two sentences beginning with a noun phrase.

**Lesson 11C** — Name five extreme adjectives.

**Lesson 11C** — Write three third conditional sentences.

**Lesson 11D** — Give two expressions for making recommendations.

**Lesson 12A** — Name two phrases with *go for* and two with *go on*.

**Lesson 12A** — Write three sentences that could come before "So would I," "Neither did I," and "I haven't."

**Lesson 12B** — Name three things you can find in an airport.

**Lesson 12C** — Write three sentences about experiences you haven't had. Use modals of deduction, e.g., *Skiing must be fun.*

**Lesson 12C** — Write three sentences about what people are doing now. Use modals of deduction, e.g., *My sister might be having dinner.*

**Lesson 12D** — Write three sentences using *fortunately*, *unluckily*, and *hopefully*.

111

## GRAMMAR PRACTICE

### 1A Simple present and present continuous; action and state verbs

▶ 1.2

I **check** my e-mails every morning.
I **need** to access the Internet.
My sister **has** a new job.
I**'m replying** to your message right now.
**Are** you **enjoying** your vacation?
My parents **are having** breakfast.

### Simple present

We use the simple present to talk about things that are always true.
*They speak Portuguese in Brazil.  The sun sets in the west.*
We also use the simple present to talk about regular routines.
*I start work at 8:45.  My brother gets up at 6:30 every day.*
We often use the simple present with frequency adverbs and expressions.
*We never go shopping on Saturdays.  They often go to the beach on the weekend.*

### Present continuous

We use the present continuous to talk about actions that are happening now.
*He's speaking to his sister on Skype right now.  I'm waiting for you at the bus stop.*
We also use the present continuous to talk about actions that are temporary.
*She's living with her parents at the moment.  I'm studying economics this year.*

### Action and state verbs

We can use the simple present and present continuous with verbs that describe an action.
*I play soccer on Wednesday evenings.*
*I'm playing a soccer game on my computer right now.*
We usually use the simple present, not the present continuous, with verbs which describe a state.
*She doesn't like her new haircut.* NOT ~~She isn't liking her new haircut.~~
*I don't understand. What do you mean?* NOT ~~I'm not understanding. What are you meaning?~~
*I own a car.* NOT ~~I'm owning a car.~~

| state verbs | |
|---|---|
| feelings | like, love, hate, want, prefer, need |
| | *Enjoy* is used in the continuous tense: *I'm enjoying the party.* |
| thoughts and opinions | know, believe, remember, forget, understand, think, feel, consider, realize, expect, agree, suppose, doubt, mean |
| states | be, have (possess), exist, seem, appear, belong, own, matter |
| senses | taste, sound, look, feel, hear, smell |

**Look!** Some verbs can be both action and state verbs, with different meanings.
*I'm thinking about my vacation.* (the action of thinking = action verb)
*I think this website is the best.* (an opinion = state verb)
*He's having steak and French fries.* (the action of eating = action verb)
*He has a white sports car.* (a possession = state verb)
*I'm feeling happy.* (the action of having an emotion = action verb)
*It feels soft.* (the sense = state verb)

---

1 Choose the correct options to complete the sentences.
  1 They *don't want / aren't wanting* to go swimming today because it's too cold.
  2 I *prefer / 'm preferring* this coffee – it *tastes / 's tasting* much better than that coffee.
  3 I can't talk to you right now. We *have / 're having* lunch.
  4 Why *do you wait / are you waiting* for the bus? There aren't any buses after midnight!
  5 I *don't understand / 'm not understanding* this movie because they're speaking too fast.
  6 We *think / 're thinking* all museums should be free.
  7 He *works / 's working* in the library this morning.
  8 That suitcase *belongs / is belonging* to me.

2 Complete the sentences with the simple present or present continuous form of the verbs in parentheses.
  1 I _____ (talk) to my boss at the moment. Can I call you back in five minutes?
  2 They _____ (send) me a birthday card every year.
  3 I _____ (leave) the office now. I'll call you later.
  4 You look really tired. I _____ (think) you _____ (need) to go to bed now.
  5 I'm so hungry! I _____ (think) about dinner.
  6 I can't talk now. I _____ (study) in the library.
  7 I _____ (stay) at my best friend's house at the moment.
  8 My Internet connection _____ (not work) today.

3 Complete the text with the correct form of the verbs in parentheses.

I ¹_____ (not understand) why some people ²_____ (believe) that we ³_____ (talk) to each other much less than in the past. I ⁴_____ (own) a smartphone, and I ⁵_____ (use) it all the time. I ⁶_____ (send) messages to my friends several times a day, and I often ⁷_____ (call) them to talk. It's true that we ⁸_____ (have) very busy lives nowadays and that we ⁹_____ always _____ (not speak) face-to-face. It ¹⁰_____ (seem) to me that electronic devices ¹¹_____ (make) our lives much easier. For example, I ¹²_____ (write) this blog now while I ¹³_____ (sit) on the train.

◀ Go back to page 5

GRAMMAR PRACTICE

# 1C  Question forms

> ▶ 1.7
>
> **Do** you **speak** German?
> **Could** we **sit** here, please?
> **When does** class start?
>
> **Who told** you that story?
> **How many people work** at your company?
> **What are** you **talking about**?

## Yes/No questions

To make a question with a *Yes* or *No* answer, we put the verb *be* or an auxiliary or modal verb before the subject. For the simple present and simple past, we use *do/does* and *did*, with the base form of the main verb.

| statement | question |
| --- | --- |
| He's from the U.S. | Is he from the U.S.? |
| They've been to China. | Have they been to China? |
| We were watching TV. | Were you watching TV? |
| She'll win the game. | Will she win the game? |
| I can speak Italian. | Can you speak Italian? |
| They like tea. | Do they like tea? |
| He plays tennis well. | Does he play tennis well? |
| We went to Paris. | Did you go to Paris? |

## Object questions

In most *wh-* questions, the question word or phrase (*who, what, why, how many, what type of*, etc.) is the object of the verb. In object questions, we use an auxiliary verb before the subject, like in *Yes/No* questions.

| question word | auxiliary verb | subject | main verb |
| --- | --- | --- | --- |
| Where | do | you | live? |
| Who | did | she | meet? |
| Why | have | they | come? |
| What | are | you | doing? |
| When | will | you | arrive? |
| How long | can | you | stay? |

## Subject questions

In subject questions, the question word asks about the subject. We use the affirmative form of the verb, so in present and simple past tenses, we don't use *do/does/did*.

| question word | main verb |
| --- | --- |
| Who | bought those flowers? NOT ~~Who did buy those flowers?~~ |
| What | happened in 1999? NOT ~~What did happen in 1999?~~ |
| Which animal | makes a noise like that? NOT ~~Which animal does make a noise like that?~~ |

## Questions with prepositions

When the main verb needs a preposition (*look for, talk to, wait for, come from, think about*, etc.), we normally put the preposition at the end of the question.

*What are you looking for?* NOT ~~*For what are you looking?*~~
*Who was she talking to?* NOT ~~*To who was she talking?*~~
*Who did you go to the movies with?* NOT ~~*With who did you go to the movies?*~~

**1**  Put the words in the correct order to make questions.

1  your friend / work / does / near here / ?
_____

2  like / you / do / going / to concerts / ?
_____

3  was / running / she / why / ?
_____

4  can / tell / you / a secret / I / ?
_____

5  come / from / which / country / you / do / ?
_____

6  speak / more slowly / you / could / ?
_____

7  you / see / did / at the party / who / ?
_____

8  which / to / movie theater / go / you / did / ?
_____

9  from / where / does / he / come / ?
_____

10  looking / who / she / for / was / ?
_____

**2**  Write subject questions for the statements.

1  Which team _____ ?
   Argentina won the game.
2  Who _____ ?
   Alexander Graham Bell invented the telephone.
3  How many students _____ ?
   More than 40 students study here.
4  What _____ to the phone?
   Something strange happened to the phone. Now it's not working.
5  Which movie _____ ?
   The movie we saw last week won the Oscar for Best Picture.
6  Who _____ ?
   A guy named Jacques lives here.

**3**  Write questions for the underlined answers.

1  I spoke to <u>Jessica</u> in the park.
_____

2  He gave Mike <u>a book</u>.
_____

3  <u>Carlo and Mira</u> went to the party.
_____

4  We arrived at <u>4 p.m.</u>
_____

5  <u>The twins</u> drank all the orange juice.
_____

6  She was watching <u>a horror movie</u>.
_____

7  I'm waiting for <u>Toni</u>.
_____

8  <u>Jen</u> works in that building.
_____

◀ Go back to page 9

113

# GRAMMAR PRACTICE

## 2A Narrative tenses

 2.2

Last week, we **bought** a new car.
It **was snowing**, and people **were hurrying** home from work.
I **was cooking** dinner when someone **knocked** on the door.
It **had stopped** raining before we **left** the party.
I **was** disappointed because my friends **had forgotten** my birthday.

A narrative describes past events. We often use the simple past, the past continuous, and the past perfect in a narrative.

### Simple past

We use the simple past to describe the main events in a narrative. These are completed actions in the past.

*Mike opened the door and saw a package on the floor. He picked it up and opened it. He couldn't believe what he saw!*

Remember that many simple past verbs are irregular. For a full list of irregular verbs, see page 175.

### Past continuous

We use the past continuous to describe the background events in a narrative.

*One fall afternoon, I was sitting in the kitchen.*
*Last night, it was raining, and we were watching TV on the sofa.*

We also use the past continuous to describe an action that was in progress when a completed action happened.

*She was having breakfast when someone knocked on the door.*
*I was taking a shower when the phone rang.*

We often use *when* and *while* to connect past events.

*I was walking along the beach when I found a wallet.*
*While they were waiting for the bus, it started to rain.*

### Past perfect

We use the past perfect to describe an action that happened before another action in the past.

*I called James at his office, but he had already gone home.*
*They decided to go for a drive in Paul's new car. He had bought it only two days before.*

**Look!** We can use the three narrative tenses with *when*, with different meanings.
*When she arrived, we had dinner.* = First she arrived, and then we had dinner.
*When she arrived, we were having dinner.* = She arrived during dinner.
*When she arrived, we had already had dinner.* = First we had dinner, and then she arrived.

1 Choose the correct options to complete the sentences.
  1 While Tina *rode a bike / was riding a bike* to work, she *was dropping / dropped* her purse.
  2 When I closed the door, I *was realizing / realized* that I *left / had left* my keys inside the house.
  3 We *watched / were watching* a movie when we *were hearing / heard* a strange noise outside.
  4 When John *had gotten / got* home, we told him what *had happened / was happening* earlier that afternoon.
  5 When they *were arriving / arrived*, the concert *already began / had already begun*.
  6 It was a hot summer's day. We *sat / were sitting* in the garden, and the sun *was shining / shone*.
  7 When the movie *was ending / ended*, the children *went / were going* straight to bed.

2 Complete the sentences with the correct past tense of the verbs in parentheses.

  1 I _____ (take) my umbrella with me because I _____ (see) the weather forecast earlier.
  2 She _____ (read) the whole book while she _____ (wait) for me.
  3 While Maria _____ (make) dinner, David _____ (take out) the garbage.
  4 I _____ (call) the police right away when I _____ (saw) the broken window.
  5 She _____ (start) laughing when she _____ (see) his new hat.
  6 I _____ (not want) to see that movie because I _____ (see) it twice before.
  7 Anna _____ (live) in San Francisco when she _____ (finish) her first novel.

3 Complete the text with the correct past tense of the verbs in the box.

  | arrive   ring   leave   put   answer   walk   drive   buy |

Last Friday, I went to the supermarket to buy a cake for a friend's party. It was really busy as people ¹_____ food for the weekend. While I ²_____ back to my car, my phone ³_____. I ⁴_____ the cake on the roof of my car and ⁵_____ the phone. After the call, I ⁶_____ to the party, but I didn't realize that I ⁷_____ the cake on my car! Luckily, it was still there when I ⁸_____!

◀ Go back to page 13

# GRAMMAR PRACTICE

## 2C *used to* and *usually*

▶ 2.11

My mom **used to have** long hair, but now it's much shorter.
I **didn't use to like** seafood, but now I often eat it.
**Did** you **use to play** the violin?
I **never used to watch** TV in the evenings.
We **usually go** for a walk after dinner.

### used to

We use *used to* + base form to talk about habits or situations that were true in the past, but are not true now. They can be states or actions.

*I used to hate classical music, but now I love it.* (hate = state)
*She used to go swimming every day.* (go swimming = action)

We form the negative and questions like other regular verbs in the simple past.

*I didn't use to like classical music.* NOT *I didn't used to like classical music.*
*Did you use to live on this street?* NOT *Did you used to live on this street?*

We often use a mixture of *used to* and the simple past when we describe past situations. It sounds unnatural to use *used to* with every verb.

*I used to get a lot of exercise when I was in school. I played tennis every weekend, and I went swimming three or four times a week.*

We use the simple past, not *used to*, when we talk about things that happened only once, or when we say how many times something happened.

*I got a job five years ago.* NOT *I used to get a job five years ago.*
*We went to Rio three times when I was young.* NOT *We used to go to Rio three times when I was young.*

We often use *never used to* instead of *didn't use to*.

*He never used to call me but now he calls every day.*
*The neighbors never used to make so much noise!*

### usually

*Used to* only refers to the past. We use *usually* or *normally* + simple present to talk about situations and habits which are true now.

*On Sundays, I usually have eggs for breakfast.* (present habit)
*On Sundays, I used to have eggs for breakfast.* (past habit)

**Look!** We can also use *usually* in the past. It has a similar meaning to *used to*.
*We usually had dinner together every evening.*
*We used to have dinner together every evening.*

1 Complete the sentences with the correct form of *used to* or the simple past and the verbs in parentheses. Use *used to* if possible.

1 I _____ my brother and sister regularly, but now we all live in different cities. (see)
2 How _____ to work before you had a car? (you/get)
3 They _____ each other when they were in school, but now they're getting married! (not like)
4 He _____ much money, but now he's rich. (not have)
5 We _____ with our friends more often when we lived in Miami. (get together)
6 Where _____ before you moved here? (you/live)
7 I _____ to reggae music, but now I love it. (never listen)
8 Jon _____ his British friend twice last year. (visit)
9 I used to sing when I was a child, and I _____ the guitar, too. (play)
10 We _____ in Los Angeles in 2012. (get married)

2 Complete the text with *usually* or the correct form of *used to* and a verb from the box.

not have   go (x2)   arrive   work (x2)

Six months ago, Sarah Thornton left her job in the city and moved to a small town in the country because she wanted a quieter life. "I
¹_____ sixteen hours a day, six days a week," she says. "It was very difficult. I
²_____ home exhausted at around 11 p.m. I ³_____ time for hobbies in the evening, and I didn't see my friends much," she says. "But now I'm happier. I ⁴_____ an eight-hour day now, so I have much more free time. It was strange living in the country at first. In the city, I ⁵_____ to concerts or go shopping on Sundays. There's nothing like that here. Now, I
⁶_____ running or do other outdoor activities every evening."

◀ Go back to page 17

115

GRAMMAR PRACTICE

## 3A Future forms: present continuous, *be going to*, and *will*

 3.4

We**'re taking** the bus to the airport at 6 a.m. tomorrow.
I**'m going to start** learning Japanese this year.
I**'ll make** you a cup of tea, if you want.
I**'ll call** you tonight.
**Should we go** for a walk?
**Should I put** some music on?

### Present continuous

We use the present continuous to talk about future plans. We usually specify when or where the event will take place.

*I'm meeting Sarah at the movies at 8:30 p.m.*
*We're flying to Miami tomorrow.*
*They're getting married next year.*

We usually use the present continuous to ask people about their plans.

*Are you doing anything tomorrow afternoon?*
*When are you going to the supermarket this week?*
*What are you doing this weekend?*

### be going to

We use *be going to* to talk about future plans and intentions.

*I'm going to call my mother tonight.*
*When are you going to buy a new car?*

The present continuous and *be going to* have similar meanings, but the present continuous often refers to the more immediate future.

*We're going to New York this summer!* = It's a definite plan and will happen soon.
*We're going to go to New York when we have the money!* = It's a plan, but it may be further in the future.

### will

We use *will* when we make an offer, promise, or instant decision.

*We'll take you to the airport, if you'd like.*
*I will do the dishes before I go out, I promise!*
*It's really hot in here. I'll open the window.*

> **Look!** We don't use *will* to talk about plans and intentions that are already decided.
> *I'm going to fly / I'm flying to New York on Tuesday.* NOT ~~I'll fly to New York on Tuesday.~~

### should

We can use *should* as a question with *I* or *we* to make offers and suggestions.

*Should I take you to the airport?*
*Should we go to that new restaurant by the beach?*

---

1 Choose the correct options to complete the sentences.
1 Next weekend,
  a we're going to have a party.
  b we'll have a party.
2 They're staying at a hotel near the beach next week,
  a and they've reserved a room for six nights.
  b but they haven't found a hotel yet.
3 Oh no, there's coffee all over the floor! Don't worry,
  a I'll clean it up in a minute.
  b I'm cleaning it up in a minute.
4 He's definitley leaving early tomorrow morning,
  a so he's called a cab for 6 a.m. to go to the station.
  b but maybe he'll stay until lunchtime.
5 I've made plans to see Sophie next week.
  a We're meeting at 2:30 on Wednesday.
  b We'll meet at 2:30 on Wednesday.

2 Complete the sentences with the present continuous, *be going to*, or *will*. Use the words in parentheses. There may be more than one answer.

1 I _____ (do) the ironing this week if you want.
2 We _____ (meet) Linda at 7:30 p.m. at the station. Don't be late!
3 I'm sorry, but I can't talk now. I _____ (give) you a call when I get home – I promise!
4 What _____ (you/do) on Saturday? _____ (we/go shopping)?
5 A Sarah's not here right now. Can I take a message?
  B No, thanks – I _____ (send) her a text.
6 I've decided I _____ (work) hard next year. I want to get good grades on my exams.
7 They _____ (arrive) at 11 a.m. – Jack's waiting at the station for them now.
8 I _____ (get) some exercise this weekend. I might play tennis, or I might go running.
9 A Do you want a salad or French fries with your hamburger?
  B I _____ (have) French fries, please.
10 Don't worry – I _____ (not tell) anyone your secret.
11 Jon wants to live closer to his family, so he _____ (move) in the next few years.
12 _____ (you/drive) into town later? Can I come with you?

◀ Go back to page 23

**GRAMMAR PRACTICE**

# 3C Defining and non-defining relative clauses

▶ 3.9

That's the man **who lives next door to us**.
That's the couple **that's always arguing**.
She's the woman **whose husband works for the government**.
That's the guy **I sit next to in class**.
My uncle lives in Los Angeles, **which is a really expensive city**.
My neighbors, **who have five children**, are really noisy.

A relative clause gives us more information about the subject of the main clause. We usually start a relative clause with a relative pronoun. We use:
– *who* or *that* for people
– *that* or *which* for objects
– *whose* + noun for possession
– *where* for places

## Defining relative clauses

We use a defining relative clause to say which person, thing, or place we are talking about.

*He's the man who I saw yesterday.*
*That's the phone that I want for my birthday.*
*She's the girl whose mother is a famous journalist.*
*That's the restaurant where we had dinner last week.*

We can omit *who*, *that*, and *which* when the verbs in the main clause and the relative clause have a different subject.

*He's the man (who/that) I met on vacation.*
*She lost the book (that/which) I lent her.*

We can't omit the relative pronoun when it is the subject of the relative clause.

*She's the woman who speaks French.* NOT ~~She's the woman speaks French.~~

## Non-defining relative clauses

A non-defining relative clause gives us extra information about something in the main clause. It doesn't identify what we are talking about. If we omit this clause, the sentence still makes sense.

We add a comma before a non-defining relative clause.
*This is my younger brother Ricardo, who lives in Washington D.C.*
*That's Tony's new sports car, which he bought in London last week.*
*Right now, Jen's on vacation in São Paulo, where her friend Maria lives.*

Sometimes we add a non-defining relative clause in the middle of a sentence. This is more common in written English.
*The hotel, which has over 200 rooms, is just 150 m. from the main square.*

We can't use *that* in non-defining clauses. We use *who* for people or *which* for things. We can't omit the relative pronoun.

> **Look!** Notice the difference in meaning between the sentences below.
>
> *The students who passed the exam received a certificate.*
> This means that not all the students passed. Only the students who passed received a certificate.
>
> *The students, who passed the exam, received a certificate.*
> This means that all the students passed, and they all received a certificate.

**1 A** Complete the sentences with the correct relative pronouns.

1 That's the man _____ I spoke to yesterday.
2 The mayor, _____ is in New York for a meeting, didn't answer the journalist's question.
3 It's a story about a man _____ dog saves his life.
4 It's the store _____ we were talking about yesterday.
5 He lives on South Street, _____ is near my office.
6 Michelle's the person _____ normally deals with computer problems.
7 In July, I'm going to stay with my cousin Sara, _____ lives in Mexico.
8 That's the hospital _____ I was born.

**B** Check (✔) the sentences in A where it's possible to omit the pronoun.

**2** Complete the second sentences so they mean the same as the first sentences. Use relative clauses.

1 We went to Bella Pizza. We had lunch there.
*We went to Bella Pizza, where we had lunch.*
2 Luke gave me a really interesting book yesterday. I'm reading it now.
Luke gave me a really interesting book yesterday, _____ .
3 Look at that car. My uncle wants one.
Look. That's the car _____ .
4 Can you see the park over there? We're meeting there tomorrow.
That's the park _____ tomorrow.
5 This is Mark. You met his brother last night.
This is Mark, _____ last night.
6 A man left a message for me this morning. What was his name?
What was the name of the man _____ ?

**3** Complete the text with phrases a–f and the correct relative pronoun.

a are both younger than me
b we used to do together
c I grew up
d backyard was much bigger
e lived on our street
f I shared with my brothers

My parents still live in the house [1]_____ .
I miss that house. My two brothers, [2]_____
used to annoy me, but I miss some of the things
[3]_____ . I also miss seeing the other kids
[4]_____ . Although it was an old house, it was
really comfortable. My bedroom, [5]_____,
was cool even in the summer. We only had a small
backyard, but we spent a lot of time playing with the boys
next door, [6]_____ than ours.

◀ Go back to page 27

117

# GRAMMAR PRACTICE

## 4A Quantifiers

 4.2

There 's **not much** traffic in my village. Do you have **a few** minutes to talk?
There are **a lot of** stores in the mall. I have **no** time to see him today.
There are **too many** buses downtown.
We do**n't** have **enough** places for young people to go.

### Small quantities

We use *a little* before uncountable nouns and *a few* before countable nouns.

*Can I have a little sugar in my coffee, please?*
*I'm busy right now. Can I call you back in a few minutes?*

We use *not much* and *not many* in negative sentences. We use *not much* before uncountable nouns and *not many* before countable nouns.

*There isn't much milk. Can you get some more, please?*
*I don't have many friends on Facebook.*

We also use (very) *little* and *few* (without *a*). They mean *not much* and *not many*.

*They speak very little English.* = *They don't speak much English.*
*She has very few friends in New York.* = *She doesn't have many friends in New York.*

### Large quantities

We use *a lot* (*of*) and *lots* (*of*) in affirmative statements before uncountable and countable nouns. We use *a lot of* before nouns, and *a lot* without a noun.

*I have lots of friends in the U.S.   She reads a lot of books. She reads a lot.*

We use *plenty of* to say there is enough or more than we need.

*Don't worry – we have plenty of time before the train leaves.*

> **Look!** In questions, we use *a lot of* before uncountable nouns and *many* or *a lot of* before countable nouns.
> *Was there a lot of snow last year?   Have you invited many people?*

### Zero quantity

We use *not any*, *no*, or *none* before uncountable and countable nouns. We use *none* in short answers.

*I have no money.* = *I don't have any money.*
*There are no tickets left.* = *There aren't any tickets left.*
*How many students got 100% on the exam?   None.*

### More than you need or want

We use *too*, *too many*, and *too much* to mean "more than is necessary or good."

*You've put too much sugar in my coffee.*
*There are too many people on this bus. It's too crowded.*

We use *enough* to mean "the right amount" or "sufficient." We can also use *not enough* to mean "less than is necessary" or "less than is good."

*I have enough money for a vacation.   There aren't enough parking lots here.*

> **Look!** We generally put *enough* before a noun, but after an adjective.
> *There are enough cookies for everyone.* NOT ~~There are cookies enough for everyone.~~
> *The box isn't big enough for all those books* NOT ~~The box isn't enough big for all those books.~~

---

**1** Choose the correct options to complete the sentences.
  1 Riding a bike in New York is dangerous because there are too *many* / *much* cars on the streets.
  2 Julia has *plenty of* / *lots* money, so she buys new clothes every week.
  3 There's usually *a lot of* / *few* snow in Sweden at this time of year.
  4 Do you have *little* / *a little* free time today so we can have a meeting?
  5 There aren't *enough parks* / *parks enough* in my town.
  6 Michael's an only child – he has *no* / *not* brothers or sisters.
  7 *Lots* / *Much* of my friends are married now, but *a few* / *a little* are still single.
  8 There isn't *any* / *no* bread left, so could you get some from the supermarket?
  9 I can't do this crossword – it's *too* / *too much* difficult for me.
  10 **A** How much ice cream is there in the fridge?
      **B** *Any.* / *None.*

**2** Read the text. Correct the eight mistakes.

A lot my friends take city vacations, but I can't understand why they want to spend their time off in a city. Most cities are too busy and too noisy. In a crowded city, there isn't space enough because there are always too much people around you. Of course, there are plenty things to buy – but that means that I don't have many money left after spending a little days in a city. I prefer to go to the country or to a beach town, somewhere where there is none traffic and where I can have a few time to myself to think and relax.

◀ Go back to page 31

## 4C Comparatives and superlatives, as … as

 4.14

My bedroom is **brighter than** the living room.
The first floor apartment is **less expensive than** the second floor apartment.
This is by far **the safest** suburb of the city.
The countryside around here is **the most beautiful** in the whole country.
My house is**n't as big as** my brother's house.

### Comparatives

We use comparative adjectives + *than* to compare two things, people, places, etc. With one-syllable adjectives, we add *-er*. With two-syllable adjectives ending in *-y*, we change the *y* to *i* and add *-er*. For adjectives with more than two syllables, we use *more* or *less*.

*Her house is smaller than yours.*   *English is easier than Russian.*
*Hotels in Tokyo are more expensive than in Madrid./Hotels in Madrid are less expensive than in Tokyo.*

We can use *a bit*, *a little*, or *slightly* before a comparative to say there is a small difference, and *a lot*, *much*, or *far* to say there is a big difference.

*My new apartment is a bit bigger than my old one.*
*I'm in much better shape than I used to be.*

### Superlatives

We use superlative adjectives to say that something is more or less than all the others in a group. With one-syllable adjectives, we put *the* in front and add *-est*. With two-syllable adjectives ending in *-y*, we change the *y* to *i* and add *-est*. With adjectives of more than two syllables, we use *the most* or *the least*.

*He's the oldest player on our team.*   *This is the funniest comedy on TV.*
*That's the most expensive hotel in Paris./That's the least economical place to stay.*

*The* can be replaced with a possessive adjective.

*It's her best album.*

We can put *by far* before a superlative to make it stronger.

*Lima is by far the biggest city in Peru.*

**Look!** We usually use *in* before places and groups of people, not *of*.
*She's the best player in the world.*   *He's the youngest person in my family.*

We often use the superlative with the present perfect + *ever* and *one of the*.

*That's the strangest movie I've ever seen.*
*This is one of the best restaurants in town.*

With one-syllable adjectives ending in consonant-vowel-consonant, we double the final consonant and add *-er / -est*.

*big – bigger – biggest   hot – hotter – hottest*

Some adjectives have irregular comparative and superlative forms.

*good – better – best   bad – worse – worst   far – farther/further – farthest/furthest*

### (not) as … as

We use *as … as* to say that two things are the same and *not as … as* to say that two things are different. We can use *just* with *as … as* to emphasize a similarity.

*Today, Boston is just as warm as Mexico City.*
*In the winter, Amsterdam isn't as cold as Moscow.*

---

**1** Complete the sentences with the words in parentheses. Use the correct form of the adjectives. Add any other words you need.

1. The bed in my hotel room is _____ as my bed at home. (just, comfortable)
2. _____ apartments are downtown. (expensive)
3. Jamie's new car isn't _____ as his old one. (big)
4. Susan lives in one of _____ parts of town. (nice)
5. Learning Spanish isn't as _____ learning Japanese. (difficult)
6. It's one of _____ books I've ever read. (funny)
7. Miami is _____ from New York than from Washington D.C. (a lot, far)
8. In January, Rio de Janeiro is usually _____ Buenos Aires. (slightly, hot)
9. That was _____ game I've ever seen. (by far, bad)
10. Mexican food is _____ British food. (a lot, spicy)

**2** Complete the second sentences so they mean the same as the first sentences.

1. John and James are both 1.70 m. tall.
   John is _____ James.
2. This restaurant is much better than the others in town.
   This is by _____ in town.
3. My new phone was much more expensive than my laptop!
   My laptop was _____ expensive _____ my new phone!
4. The class tomorrow starts at 9:10 instead of the usual time of 9:15.
   The class tomorrow starts a _____ usual.
5. This is the cheapest watch I could find.
   This watch is the _____ expensive I could find.
6. I've never seen a nicer beach before.
   This is _____ that I've _____ .
7. His last movie is funnier than this one.
   This movie _____ funny as his last one.
8. Jill and Maura are sisters. Maura is 19 and Jill is 18.
   Jill is _____ her sister.

◀ Go back to page 35

119

## GRAMMAR PRACTICE

### 5A  Zero and first conditional; future time clauses

 5.5

**If** you **borrow** money, you **need** to pay it back.
**If** I **ask** my bank manager for a loan, he**'ll say** no.
**Tell** me **if** you **need** some cash.
You **can't open** an account **unless** you**'re** over eighteen.
I **won't be** able to go shopping **until** I **get** paid this Friday.
I**'ll lend** you some money **after** I **go** to the ATM.

### Zero conditional

We use the zero conditional to talk about routines or situations that are generally true, including facts. We use the simple present, in both the *if* clause and the main clause.

*If I have time, I normally go for a walk on my lunch break.*
*I usually ride my bike to work if it's a nice day.*
*If you heat ice, it melts.*

### First conditional

We use the first conditional to talk about the result of a possible action. We form the *if* clause with *if* + simple present and we usually form the main clause with *will* + base form.

*If we take the bus, we'll get there more quickly.*
*If John doesn't leave now, he won't get to school on time.*
*You'll be tired tomorrow if you don't go to bed now.*

We can put either clause first with no change in meaning. However, if we put the main clause first, we don't use a comma between the two clauses.

*If it's nice this weekend, we'll go camping.*
*We'll go camping if it's nice this weekend.*

We can use the imperative in the main clause.

*If you see Matthew tomorrow, tell him about the party.*

We can use *unless* to talk about possible future events. It means the same as *if* + *not*.

*Unless you work harder, you won't pass your exams.* = *If you don't work harder, you won't pass your exams.*

### Future time clauses

We use the simple present, not *will* + base form, after words and phrases like *when*, *until*, *before*, *after*, and *as soon as* when we are referring to the future.

*I'll buy a new phone when this one stops working.*
*She won't call you back until she finishes her homework.*
*Before we go out, I'll take a quick shower.*
*We'll wash the dishes after we have lunch.*
*I'll call you as soon as we arrive at the airport.*

---

**1** Choose the correct options to complete the sentences.
1  You can't come to the party *if* / *unless* you're invited.
2  I'll call you *until* / *as soon as* I get my test scores.
3  They'll cancel the flight *if* / *unless* the weather is bad.
4  I'll get a job *when* / *until* I finish school.
5  She'll stay with us *until* / *unless* summer vacation finishes.
6  He'll worry *if* / *when* you don't call him.

**2** Complete the sentences with the correct form of the verbs in parentheses.
1  Plants _____ (die) if they _____ (not get) enough water.
2  If you _____ (not save) money now, you _____ (not have) enough to go on vacation.
3  I think I _____ (get) some coffee before the meeting _____ (start).
4  If I _____ (get) lost when I'm in a foreign city, I usually _____ (ask) someone for directions.
5  I _____ (send) you a text as soon as Helen _____ (arrive).
6  We _____ (not play) tennis unless the weather _____ (improve).
7  My brother _____ (be) excited if his team _____ (win) the game tonight.
8  I _____ (make) dinner after this movie _____ (finish).

**3** Complete the ad with the correct form of the verbs in the box.

| go   have (x2)   want   not pay |
| open   be (x2)   prefer   not have |

At **MegaBank**, we know that people ¹_____ speaking to a member of staff if they ²_____ questions about their account. But we also understand that if people ³_____ busy lives, they ⁴_____ time to visit or call their bank. That's why **MegaBank** has a new chat app. As soon as you ⁵_____ the app, someone ⁶_____ available to talk to you. If you ⁷_____ to know more, ⁸_____ to our website. You ⁹_____ a penny to download the app if you ¹⁰_____ a **MegaBank** customer!

◀ Go back to page 41

## 5C Predictions: *will*, *be going to*, *may/might*

 5.9

I'm sure Emily **will love** her present.
I **don't think** we**'ll have** time to go to the museum today.
There are lots of people here. It**'s going to be** a great party!
It **might rain** later this afternoon.
We **may not stay** at home for Thanksgiving this year.

### *will*

We use *will* and *won't* to make predictions about the future, based on our personal opinions. We often use phrases like *In my view/opinion ...* , *I think/feel (that) ...* , *I expect (that) ...*, and *I'm sure (that) ...* before *will* and *won't*.

*In my view, Germany will win the next World Cup.*
*It won't be easy for her to find a cheap apartment in the city.*

We often use *Do you think ... ?* to ask someone to make a prediction.
*Do you think she'll like her present?*

**Look!** To make a negative prediction with *will*, we normally use the negative form of *think*, followed by *will*.
*I don't think he'll get the job.* NOT *I think he won't get the job.*

### *be going to*

We use *be going to* to make predictions that we are sure about, based on something we can see or something that we know.

*Look at how full the parking lot is. The mall's going to be really busy.*
*Everyone says Toronto is an amazing city – you're going to have a great vacation.*

### *probably* and *definitely*

We use the adverbs *probably* and *definitely* to make a prediction with *will* or *going to* less certain or more certain.

*He'll probably buy a new car next year.*
*He's probably going to buy a new car next year.*
*Sarah will definitely go to college.*
*She's definitely going to go to college.*

**Look!** We use *probably* and *definitely* after *will* but before *won't*.
*It'll probably rain when we're on vacation.*
*I definitely won't miss the party.*

### *may/might*

We use *may (not)* or *might (not)* + base form to say that a prediction is possible. They mean "maybe" or "perhaps."

*We may not go on vacation this year.* = Perhaps we won't go on vacation this year.
*It might rain later, so take an umbrella.* = Maybe it will rain later, so take an umbrella.

## GRAMMAR PRACTICE

1 Choose the correct options to complete the sentences.
1 Look at those dark clouds. It *will* / *'s going to* rain!
2 I *'m going to* / *might* be home before seven, but it depends on the traffic.
3 The score is 10–0! Our team *is going to* / *will* win the game.
4 Jane *will definitely* / *definitely will* be at the concert. She bought her ticket months ago.
5 He's studying really hard at the moment. He *might* / *'s going to* pass the exam easily.
6 I'm sure you *might* / *'ll* enjoy the movie.
7 It *will* / *may* snow tonight. There's a 50% chance of snow according to the weather forecast.
8 We're arriving at midnight, so I *think we won't* / *don't think we'll* have time to go for dinner.
9 She doesn't think they *'ll* / *won't* move next year.

2 Complete the second sentences so they mean the same as the first sentences. Use the words in parentheses.
1 Perhaps she will win the Olympic gold medal.
   She _____ the Olympic gold medal. (win)
2 I'm absolutely sure that Mark won't pass his driving test.
   Mark _____ his driving test. (fail)
3 We probably won't have time to visit you this month.
   I _____ have time to visit you this month. (think)
4 I'm sure there will be a party this weekend.
   There _____ a party this weekend. (definitely)
5 The weather's awful. Maybe the train will be late.
   The train _____ on time because of the awful weather. (arrive)
6 You'll definitely learn a lot in this course.
   I _____ learn a lot in this course. (sure)
7 It's possible that it will rain later today.
   It _____ later today. (might)
8 We're not going to get to the airport on time with this traffic.
   I _____ get to the airport on time with this traffic. (think)

◀ Go back to page 45

121

## GRAMMAR PRACTICE

### 6A Present perfect and simple past, *already, yet, recently*

 6.2

I **'ve never been** fired from a job.
Ivan **has already finished** work, and it's only 3 p.m.
I **'ve heard** that Simona is leaving the company.
My dad **has been** retired **for** twelve years.
I **'ve been** to Australia twice. I last **went** there two years ago.

### Present perfect

We form the present perfect with *have/has* + past participle. We use it:

- to talk about experiences in our lives.
  *I've been to the U.S. three times.   I've never eaten Mexican food.
  Have you ever traveled abroad for work?   She's seen this movie before.*

- to talk about something that happened earlier than we expected, or didn't happen when we expected, with *already, yet,* and *still.*
  *I've already spoken to Tony.
  Have you written that report yet?   I haven't finished it yet. / I still haven't finished it.*

- to talk about the duration of a situation that started in the past and is still true now, with *for* and *since.*
  *I've worked here for ten years.   She's lived here since 1985.*

### Present perfect or simple past?

We use the present perfect to talk about the past from the perspective of the present.

*This is the best book I've ever read.* (in my life until now)
*I've lived in London for five years.* (I still live there.)

In addition to the adverbs above, we often use the present perfect with words and time expressions such as *so far, this morning, today, this week,* and *this year.*

*I've seen my friend twice this year.
He's only read one chapter of the book so far.*

We use the simple past to talk about completed actions in the past, and <u>when</u> they happened. We often use the simple past with words and past time expressions such as *yesterday, last Saturday, last week, in 2014, five years ago, What time … ?, When … ?*

*I lived in London for five years.* (I don't live there now.)
*We had a great vacation.* (We're not on vacation now.)
*I read that book last summer.   I got home two hours ago.   When did you arrive?*

We use the present perfect or simple past to talk about something that happened a short time ago with *recently.*

*We('ve) recently moved to a new office.*

We usually use the simple past with just.

*I just saw your text message.*

### Present perfect and simple past

We often ask a question or say something in the present perfect and then give more information in the simple past.

*Have you ever met Ana's sister?
Yes, I've met her. I talked to her at Ana's birthday party last month.*

*Do you know anything about Lima?
Yes, I've been to Lima, so I know it pretty well. I went there last year.*

> **Look!** *Ian's been to Lima* means he went to Lima and came back home.

---

**1** Choose the correct options to complete the sentences.
 1 I've been to the movies three times *this / last* week.
 2 Sarah *has spoken / spoke* to me yesterday.
 3 *Have you seen / Do you see* Maria recently?
 4 *Do you plan / Have you planned* your vacation yet?
 5 *I never went / I've never been* to Moscow.
 6 *I've visited / I visited* lots of beautiful places when I was in Argentina last year.
 7 This is the most difficult job *I've ever had / I ever had.*
 8 Sorry, I *haven't cooked / don't cook* dinner yet. I hope you aren't hungry.
 9 Her plane *has arrived / arrived* at 10:45.
 10 What *have you thought / did you think* of the movie?

**2** Check (✓) the sentences if they are correct. Then correct the incorrect sentences.
 1 Tom just moved to Bogotá. _____
 2 I've broken my leg six months ago. _____
 3 He works here since 2016. _____
 4 Michael has worked really hard this year. _____
 5 Have you lived here since five years? _____
 6 When have they gotten married? _____
 7 Have you spoken to Maria about the party yet? _____
 8 This is the best pizza I ever had. _____
 9 I've seen John in the park yesterday. _____
 10 Have you enjoyed the game last night? _____

**3** Complete the text with the verbs and adverbs in parentheses. Use the simple past or present perfect.

I love my job. I ¹_____ (be) a wedding photographer for two years. At first it was hard. Photography is a competitive industry, and you need experience. I ²_____ (not get) many assignments in my first year, but recently I ³_____ (become) really busy. I ⁴_____ (already, have) ten weddings this year! I ⁵_____ (work) in a lot of beautiful places – I ⁶_____ (just, do) a wedding at a palace. But things don't always go well. One colleague ⁷_____ (delete) all the wedding photos the day after his first wedding! Another colleague ⁸_____ (still, not receive) the money from a wedding that she ⁹_____ (do) last year. Thankfully, nothing like that ¹⁰_____ (happen) to me yet.

◀ Go back to page 49

## 6C Present perfect continuous and present perfect

▶ 6.15

I've **been studying** Spanish **for** 25 years.
She**'s been playing** tennis **since** 12:30.
My shirt's dirty because I've **been painting** my bedroom.
I**'ve known** Ed my whole life, but we've only **been going out** for three months.

### Present perfect continuous

We use the present perfect continuous to talk about longer or repeated actions that started in the past and are still true now. We form the present perfect continuous with the auxiliary verb *have* + *been* + *-ing* form of the main verb.

*We've been waiting for the bus for 45 minutes.*
*He's been coming to this restaurant since 2015.*

We often use *How long ... ?*, *for*, *since*, and time phrases like *this morning*, *today*, *this month*, *all year* with the present perfect continuous.

*How long has she been waiting?*
*He's been playing that computer game for four hours/since ten o'clock.*
*I've been taking the bus to work all week because my bike is broken.*
*Sam's been going to the gym a lot this year.*

We also use the present perfect continuous to talk about longer or repeated actions that have recently finished. These actions can have a result in the present.

*You look hot! What have you been doing?*
*I'm hot because I've been sitting in the sun.* (result = I'm hot)
*The grass is wet because it's been raining.* (result = the grass is wet)

### Present perfect

We don't use the present perfect continuous with state verbs. To talk about states that started in the past and continue in the present, we use the present perfect.

*How long has Matt had his car?* NOT ~~How long has Matt been having his car?~~
*Matt's had his car since last September.* NOT ~~Matt's been having his car since last September.~~
*I've known my neighbors for a long time.* NOT ~~I've been knowing my neighbors for a long time.~~

> **Look!** We can use both the present perfect and the present perfect continuous with action verbs and *How long ... ?*, *For ... ,* and *Since ... .* The meaning is the same.
> *How long have you lived here?*
> *I've lived here since 1980.*
> *How long have you been working here?*
> *I've been working here for seven years.*

## GRAMMAR PRACTICE

1 Complete the sentences with the present perfect continuous form of the verbs in parentheses.
  1 James _____ to the gym every day for the last four weeks. (go)
  2 How long _____ for that company? (you/work)
  3 He _____ much time at home because he's been so busy at work. (not spend)
  4 I _____ to this park since I was a child. (come)
  5 How long _____ for a cab? (you/wait)
  6 What horrible weather! It _____ all morning. (rain)
  7 Why do you never answer your phone? I _____ you all evening. (call)
  8 You _____ computer games all evening. Go and do your homework now! (play)

2 Choose the correct options to complete the sentences.
  1 How long have you *known / been knowing* Anne?
  2 *I'm training / I've been training* for the marathon for the last six months.
  3 I've *loved / been loving* you since the first time I met you.
  4 She's *talking / been talking* on the phone to her boyfriend for over an hour now.
  5 Silvia *is doing / has been doing* her homework all morning.
  6 I've *owned / been owning* this apartment since 2010.
  7 How long are *you coming / have you been coming* to this gym?
  8 *We're going / We've been going* to yoga classes for six months.

◀ Go back to page 53

# GRAMMAR PRACTICE

## 7A The passive

>  7.4
>
> Thousands of movies **are made** every year.
> The main character **was played** by Emily Blunt.
> The book **has been made** into a movie.
> He **was being interviewed** for the role when I called him.
> Her new movie **will be released** later this year.

In active sentences, the focus is on the person or thing that does the action.

*My friend Robert is repairing my bike.*
*Maria Jones wrote that book.*

In passive sentences, the focus is on the action itself or on the thing that the action affects.

*My bike is being repaired by my friend Robert.*
*That book was written by Maria Jones.*

We often use the passive if we don't know who did the action, or if it isn't important who did the action.

*The window was broken last night.*
*Over a million cars are made here every year.*

We can use *by* in a passive sentence to say who does an action. We often use by when the person who does the action is new information.

*The Harry Potter books are popular all over the world. They were written by J. K. Rowling.*

We form the passive with a form of the verb *be* + past participle. We can use the passive with all tenses, forms, and modal verbs.

|  | active | passive |
|---|---|---|
| simple present | I usually clean it every day. | It is usually cleaned every day. |
| simple past | They arrested him this morning. | He was arrested this morning. |
| present perfect | They've completed the project. | The project has been completed. |
| present continuous | He is feeding the cat. | The cat is being fed. |
| will | We will finish the report. | The report will be finished. |
| past continuous | They were repairing the road. | The road was being repaired. |
| modal verbs | You should answer all the questions. | All the questions should be answered. |

We make negatives and questions in the usual way with the negative form or the question form of the verb *be*.

*He wasn't arrested.*
*Was he arrested?*
*It hasn't been completed.*
*Has it been completed?*

1 Choose the correct options to complete the sentences.
  1 She will *be met / meet* at the airport by the Prime Minister.
  2 Picasso *was painted / painted* "Guernica" in 1937.
  3 A new library is *being built / building* at the university.
  4 The movie *directed / was directed* by Christopher Nolan.
  5 The band has *sold / been sold* over 2 million copies of their new album.
  6 Tickets for their next concert can *buy / be bought* online.
  7 They were *being built / building* a new airport when I lived in Warsaw.
  8 All the doors should *lock / be locked* when you leave the building.
  9 These days, most of the world's computers *are made / make* in China.
  10 I'm not sure where the next Olympic Games will *hold / be held*.

2 Rewrite the sentences in the passive.
  1 He wrote the book in 2007.
    _____ in 2007.
  2 They have sold all the tickets for the concert.
    All the tickets for the concert _____ .
  3 Can you watch that movie on Netflix?
    _____ that movie _____ on Netflix?
  4 They're making a lot of science-fiction movies these days.
    A lot of science-fiction movies _____ these days.
  5 They aren't going to release their new game until next year.
    Their new game _____ until next year.
  6 They make cars at that factory.
    Cars _____ at that factory.
  7 When we arrived at the hotel, they were cleaning our room.
    When we arrived at the hotel, our room _____ .
  8 They will send the information to you soon.
    The information _____ to you soon.
  9 They repaired my TV last week.
    My TV _____ last week.
  10 The fire completely destroyed the hotel.
    The hotel _____ by _____ .

124

◀ Go back to page 59

# 7C Modals of ability and possibility

▶ 7.10

I **could ride** a bike when I was four years old.
We **couldn't watch** our favorite show because the TV broke.
I**'ll be able to go** on tour with my band when I finish college.
I **wasn't able to go** to the concert because I was sick.
My dad **hasn't been able to play** squash since he hurt his knee.

## can and could

We use *can/can't* and *could/couldn't*:

- to say that somebody has or had the ability to do something.
  *He can play the piano really well.*
  *I couldn't drive five years ago.*

- to say that it is or was possible to do something.
  *I have my car here, so I can drive you to the station.*
  *I can't talk to you right now – I'll call you tonight.*
  *I couldn't use my cell phone when I was in the country – there was no signal.*

- with verbs of the senses, such as *hear* and *see*.
  *I can't hear you very well. Please speak more loudly.*
  *It was very foggy, and I couldn't see the cars in front of me.*

## be able to

We also use *be able to* + base form to talk about ability and possibility. It sounds a little more formal than *can* or *could*. We can use *be able to* with all tenses, forms, and with modal verbs.

*Are you able to speak any foreign languages?*
*I wasn't able to finish the report yesterday.*
*She's never been able to swim very well.*
*Sorry, but I won't be able to come to the party tonight.*
*We love being able to sleep late on weekends.*
*I'd like to be able to speak Italian.*

> **Look!** We can't use *can* with most tenses, structures, or modal verbs. We use *be able to*, instead.
> *I will be able to go to college if I pass my exams.* NOT ~~I will can go to college…~~
> *I'd like to be able to play the guitar.* NOT ~~I'd like to can play the guitar.~~

We can use both *would you be able to* or *could you* to make polite requests.
*Could you open the window, please?*
*Would you be able to pick up some milk later?*

## GRAMMAR PRACTICE

1. Choose the correct options to complete the sentences.
   1. I *can't / couldn't* speak to my father yesterday.
   2. I've *been able to / could* paint since I was a child.
   3. I'm sorry, but I won't *can / be able to* meet you for lunch tomorrow.
   4. Have you *could / been able to* speak to John yet?
   5. I love *can / being able to* stay in bed all morning.
   6. Maria says she'll *can / be able to* come for dinner.
   7. I'd like to *be able to / can* speak Chinese.
   8. You should *can / be able to* find a cab outside.

2. Complete the sentences with affirmative (+) and negative (–) forms of *be able to*.
   1. I'd love _____ walk to work, but it's too far away. (+)
   2. I _____ make any calls on my phone since yesterday. (–)
   3. I'm afraid that I _____ come to the meeting tomorrow. (–)
   4. The doctor _____ see you yesterday, but he's free today. (–)
   5. If I finish all my work today, I _____ go out tonight. (+)
   6. I've always _____ make new friends easily. (+)

3. Complete the text with the correct form of *can*, *could*, or *be able to* and the verbs in parentheses. There may be more than one answer.

My dad's Irish, my mom's Mexican, and I grew up in Belgium, so I've always [1]_____ (speak) different languages, plus I studied Russian and Swedish in college. At first, learning Russian was difficult as I [2]_____ (not understand) the alphabet, but I speak it well now. I travel a lot for my job, and I really love [3]_____ (talk) to local people in restaurants and markets – in my opinion, you [4]_____ (not get) to know a country if you don't make an effort to understand its language. I'd like to learn Mandarin as I'm going to Beijing for work next year. There's a Mandarin course at my local language school in May, so I'll [5]_____ (take) classes, and this time next year, I might [6]_____ (have) a conversation when I go to the market in Beijing!

◀ Go back to page 63

# GRAMMAR PRACTICE

## 8A Tag questions

 8.7

You don't live in Chicago, **do you**?
Emma went to Harvard, **didn't she**?
Your parents weren't at the party last weekend, **were they**?
I'll see you tomorrow at the concert, **won't I**?
You've never been to Canada, **have you**?
They should be here by now, **shouldn't they**?

We often use a statement with a tag question when we think we know something but we want to check.

*You're from Mexico, aren't you?* = I think you're from Mexico. Is that right?
*He doesn't speak Arabic, does he?* = I don't think he speaks Arabic. Is that right?

We also use tag questions to start a conversation or to encourage somebody to speak.

*It's a hot day, isn't it?*
*You've just bought a new car, haven't you?*

With affirmative statements, we use a negative tag question. With negative statements, we use an affirmative tag question.

| + | − |
|---|---|
| His name was Juan, | wasn't it? |
| It will be sunny later, | won't it? |

| − | + |
|---|---|
| We aren't late, | are we? |
| They didn't come, | did they? |

To form a tag question, we use an auxiliary or modal verb followed by a pronoun. If the statement already contains an auxiliary or modal verb, we use it in the tag question.

*We're meeting at 8:30, aren't we?*
*It won't rain this afternoon, will it?*
*The children should go to bed early tonight, shouldn't they?*
*Sara can't play volleyball with us on the weekend, can she?*
*Tim hasn't lived here very long, has he?*

In the present or simple past, we make the tag question using *do*, *does*, or *did*.

*They like Italian food, don't they?*
*The waiter speaks Spanish, doesn't he?*
*Sami spent three months in Beijing, didn't he?*
*You didn't like that concert, did you?*

**Look!** We only use pronouns in tag questions. All names and nouns change to *he*, *she*, *it*, or *they*.
John plays tennis, doesn't he? NOT ~~John plays tennis, doesn't John?~~
Paris is very expensive, isn't it? NOT ~~Paris is very expensive, isn't Paris?~~

1 Match statements 1–10 with tag questions a–j.
   1 Mark's coming tonight, _____
   2 Michael's been to Paris before, _____
   3 We shouldn't come early, _____
   4 You'll help me tonight, _____
   5 Tom and Dan can't speak Chinese, _____
   6 You like soccer, _____
   7 Sarah called you this morning, _____
   8 Karl isn't here, _____
   9 She didn't pass her exams, _____
   10 The exam won't be easy, _____

   a didn't she?
   b don't you?
   c is he?
   d isn't he?
   e should we?
   f will it?
   g did she?
   h hasn't he?
   i won't you?
   j can they?

2 Complete the sentences with tag questions.

   1 Surfing's an exciting sport, _____ ?
   2 They're going to lose, _____ ?
   3 Tina hasn't left yet, _____ ?
   4 You don't know the rules, _____ ?
   5 You went running on the weekend, _____ ?
   6 Steven is working tonight, _____ ?
   7 It wasn't a great game, _____ ?
   8 We can go out for dinner tonight, _____ ?
   9 The Jamaicans won't win this race, _____ ?
   10 We have to show our passports, _____ ?
   11 You've been waiting for ages, _____ ?
   12 You used to go to that school, _____ ?

126 ◀ Go back to page 67

GRAMMAR PRACTICE

# 8C Modals of obligation and advice

▶ 8.13

You **have to take off** your shoes before you go into the temple.
Visitors **must park** only in the visitor parking lot.
We **don't have to work** today. It's Saturday.
You **can't give** chocolate to the dog. It's very bad for him.
I **had to go** to the doctor because I was having stomach pains.
You **should have** a more balanced diet.

## have to and must

We generally use *have to* to talk about obligation and rules. In written rules, and in very strong statements, we can also use *must*.

*I have to drive to the station because my wife's waiting for me.*
*You have to buy a ticket before you leave the parking lot.*
*You have to/must take your passport with you when you travel abroad.*

We normally don't use *must* in conversation unless the obligation is very strong.

*You must see a doctor immediately!*

There is no past or future form of *must*, and we don't usually use *must* in questions. In these cases, we use a form of *have to* instead.

*Yesterday I had to work until 8 p.m.*
*He'll have to find a job when he finishes college next year.*
*Do we have to do all the exercises or just the first one?*

## don't have to or can't?

*Don't have to* and *can't* have very different meanings. We use *don't have to* to say that something isn't necessary.

*You don't have to pay to go by bus. Public transportation is free on Sundays.*

We use *can't* to say something is prohibited.

*You can't speak during the exam.*

> **Look!** In spoken English, we can use *can't* or *not allowed to* to say that something isn't permitted because of a rule or a law. In written English, we use *not allowed to*.
> *You can't take photos inside the art gallery* (spoken).
> *Visitors aren't allowed to take photos inside the art gallery* (spoken or written).

## should/shouldn't

We use *should* to give advice and recommendations or to say if we think that something is a good idea or a bad idea.

*You should go to the gym two or three times a week.*
*You shouldn't eat so much fast food.*

1 Choose the correct options to complete the sentences.

1 It's after midnight. I think you *can / should* go home by taxi.
2 I'm sorry I'm late. I *should / had to* take my sister to the airport.
3 I haven't seen Helen for ages. I *can / have to* call her soon to catch up.
4 You *can't / don't have to* come to the supermarket with me. I can go by myself.
5 I *don't have to / can't* go to work early today because my first meeting starts at 11 a.m.
6 You *shouldn't / have to* eat so fast – it's bad for your digestion.
7 You *don't have to / can't* park your car in front of that garage.
8 We *don't have to / can't* drive downtown. There's a very convenient bus.
9 My children *have to / can* wear a school uniform.
10 All arriving passengers *must / can* have their passports ready.

2 Complete the second sentences with the correct form of *have to*, *can*, or *should* so they have the same meaning as the first sentences. There may be more than one answer.

1 It's not necessary to hurry – there's plenty of time.
We _____ to hurry – there's plenty of time.
2 You aren't allowed to use your phone in the library.
You _____ use your phone in the library.
3 It's not a good idea to drink coffee before you go to bed.
You _____ drink coffee before you go to bed.
4 It will be necessary to stay at the airport hotel because we have an early flight.
We _____ stay at the airport hotel because we have an early flight.
5 I think it's really important for me to visit Grandma tomorrow because it's her birthday.
I really _____ visit Grandma tomorrow because it's her birthday.
6 I think it's a good idea for us to buy a bigger car.
We _____ buy a bigger car.
7 You aren't allowed to ride a motorcycle without a helmet.
You _____ ride a motorcycle without a helmet.
8 Last week, it was necessary for me to go to the hospital for a check-up.
Last week, I _____ go to the hospital for a check-up.
9 I think it's really important for us to invite Bill and Donna for dinner soon.
We really _____ invite Bill and Donna for dinner soon.
10 It's not necessary to pay to enter that museum – it's free.
You _____ pay to enter that museum – it's free.

◀ Go back to page 71

127

## GRAMMAR PRACTICE

### 9A Uses of *like*

> ▶ 9.5
>
> I **don't like eating** takeout.
> **Would** you **like** a cup of tea?
> Saul is **just like** his dad.
> That **sounds like** a good idea.
> What**'s** Japanese food **like**?
> What **does** your new girlfriend **look like**?

#### *like* + verb or noun

We use the verb *like* + -ing or + noun to talk about preferences. We can also use *like* + infinitive.

*I like listening/to listen to music.*
*Did he like the concert?*
*I think he'll like the food in that restaurant.*
*I didn't like that dessert.*

#### *would like*

We use *would like* + infinitive or + noun to make polite offers and requests. We also use *would like* to talk about something we want to have or do. It is more polite than using the verb *want*. We usually contract it to *I'd/we'd like*.

*Would you like a glass of water?*
*Would you like to sit down?*
*I'd like a chicken salad, please.*
*I'd like to go to Paris one day.*
*We'd like to try that Italian restaurant.*

#### *like* (preposition)

We also use *like* as a preposition. It means "similar to." *Just like* means "exactly the same as."

*Sarah is like her mother.* = Sarah and her mother have a similar personality.
*His car is just like mine.* = His car is exactly the same as mine.

We often use the preposition *like* with verbs of the senses (*look, sound, taste, feel, smell*, etc.) and the verb *seem*. For verbs of the senses, we can use *just like* if something is exactly the same.

*Your perfume smells like lemon.*
*That seems like a good idea.*
*This tastes just like chicken!*

We use the phrase *feel like* + -ing to mean "want to do," especially when we're making plans.

*What do you feel like doing tonight?* = What do you want to do tonight?
*I don't feel like going to the movies.* = I don't want to go to the movies.

#### What ... like?

We use *what* + *be like* to ask for a description of something or someone.

*What was the movie like?*
*What's that new restaurant like?*

> **Look!** We use *What's he/she like?* to ask about someone's character or personality, not his or her appearance. We use *What does he/she look like?* to ask about someone's appearance.
> *What's Tanya like?*
> *She's very nice, but she's rather shy.*
> *What does she look like?*
> *She's very pretty, and she has short brown hair.*

1 Put the words in the correct order to make sentences and questions.

 1 party / what / Sarah's / like / was / ?
 _____
 2 in / like / park / my / having / I / the / lunch
 _____
 3 feel / going / you / like / do / tonight / out / ?
 _____
 4 this / like / to / movies / weekend / to / I'd / the / go
 _____
 5 brother / like / Martina's / does / what / look / ?
 _____
 6 coffee / you / a / like / of / would / cup / ?
 _____
 7 teacher / is / new / like / what / your / English / ?
 _____
 8 bigger / move / a / Maria / like / to / would / to / apartment
 _____
 9 Beyoncé / like / just / she / sounds
 _____
 10 please / reserve / like / double / a / room / I'd / to
 _____

2 Complete the conversation with the words in the box.

| sounds   feel (x2)   I'd   do   would   like (x2) |

A Hi, Julia. Are you hungry? [1]_____ you like to go somewhere for lunch?
B Sure. Where do you [2]_____ like going?
A [3]_____ you like Greek food?
B No, I don't, not really. I think I'd [4]_____ to go to an Italian place. I [5]_____ like having pizza today.
A That [6]_____ like a good idea. What about Luigi's, then?
B I've never been to Luigi's. What are their pizzas [7]_____?
A They're delicious! But I had one last week, so today I think [8]_____ like to have a pasta dish.
B Great. Let's go!

◀ Go back to page 77

## 9C -ing forms and infinitives

▶ 9.11

**Eating out** every week can be expensive.
I always go running **after coming** home from work.
That woman **keeps looking** at me. Do you know her?
It's really important **to leave** a tip in the U.S.
I decided **to become** a vegetarian three years ago.
I called the restaurant **to reserve** a table for lunch.

We use the *-ing* form:
- as the subject of a sentence.
  *Cooking is one of my favorite hobbies.*
- after prepositions and phrasal verbs.
  *We're thinking of going out for a meal.*
  *She's looking forward to trying that restaurant.*
- after some verbs, including *enjoy, feel like, finish, hate, keep, like, love, (don't) mind, miss, prefer, recommend, spend time, suggest.*
  *I love trying new food.*
  *I prefer cooking at home to eating out.*

We put *not* before an *-ing* form to make a negative.
*I love not having to get up early on the weekend.*

We use the infinitive with *to*:
- after adjectives.
  *It's easy to cook this kind of food.*
  *It's expensive to eat out in this city.*
- after some verbs, including *afford, agree, decide, expect, forget, help, hope, learn, need, offer, plan, promise, refuse, want.*
  *We decided to go out for coffee.*
  *Julie offered to cook me dinner.*
- to give a reason.
  *I went to the supermarket to get some food for the party.*

We put *not* before an infinitive to make a negative.
*He promised not to make the same mistake again.*

**Look!** We can use the verbs *begin, continue,* and *start* with an *-ing* form or an infinitive, without any change in meaning.
*He started running. / He started to run.*
We can also use the verbs *prefer, hate, like,* and *love* with an *-ing* form or an infinitive, without any change in meaning.
*I hate doing homework on weekends. / I hate to do homework on weekends.*

With some verbs, we use an object before the infinitive.
*Carl asked her to marry him.*
*He told Sara to call him.*
*They want me to go with them.*
*I would like you to help me with the dinner.*
*We expect him to pass the exam.*

---

**GRAMMAR PRACTICE**

1 Choose the correct options to complete the sentences.
   1 It was hard *to find / find* your house because it doesn't have a number.
   2 Jackie suggested *to go / going* to see a movie tonight.
   3 I offered *to help / helping* my brother with his homework.
   4 We went outside *for getting / to get* some fresh air.
   5 *Live / Living* downtown is very expensive.
   6 I don't mind *getting up / to get up* early in the morning.
   7 I decided to give up *to eat / eating* sugar for a week.
   8 *Growing / To grow* up in the country was great.
   9 I'm tired of *going / to go* to the same restaurant all the time.
   10 I would love *speaking / to speak* English as well as you.

2 Complete the conversation with the correct form of the verb in parentheses.

A Hey, Mike. Do you want [1]_____ (do) something tonight?
B Sure. How about [2]_____ (go) to see that new sci-fi movie at the old theater in town?
A But it's so hot today. [3]_____ (sit) in a hot movie theater doesn't sound like much fun! I think I'd prefer [4]_____ (be) outdoors.
B OK, do you feel like [5]_____ (go) to that concert in the park?
A Great idea. Do you mind [6]_____ (give) me a lift?
B No, of course not. I'll come get you when I finish [7]_____ (clean) the kitchen.
A OK, thanks. Don't forget [8]_____ (bring) my jacket. Remember, I left it in your car last week.

◀ Go back to page 81

# GRAMMAR PRACTICE

## 10A Reported speech

> ▶ 10.4
>
> He **said that he knew** where the burglar lived.
> The police **told us that they had arrested** someone for the crime.
> I **asked Emma if she could** help me with my homework.
> The police officer **asked me where I had been** the night before.

We use reported speech to say what someone said.

Direct speech: *"I live downtown."*
Reported speech: *She said (that) she lived downtown.*

In reported speech, we usually change the tense of the verbs:

- simple present → simple past
  *"I work in a bank."* → *He said (that) he worked in a bank.*
- present continuous → past continuous
  *"The train is arriving."* → *Sara said (that) the train was arriving.*
- present perfect → past perfect
  *"I've finished work."* → *Mike told me (that) he'd finished work.*
- simple past → past perfect
  *"I lost my keys."* → *She said (that) she'd lost her keys.*

Some modal verbs also change in reported speech.
*"I can speak French."* → *Luke said (that) he could speak French.*
*"I'll see you tonight."* → *Lisa said (that) she would see us tonight.*
*"We may get married."* → *Sarah told me (that) they might get married.*
*"We have to buy her a present."* → *They said (that) they had to buy her a present.*

The following modal verbs don't change in reported speech: *would, could, might,* and *should*.

### Reported statements

The most common verbs that we use to report statements are *say* and *tell*. When we use *say*, we don't usually specify the person who was spoken to.
*He said that he was Spanish.* NOT *He said me that he was Spanish.*
When we use *tell*, we always specify the person who was spoken to.
*He told me that he was Spanish.* NOT *He told that he was Spanish.*
We often use *that* after *said* and *told* but it isn't essential.

### Reported questions

We report a *Yes/No* question with the following structure:
subject + *asked* + (object) + *if* + subject + affirmative verb form + rest of sentence.
*"Do you want ice cream?"* → *She asked (me) if I wanted ice cream.*
*"Is this your car?"* → *He asked (me) if it was my car.*
When we report *wh-* questions, we include the question word(s) instead of *if*.
*"Why did you call me?"* → *She asked (me) why I had called her.*
*"When will you buy a car?"* → *They asked (us) when we would buy a car.*

> **Look!** In reported speech, we change pronouns and words referring to time and place if the sentence is reported on a different day or in a different place.
> *"I'm coming tomorrow."* → *She said she was coming the next day.*
> *"We visited him yesterday."* → *They said they had visited him the day before.*
> *"I'll wait for you here."* → *He said he'd wait for us there.*

1 Complete the sentences with reported speech.
  1 "I'll see you at eight o'clock."
    Mike told me _____ at eight o'clock.
  2 "I'm seeing Maria this weekend."
    She said _____ Maria this weekend.
  3 "I've lost my phone."
    Martin said _____ phone.
  4 "I can't speak Portuguese."
    Susan told them _____ Portuguese.
  5 "I bought a new car last week."
    She told me _____ before.
  6 "Do you like going to the movies?"
    He asked her _____ going to the movies.
  7 "Why didn't you wait for me last night?"
    She asked me _____ last night.
  8 "Can you buy me this red dress?"
    She asked me _____ the red dress.

2 Complete the story. Look at the direct speech below and use reported speech in the story.

  "He used his own car to drive to and from the bank."
  "He forgot to change his black T-shirt with his name on it."
  "Do you recognize the man in this photograph?"
  "He's the man who robbed the bank this morning."
  "We can't afford to pay the rent for our home any more."
  "I didn't tell my wife about the robbery."
  "I borrowed the money."

  It only took Denver police five hours to find the man who had robbed the Wells Fargo bank. But they had a little help from the robber! Police said that the suspect ¹_____ his own car to drive to and from the bank. They also said that he ²_____ to change his black T-shirt with his name on it before robbing the bank.

  Police soon identified the man from the license plate on the car and printed a photograph of him. When they went to the bank and asked a bank worker ³_____ the man in the photograph, she said that he ⁴_____ the man who ⁵_____ the bank that morning. Later they found his car at a hotel nearby and arrested him in his room. The suspect said that he and his wife were staying at the hotel because they ⁶_____ afford to pay the rent for their own home any more. He said that he ⁷_____ his wife about the robbery. Instead he told her that ⁸_____ the money.

130

◀ Go back to page 85

## GRAMMAR PRACTICE

# 10C Second conditional, *would, could,* and *might*

▶ 10.11

**If** I **argued** with my best friend, I**'d be** sad.
I**'d visit** you every year **if you lived** near the coast.
**If** I **could speak** Spanish, I**'d go** traveling in South America.
**If** I **won** the lottery, I **might give** all the money to charity.
**If** I **were** you, I**'d update** my résumé.

We use the second conditional to talk about impossible or very unlikely hypothetical situations in the present or future and their consequences.

**Impossible situation**
*If I were rich, I'd buy a big house by the sea.* (I'm not rich, so it's impossible for me to buy a big house by the sea.)

**Unlikely situation**
*If my new phone stopped working tomorrow, I'd take it back to the store.* (It's a new phone, so this probably won't happen.)

We form the *if* clause with *if* + simple past, and we form the main clause with *would* + base form. The *if* clause can come either at the beginning or at the end of the sentence with no change in meaning.

*If you went to bed earlier, you wouldn't feel so tired.*
*You wouldn't feel so tired if you went to bed earlier.*

We can also use *could* or *might* in the main clause to say that something would be possible.

*If we lived by the sea, we could go swimming every day.*
*If you asked John more politely, he might help you.*

With the verb *be*, we often use *were* instead of *was* in the *if* clause with *I*, *he*, *she*, and *it*. We often use *were* in the phrase *If I were you* … to give advice.

*If Adam were here, he would fix your computer.*
*If I were you, I'd take a cab to the airport.*

**Look!** Don't use *would* in the *if* clause.
*If I had more time, I'd learn the saxophone.* NOT ~~If I would have more time, I'd learn the saxophone.~~

## Second conditional or first conditional?

We use the first conditional when we think a future event is likely. We use the second conditional when we think a future event is less likely.

*If it rains tomorrow, we'll go shopping.* (It often rains here, so it might rain.)
*If it rained tomorrow, we'd go shopping.* (It probably won't rain.)

---

**1** Complete the second conditional sentences with the correct form of the verbs in parentheses.

1 If I _____ (live) downtown, I _____ (walk) to work.
2 This city _____ (be) much nicer if there _____ (be) less traffic on the streets.
3 If you _____ (get up) a bit earlier, you _____ (not be) late for work so often.
4 If we _____ (have) a bigger car, we _____ (can) take more things on vacation with us.
5 What _____ (you/do) if someone _____ (steal) your car?
6 I _____ (play) basketball if I _____ (be) a bit taller.
7 If I _____ (be) you, I _____ (ask) my boss for a promotion.
8 If you _____ (not spend) so much money on clothes, you _____ (be able to) afford a new phone.

**2** Complete the second sentences. Use the second conditional to link the situations in the first sentences.

1 I'm lazy. I always get bad grades in school.
 *If I wasn't lazy, I wouldn't always get bad grades in school.*
2 I have a small bedroom. I don't have enough space for all my books.
 If I _____ , _____ enough space for all my books.
3 It's so hot today. I can't concentrate on my work.
 If _____ , _____ on my work.
4 I don't get any exercise. I'm so out of shape.
 If I _____ , _____ so out of shape.
5 I feel tired. I can't play tennis this afternoon.
 If I _____ , _____ this afternoon.
6 I drink coffee in the evening. I don't sleep well.
 If I _____ , _____ better.

**3** Complete the sentences with the correct form of the verbs in parentheses. Use the first or second conditional.

1 If we _____ (leave) now, we'll get there on time.
2 What would you do if you _____ (win) $1,000?
3 If you _____ (have) a car, you could drive to work.
4 _____ (you/go) to college if you get good grades this year?
5 If he _____ (ask) her to marry him, what would she say?
6 We'll play tennis later if it _____ (stop) raining.
7 I _____ (not accept) that job if they offered it to me.
8 If they win, they _____ (be) the champions.

◀ Go back to page 89

131

# GRAMMAR PRACTICE

## 11A Articles

>  11.3
>
> My best friend is **an architect**.
> You're **the funniest** person I know.
> They sent him to **prison** for six years.
> We go on vacation **three times a year**.
> I'm going to **the Czech Republic** soon.
> **Floods** are common in this country.

### Indefinite article (*a/an*)

We use *a/an* with singular, countable nouns:

- to talk about something or somebody for the first time.
  *Suddenly, a man ran out of the bank.*
- to describe something or somebody.
  *It's a beautiful building.   She's a really funny person.*
- to talk about a person's job.
  *He's a computer programmer.   She works as an accountant.*
- in frequency and measurement expressions.
  *I go to the gym twice a week.   He was driving at over 150 km. an hour.*

### Definite article (*the*)

We use *the*:

- to talk about something we've already mentioned, or when it's clear which particular thing or person we're talking about.
  *I saw a man and a woman looking at a map. The man asked me for help.*
  *That restaurant looks nice, but the prices are very high.* (This clearly means the prices in the restaurant.)
- when we use a defining relative clause to define a noun.
  *That's the boy who stole my bike.*
- when there's only one of a thing.
  *The sun went behind the clouds.   I reserved our hotel on the Internet.*
- with superlative adjectives and ordinal numbers (*first, second, third,* etc.).
  *She was the first person I met at the party.*
- with the names of rivers, seas, oceans, and groups of islands.
  *London is on the River Thames.   We're flying over the Pacific Ocean.*
  *Last year I went to the Galápagos Islands.*
- before countries that include the words *United, Republic,* and *Kingdom,* or are plurals.
  *I'd love to visit the U.S.*

### No article (zero article)

We don't use an article:

- to talk about things in general (with plural or uncountable nouns).
  *Houses are more expensive than apartments.* (houses and apartments in general)
  *Sugar is bad for you.* (sugar in general, and not the sugar in this packet)
- with some places where we work, live, study, or do other specific activities, such as *work, school, college, prison, church*. We usually use them with no article after a preposition.
  *I stayed (at) home all day.   Chris is in college in Boston.*
- before *next/last* + *day, week, month, year,* etc.
  *I saw him last week.   We'd like to stay in the same hotel next July.*
- with most names of streets, towns, cities, countries, and continents.
  *He lives on Pine Street.   We're going to New York next week!*
  *I hope to visit Australia one day.*

1 Choose the correct options to complete the sentences.
  1 That was *the / –* best movie I've ever seen!
  2 I go running three times *a / the* week.
  3 I have to go to *– / the* work now. I'll call you later.
  4 Look at *a / the* moon – it's really bright tonight.
  5 A What do you do?   B I'm *a / –* student.
  6 I don't like *the / –* rock music.
  7 The president arrives in *the / –* France on Monday.
  8 Most people now use *– / the* smartphones.
  9 There was *a / –* man selling ice cream outside.
  10 I hope to see you *the / –* next week.

2 Complete the sentences. Add *the* or leave a blank (no article).
  1 _____ food in this restaurant is amazing!
  2 _____ basketball is one of _____ most popular sports in _____ world.
  3 In _____ U.S., _____ tornadoes are pretty common in the Midwest.
  4 _____ girl who gave me those flowers was about ten years old.
  5 I'd like to talk to _____ manager of _____ hotel, please.
  6 _____ boys are usually taller than _____ girls.
  7 I often listen to _____ music while I'm studying.
  8 _____ hotel where I stayed had a beautiful view of _____ sea.

3 Complete the text. Add *a, an,* or *the* or leave a blank (no article).

I think that [1]_____ most beautiful place to visit in Colombia is Tayrona National Park. It's [2]_____ protected area on [3]_____ Caribbean coast, 34 kilometers from [4]_____ city of Santa Marta. There's [5]_____ amazing rainforest in [6]_____ park where you might see [7]_____ monkeys, parrots, frogs, and iguanas. I went to a magnificent beach at Cabo San Juan, which was [8]_____ perfect place to swim and to watch [9]_____ spectacular sunset over [10]_____ sea. [11]_____ tourists love going to Tayrona National Park, so if you want to avoid the crowds, [12]_____ quietest time to visit [13]_____ park is during [14]_____ off season, from February to November.

◀ Go back to page 95

## 11C Third conditional

▶ 11.6

If Emil **hadn't** stayed out all night, his parents **wouldn't have been** so furious.
I would **have come** to the party if I**'d known** about it.
If I**'d studied** more before my exam, I **might have passed**.
If you**'d called** me earlier, we **could have gone** out for dinner.

We use the third conditional to talk about hypothetical (unreal) situations in the past and their consequences.
*If I'd seen your e-mail, I would have replied to it.* (I didn't see your e-mail. I didn't reply to it.)
*If he'd taken a cab, he wouldn't have missed his train.* (He didn't take a cab. He missed his train.)

We form the *if* clause with *if* + past perfect. We form the main clause with *would have* + past participle.
*If you had come with us, you would have had a great time.*
*If the bus hadn't been late, we would have arrived at the theater before the movie started.*

The *if* clause can come either at the beginning or at the end of the sentence with no change in meaning.
*If it had been sunny yesterday, we would have gone for a walk.*
*We would have gone for a walk if it had been sunny yesterday.*

We can use *might* or *may* instead of *would* when the consequences weren't certain.
*If I hadn't arrived late to the interview, I might have gotten the job.*
*If they'd stayed longer at the beach, we may have seen them.*

We can use *could* instead of *would* to talk about hypothetical possibilities.
*If my car hadn't broken down, I could have taken you to the airport yesterday.*
*If they'd told us about the problem, we could have helped them.*

> **Look!** The contraction *'d* can mean *had* or *would* although we often don't contract *would* in the third conditional.
> *If I'd (I had) known you were in the hospital, I'd (I would) have come to visit you.*

## GRAMMAR PRACTICE

1 Complete the sentences with the correct form of the verbs in parentheses to make third conditional sentences.
  1 If you _____ (ask) me for some money, I _____ (give) it to you.
  2 We _____ (not stay) at that hotel if you _____ (not recommend) it.
  3 I _____ (go) to the party if they _____ (invite) me.
  4 If they _____ (arrive) five minutes earlier, they _____ (not miss) the flight.
  5 If you _____ (not drive) so slowly, we _____ (arrive) home an hour ago.
  6 I _____ (go) to the concert last Saturday if I _____ (know) it was free.
  7 If you _____ (take) a better map, you _____ (not get) lost.
  8 We _____ (not go) to the beach yesterday if we _____ (see) the weather forecast.

2 Write sentences about how these situations and consequences in the past would have been different. Use the third conditional.
  1 You didn't work hard last year. You didn't pass your exams.
     *If you had worked hard last year, you would have passed your exams.*
  2 There was a lot of traffic. We arrived late for the meeting.
     _____
  3 She cut her finger badly. I took her to the hospital.
     _____
  4 It was really hot yesterday. We didn't play tennis.
     _____
  5 I left my phone at home. I couldn't call you.
     _____
  6 I didn't know it was your birthday today. I didn't buy you a present.
     _____
  7 He trained hard every day. He won the race.
     _____
  8 You didn't stop at the red light. The police officer gave you a fine.

◀ Go back to page 99

**GRAMMAR PRACTICE**

# 12A *So/Neither do I*

> ▶ 12.3
>
> "I love playing golf." "**So do I.**"
> "I'd love to visit New Zealand one day." "**So would I.**"
> "I'm not very good at chess." "**Neither am I.**"
> "I couldn't go to class last week." "**Neither could I.**"
> "I haven't done my homework." "**Really? I have.**"
> "I'm going on vacation next month." "**I'm not.**"

## Agreeing

When we want to show that we agree with someone, or what he or she says is the same for us, we can use *so* or *neither* instead of repeating the whole sentence.

*I can ski pretty well.*
*So can I.* (= I can ski pretty well.)

*I don't like rap music.*
*Neither do I.* (= I don't like rap music.)

We use *so* to agree with an affirmative statement, and we use *neither* to agree with a negative statement. These are both followed by the auxiliary or modal verb from the first statement + *I*.

| | |
|---|---|
| *I'm at the airport.* | *So am I.* |
| *I can speak Spanish.* | *So can I.* |
| *I've never been abroad.* | *Neither have I.* |
| *I won't be late.* | *Neither will I.* |

If the statement is in the simple present or simple past, we use the auxiliary *do/does* or *did* to agree with the other person.

| | |
|---|---|
| *I live near the sea.* | *So do I.* |
| *I didn't like the hotel.* | *Neither did I.* |

## Disagreeing

When something that someone says isn't true for us, or what is said is different for us, we can use *I* + auxiliary or modal verb from the first statement. We often respond with *Really* first.

| | |
|---|---|
| *I don't like traveling by train.* | *Really? I do.* |
| *I've never tried mint ice cream.* | *Really? I have. It's delicious!* |

After an affirmative statement that isn't the same for us, we use *I* + negative auxiliary or modal verb, such as *I'm not. / I don't. / I didn't. / I can't. / I wouldn't.*

| | |
|---|---|
| *I really enjoyed that movie.* | *I didn't.* |
| *I love going running after work.* | *I don't. I hate running.* |

After a negative statement that isn't the same for us, we use an affirmative auxiliary or modal verb.

| | |
|---|---|
| *I didn't enjoy that movie.* | *Really? I did.* |
| *I can't help Leo with his homework.* | *I can. Don't worry.* |

**1** Complete the replies with the words in the box.

> could    did (x2)    so    would
> can    neither    have    do    'm not

1 A I love sightseeing.
  B So _____ I. It's better than lying on the beach.
2 A I've never been to Japan.
  B Neither _____ I. But I'd like to go one day.
3 A I can't swim very well.
  B Oh, I _____ . I'm a very good swimmer.
4 A I'm staying at home tonight.
  B Really? I _____ . I'm going out.
5 A I didn't like that movie.
  B _____ did I. I thought it was really boring.
6 A I'd love to go to New York one day.
  B Yes, _____ would I.
7 A I just bought a new camera.
  B So _____ I. What a coincidence!
8 A I didn't buy her a present for her birthday.
  B Neither _____ I.
9 A I'd like to watch that new reality show.
  B Yes, so _____ I.
10 A Unfortunately, I couldn't go to her party.
  B No, neither _____ I.

**2** Write replies to agree (✔) or disagree (✗) with the statements. Use *so* or *neither* or *I* + auxiliary or modal.

1 I've finished all my homework. (✔)
  *So have I.*
2 I won't go to bed late tonight.
  _____ . (✔)
3 I like going to the movies by myself.
  _____ . (✗)
4 I can't speak French very well.
  _____ . (✔)
5 I usually drive to work.
  _____ . (✔)
6 I'm going to the U.S. in the summer.
  _____ . (✔)
7 I'm not going to Luke's party.
  _____ . (✗)
8 I haven't bought my ticket yet.
  _____ . (✔)
9 I didn't enjoy reading that book.
  _____ . (✗)
10 I'd love to see her again.
  _____ . (✔)

◀ Go back to page 103

## 12C Modals of deduction

 12.11

I can't hear the children. They **must be** in bed.
I haven't seen Lukas for a few days. He **might be** on vacation.
You **might not like** this new café. They only serve coffee, not tea.
Sandra's not at work today. She **may be** sick.
It's very noisy in the apartment upstairs. They **must be having** a party.

We use modals of deduction to talk about something when we don't know if it's definitely true.

We use *must* + base form when we think that something is true.
*It must be cold outside. Everyone's wearing gloves.* (= I'm sure it's cold outside.)

We use *can't* or *couldn't* + base form when we are sure that something isn't true.
*Sally can't live here. This is a house, and she said she lived in an apartment.* (= I'm sure that Sally doesn't live here.)

We use *might* or *might not* + base form when we think it's possible that something is true, but we're not sure.
*Mark isn't answering his phone. He might be in a meeting. Or he might not have it with him.* (= It's possible that Mark is in a meeting. It's possible that he doesn't have his phone with him.)

We also use *may* or *could* + base form when we think something is possible.
*They're speaking English, so they may be British.*
*I don't know where he is. He could be at a friend's house.*

We often use the continuous form of the verb after modals of deduction when we talk about what we think is happening now.
*Tom's not in the kitchen. He must be doing his homework in his bedroom.*
*They can't be playing soccer now – it's nearly midnight!*
*She might be talking to David on the phone. He left a message for her this morning.*

**Look!** We never use *can* or contract *must not* to talk about what we think is true. The word *mustn't* has a different meaning and expresses prohibition in British English.
*Lisa has ordered tofu. She might/could be a vegetarian.* NOT ~~She can be a vegetarian.~~
*That must not be Steve's coat. It looks too small.* NOT ~~That mustn't be Steve's coat. It looks too small.~~

### GRAMMAR PRACTICE

1  Choose the correct options to complete the sentences.
   1  John didn't sleep at all last night. He *must / can't* be really tired today.
   2  Where's Lidia? She *can't / might* be at work because her office is closed today.
   3  Let's try that store over there. It *might / can* be cheaper, but I'm not sure.
   4  We *can / can't* be at the right address. There's no restaurant here.
   5  A  Is Vicki's husband from Australia?
      B  I think he *might / can't* be, but I've never asked him.
   6  I never see Max studying, so he *can't / must* be a very good student.
   7  Look, Brian *must / can* be home – the lights are on in his apartment.
   8  This *must / may* be the museum Lucy was talking about. I'm absolutely sure.
   9  That movie won three Oscars, so it *can't / must* be good.
   10 The people on the street have opened their umbrellas so it *can't / must* be raining.

2  Complete the second sentences so they mean the same as the first sentences. Use *must*, *might*, or *can't*.
   1  Luke's not here. It's possible that he's sick.
      Luke's not here. He _____ sick.
   2  I'm sure that's not Martin's car. His is much bigger.
      That _____ Martin's car. His is much bigger.
   3  Steve goes to the pool every day at this time. He's definitely swimming right now.
      Steve _____ swimming right now – he goes to the pool every day at this time.
   4  It's possible that there are still tickets available for the concert.
      There _____ tickets available for the concert.
   5  It seems impossible that this dish is very healthy – it's full of sugar.
      This dish _____ very healthy – it's full of sugar.
   6  I'm totally sure she knows Toni – I saw them talking at the party.
      She _____ Toni – I saw them talking at the party.
   7  It's possible that they're waiting for us outside.
      They _____ for us outside.
   8  I don't believe that it's snowing. It's the middle of May!
      It _____ . It's the middle of May!

◂ Go back to page 107

# VOCABULARY PRACTICE

## 1A Communication

1  ▶ 1.1 Match phrases 1–10 with definitions a–j. Listen and check.

1 get a text message/an e-mail _____
2 check your phone _____
3 reply to a text message/an e-mail _____
4 give someone a call _____
5 share something on social media _____
6 comment on a post _____
7 check Facebook/your messages _____
8 go online/access the Internet _____
9 keep in touch with someone _____
10 speak to someone face-to-face _____

a send a text message/an e-mail to a person who has sent one to you
b call someone
c receive a text message/an e-mail
d look at your phone to see messages, alerts, etc.
e give your opinion on something on social media
f look at a social media/e-mail account to see messages, alerts, etc.
g put something on social media, e.g., a photo or video
h stay in contact with someone
i have a conversation with someone in person
j connect to the Internet

2  Complete the sentences 1–9 with the words in the box.

| get  speak  share  check  reply  give  keep  comment  access |

1 Sorry, I can't talk now. Can I _____ you a call when I get home?
2 Can I borrow your laptop so I can _____ my messages?
3 I can't _____ the Internet because there's no WiFi here.
4 I had no signal on my phone, so I didn't _____ your text message.
5 My friends often _____ on my blog posts. Sometimes we have long discussions online.
6 It's easy to _____ in touch with your family when you're abroad.
7 I usually _____ my vacation photos on Facebook.
8 It's much better to _____ to someone face-to-face when you have a problem.
9 I didn't _____ to your message because I was in a meeting. Sorry.

◀ Go back to page 4

## 1C  *say*, *tell*, *speak*, and *talk*

1  ▶ 1.4 Complete the chart with *say*, *tell*, *speak*, or *talk*. Listen and check.

| 1 _____ | a language |
| speak / 2 _____ | (to someone) about something quickly/slowly/loudly |
| 3 _____ | someone (something) (someone) a lie/the truth/a story/a joke someone a secret |
| 4 _____ | hello/goodbye something (to someone) sorry/thanks/congratulations |

2  Choose the correct verbs to complete the sentences.

1 Can I *say* / *talk* to Pedro, please?
2 You need to *say* / *tell* sorry to Carl for arriving late.
3 I *told* / *said* her the good news.
4 Mary can *speak* / *talk* two languages.
5 Can I *say* / *tell* you a secret?
6 Sara *said* / *told* something really interesting.
7 Why are you *saying* / *speaking* so loudly?
8 Can you *tell* / *say* me your address, please?

3  Complete the sentences with a form of *say*, *tell*, *speak*, or *talk* and a word or phrase from the box.

| German  thanks  a secret  sorry  a great joke  to my boss |

1 I'm calling to _____ for helping me with my work yesterday.
2 I _____ Jan _____ yesterday. That was a mistake – now everyone knows it!
3 I'm having some problems at work, so I need to _____ .
4 Simon _____ me _____ this morning – it was so funny!
5 I want to learn to _____, so I'm going to take a course at a language school.
6 You were so rude to your brother. I think you should _____ him you're _____ .

136

◀ Go back to page 8

# VOCABULARY PRACTICE

## 2A -ed and -ing adjectives

1  ▶ 2.1 Match the pairs of adjectives with pictures 1–10. Listen and check.

depressed/depressing   excited/exciting   amazed/amazing   amused/amusing   disappointed/disappointing
embarrassed/embarrassing   fascinated/fascinating   annoyed/annoying   terrified/terrifying   shocked/shocking

1 _____

2 _____

3 _____

4 _____

5 _____

6 _____

7 _____

8 _____

9 _____

10 _____

2  Complete sentences 1–10 with adjectives from exercise 1.

1 I'm really scared of spiders. I find them _____ !
2 My brother always gets home late for dinner, and we all have to wait. It makes me really _____ .
3 Jamie was _____ with his grades – he was hoping to get As, but he only got Cs.
4 I'm watching a really _____ soccer game – the score's 5–5!
5 Sue thought the book about Japanese paintings was _____ . She's really into art.
6 I lost my job, then my girlfriend left me, and now I have no friends. I'm feeling _____ .
7 The people who saw the terrible accident were all _____ .
8 I fell off my chair during the job interview. My face turned bright red, I was so _____ !
9 I was _____ that my boyfriend remembered my mom's birthday because he always forgets important days.
10 Everyone in the theater was laughing, but I didn't find the movie very _____ .

◀ Go back to page 12

137

# VOCABULARY PRACTICE

## 2B Phrasal verbs

1 ▶ 2.6 Match sentences 1–9 with pictures a–i. Listen and check.

1 I hate ice skating! I always **fall over**. ____
2 Jack needs to **try on** the jeans before he buys them. ____
3 My best friend wants to **go out** with my brother. She thinks she's in love with him. ____
4 I think my brother would **break up** with her after a few days. He prefers being single. ____
5 **Hurry up**! The bus is coming! ____
6 Ana wants to **sign up** for extra English classes in college. ____
7 Prices will **go up** again next year. ____
8 My neighbors **set off** for Boston early on a long business trip. ____
9 When she got to the checkout, Eva realized she'd **run out** of money. ____

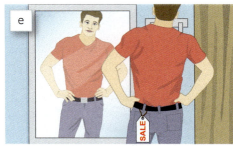

2 ▶ 2.7 Match the phrasal verbs in **bold** with definitions a–f. Listen and check.

1 I'll **pay back** the money my father lent me. ____
2 Jo left her bag at the store, so she has to **go back** to get it. ____
3 It takes a lot of patience and hard work to **bring up** children. ____
4 I haven't seen Alex for ages, but we're going to **catch up** over coffee soon. ____
5 A lot of garbage and plastic bags **end up** in the sea. ____
6 I always **look forward to** my birthday because I enjoy celebrating it. ____

a feel excited about something that is going to happen
b take care of a child until he/she is an adult
c finally be in a place or situation
d meet someone you haven't seen for a while and talk about your news
e return to a place
f return money to the person you borrowed it from

3 Complete the sentences below with the correct form of the phrasal verbs from exercises 1 and 2.

1 The price of a bus ticket _____ by 10% last month.
2 I'd planned to go to the movies with Mark, but he was sick, so I _____ going on my own.
3 My grandparents _____ my cousin after his parents died, and he lived with them until he was 18.
4 My boss is away, but when she gets back, we'll _____, and I'll tell her about the new clients.
5 I stood up very quickly and _____.
6 My colleagues have _____ for an online course in computer programming.

138 ◀ Go back to page 14

# VOCABULARY PRACTICE

## 3A Personality adjectives

1 ▶ 3.1 Complete sentences 1–9 with the adjectives in the box. Listen and check.

> easygoing   sensitive   reliable   helpful   organized   sensible   confident   friendly   anxious

1 The staff in that store is really _____ . Someone always carries my bags to my car.
2 Joe is so _____ . I could never sing in front of so many people, like he does.
3 Mike is very practical and has a lot of common sense. He's so _____ .
4 Tina's always worrying about something. I don't know why she's so _____ .

5 All of Marta's plans for next year are written in her diary. She's very _____ .
6 When Jon says he'll do something, he always does it. He's very _____ .
7 Ana understands other people's feelings. She's very _____ .
8 The students in my new class took me out for coffee on my first day. They're so _____ .
9 Sarah's always relaxed and calm, and she doesn't worry about things. She's very _____ .

2 ▶ 3.2 Which negative prefix do we use with the adjectives in the box? Put the adjectives in the correct column. Listen and check.

> ~~kind~~   patient   sensitive   reliable   helpful
> polite   friendly   honest   organized   sociable

| un- | dis- | im-/in- |
|---|---|---|
| unkind | | |

◀ Go back to page 22

## 3C Relationships

1 ▶ 3.6 Complete sentences 1–9 with the words and phrases in the box. Use the plural form if necessary. Listen and check.

> best friend   close friend   colleague   partner   couple   parents   relative   classmate   next-door neighbor

1 He knows a lot of people here, but he doesn't have many _____ .
2 I went out with some of my _____ from the office after work.
3 That one-bedroom apartment would be perfect for a _____ .
4 I have a lot of _____ who live in the U.S. – mainly cousins.
5 It's not easy these days to find a romantic _____ .
6 I still live with my _____ . It's just me, my mom and my dad.
7 The walls in my building are very thin. I can hear my _____ talking.
8 I've known Liz for ten years. She's the first person I call if I'm sad or if I have good news – she's my _____ .
9 My _____ and I have a WhatsApp group where we talk about our homework.

2 ▶ 3.7 Read sentences 1–8. Match the words and phrases in **bold** with definitions a–h. Listen and check.

1 We had a **falling out** and haven't spoken since.. _____
2 We **argue** a lot because we never agree about what to watch on TV. _____
3 I **get along well** with my neighbors – we're all good friends. _____
4 It's sometimes difficult to **get to know** new people, but I'm lucky – my classmates in college are all really friendly. _____
5 Do you know that girl? Could you **introduce** me to her? _____
6 Sam and Ben had a fight this morning. I told them to **make up**, and now everything's fine! _____
7 It's hard for me to have a conversation with my neighbors since we don't **have a lot in common**. _____
8 I **get together** with my close friends at least once a week. _____

a have a good relationship
b tell someone another person's name when they meet for the first time
c talk to someone in an angry way because you disagree
d meet and go out
e stop being friends with someone because you disagree about something
f have the same interests, experiences, opinions, etc. as someone
g become friends again
h spend time with people so you become friends

◀ Go back to page 26

139

# VOCABULARY PRACTICE

## 4A Compound nouns

1 ▶ 4.1 Complete compound nouns 1–12 with the words in the box. Listen and check.

| transportation | pedestrian | life | gallery | parking | path | department | jam | shopping | night | sports | town |

1 art _____

2 bike _____

3 _____ mall

4 _____ club

5 _____ area

6 traffic _____

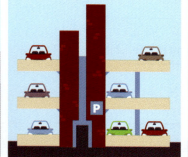
7 _____ lot

8 _____ store

9 _____ center

10 public _____

11 down_____

12 night_____

2 Complete sentences 1–12 with compound nouns from exercise 1. Use the plural form if necessary.

1 I love shopping in a _____ because you can find so many different things in one store.
2 Let's go to the new _____ near the airport – there are over 300 stores there!
3 I love the _____ in my city. It's great to be able to walk around without any cars.
4 There are lots of _____ in the old part of the city, where you can go dancing until 6 a.m.
5 That _____ has some amazing sculptures and paintings by local artists.
6 I was late for my meeting today. I drove to work, and there was a big _____ .
7 The _____ is great in my city. There are lots of clubs and places to hear music..
8 They've just opened a fantastic new gym at the _____ where I usually play tennis.
9 There aren't many _____ downtown, so it's better to take the bus than to drive.
10 There's a great _____ along the river. It's so relaxing to ride your bike there in the evening.
11 The _____ here is terrible. The buses are dirty, and they're never on time.
12 It's hard to find a good restaurant in my area. The best ones are _____ .

◀ Go back to page 30

VOCABULARY PRACTICE

## 4B Common verb phrases

1 ▶ 4.5 Complete diagrams 1–8 with the verbs in the box. Listen and check.

know   meet   lose   miss   take   catch   keep   have

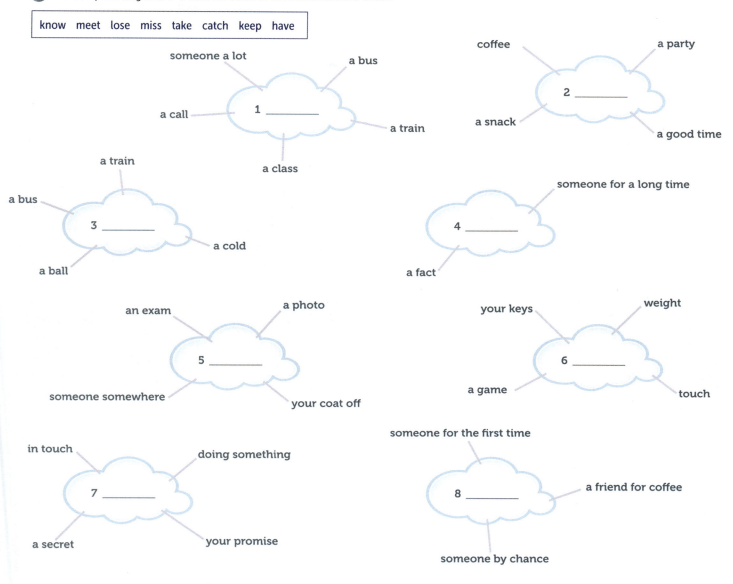

2 Choose the correct options to complete the text.

I've ¹*met / known* my friend Carl for ages. We ²*met / knew* at school when we were kids, but we ³*lost / kept in* touch for a few years when we went to different colleges. It was my fault. I ⁴*took / kept* losing my phone, so I ⁵*missed / lost* all his calls, but he ⁶*kept / took* calling, and eventually we got together and ⁷*had / took* coffee together. Since then we've ⁸*lost / kept* in touch, and we always ⁹*have / keep* a good time together. He's a great friend.

3 Complete sentences 1–7 with the correct form of the verb phrases in exercise 1.

1 Mark hasn't been eating well in college. Don't you think he's _____ ?
2 My car broke down, and my flight leaves in two hours! Can you _____ airport in your car?
3 I had breakfast ages ago, and I'm a bit hungry. Should we _____ ? I have some cheese and crackers.
4 Jon promised he would come and help me fix my car, but he never came. He didn't _____ .
5 We always _____ when the whole family gets together and put it in the family album.
6 I feel terrible. I have a sore throat and a cough. I think I've _____ .
7 I think I'm going to _____ for my birthday and invite 30 people.

◀ Go back to page 32

141

# VOCABULARY PRACTICE

## 4C Describing homes

1 ▶ 4.9 Match sentence parts 1–10 with a–j. Listen and check.

1 My new apartment has big windows, _____
2 I live in the newest part of the city, _____
3 My best friend's house has a **huge** backyard, _____
4 The windows in my old apartment were **tiny**, _____
5 His old house was **spacious**, but very **basic**; _____
6 My aunt's furniture is all from the 1970s, _____
7 Mike's new apartment is really **convenient** – _____
8 The living room has an open fire, _____
9 Tina's very fashionable, and she's a designer, _____
10 The bed in my hotel room is **comfortable**, _____

a so it was always very **dark**.
b you can walk downtown in ten minutes.
c so it's warm and **cozy** in winter.
d so we often play soccer in it.
e so it's really **bright** during the day.
f so I slept well last night.
g so my apartment is very **modern**.
h so her apartment is full of **stylish** furniture.
i it had five large bedrooms, but no central heating.
j so most of it is very **old-fashioned**.

2 Complete the texts below with the words in **bold** from exercise 1.

Sarah's apartment is only two years old, so it's very ¹_____ . It's a huge apartment – most of the rooms are ²_____, except for the kitchen, which is ³_____, so there's not much space to cook. It's on the top floor, and it has plenty of large windows, so it's very ⁴_____ . She's an architect, so the apartment looks really ⁵_____ . It's only two minutes from the nearest subway station, so it's very ⁶_____ – she can get to work in less than 20 minutes.

My parents live in a ⁷_____ house in the country with six spacious bedrooms. The windows are pretty small, which means it's very ⁸_____ . Also, since they don't have central heating, and there's only one bathroom, it's pretty ⁹_____ . They haven't bought any new furniture for years, so it's pretty ¹⁰_____ . I love their living room; in the winter, they have a real fire, so it's very ¹¹_____ . They also have two old leather sofas that are really ¹²_____ .

3 ▶ 4.10 Complete sentences 1–4 with the words in the box. Listen and check.

| village   suburbs   town   country |

1 I live in Melbourne, but my house isn't in the city. I live right outside, in the _____ .
2 I live in a place with a population of about 15,000. I live in a small _____ .
3 There are only a hundred houses where I live. I live in a _____ .
4 Where I live there are farms, fields, and lots of trees. I live in the _____ .

4 ▶ 4.11 Match words and phrases 1–8 with a–h in the picture on the right. Listen and check.

1 apartment building ____
2 basement ____
3 first floor ____
4 second floor ____
5 third floor ____
6 top floor ____
7 balcony ____
8 roof terrace ____

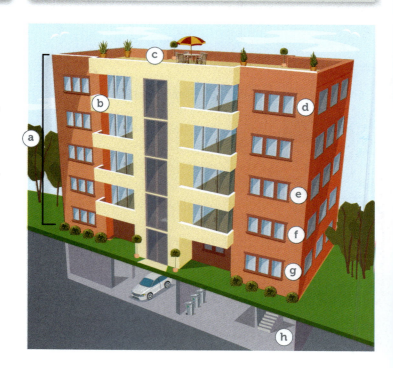

◀ Go back to page 34

# VOCABULARY PRACTICE

## 5A Money

1 ▶ 5.1 Complete sentences 1–9 with the words in the box. Listen and check.

| credit card  wealthy  broke  coins  savings account  cash |
| bills  loan  mortgage  taxes  ATM  save up |

1 The machine at the station didn't accept my _____, so we had to pay with _____.
2 I want to _____ for a car, so I put $200 into my _____ every month.
3 I needed $100, so I went to the bank. They gave me five $20 _____.
4 I got a _____ from my bank to buy my car and a _____ to buy my apartment.
5 My uncle's very _____ – he has four houses, six cars, and a boat.
6 I pay a lot of _____ to the government – about 25% of what I earn.
7 In cafés, people normally leave a tip for the waiter. A few _____ are sometimes enough if you only have coffee.
8 Jim realized he was completely _____ – he didn't even have enough money to take the bus home!
9 Can we stop at the _____? I need some money.

2 ▶ 5.2 Complete sentences 1–9 with the prepositions in the box. Listen and check.

| on (x2)  for  by  into  from  out  back  to |

1 I don't like to **lend** money _____ friends.
2 Can I **pay** _____ credit card?
3 My sister and her husband usually **spend** over $400 _____ clothes every month!
4 How much would you **pay** _____ a second-hand car?
5 I went to the ATM to **take** _____ some money.
6 Can I **borrow** $20 _____ you until tomorrow?
7 Martin shouldn't **waste** so much money _____ lottery tickets.
8 Could you **pay** _____ the money you owe me before the end of the week?
9 I **pay** $50 _____ a savings account for my grandchildren every month.

◀ Go back to page 40

## 5C Shopping

1 ▶ 5.7 Complete the online product information below with the words and phrases in the box. Listen and check.

| products  delivery  in stock  checkout  cart  item |

**Santelli Go II Mountain Bike**
$420

1 _____ (5 available) ✓
Next-day 2 _____ available  🚚  **Buy**
Go to the 3 _____ and pay.
You have one 4 _____ in your 5 _____.
Click **here** to see other Santelli 6 _____.

2A Read the review and match words 1–8 with definitions a–h.

I usually prefer ¹**in-store** shopping because I like to ²**browse** different products and see them before I choose what I want. Last month, I went shopping for a new camera. A ³**salesclerk** said there was a ⁴**special offer** on the Cam2. It's a great camera, and at $350 it was very ⁵**reasonable**. I decided to buy one, but it was ⁶**sold out**, so I ⁷**ordered it online**, instead. When the camera arrived, I realized they'd sent me the Cam1 model, instead, so I had to ⁸**return** it.

a no more left to buy ____
b take or send something back ____
c a lower price than normal ____
d bought it on the Internet ____
e a good price ____
f in a store ____
g a person who sells things in a store ____
h look at ____

B ▶ 5.8 Look at the words in **bold** in exercise 2A. Listen and repeat.

◀ Go back to page 44

# VOCABULARY PRACTICE

## 6A Work and careers (1)

1 ▶ 6.1 Complete sentences 1–11 with the correct form of the words in the box. Listen and check.

> be laid off   get a degree   take a training course   get a job
> retire   get a promotion   do an internship
> resign   look for a job   learn new skills   get experience
> get fired   do a job placement

1 Mark is so angry with his boss that he's decided to _____ . He's leaving at the end of the month.
2 Eighty workers _____ at that company last week. They lost their jobs because the company is losing money.
3 Dan _____ from his last job because he was always late.
4 I'm _____ to learn how to use the company's new software.
5 Two years after he joined the company as an assistant manager, Leo _____ . He became the manager.
6 Ed wants to _____ working in a big hotel, so he took a summer job as a receptionist in the largest hotel in Miami.
7 I'd like to _____ when I'm 60 and have a lot of time to enjoy life.
8 Before I can work as a nurse, I need to _____ in nursing, so I'm studying hard, and I hope to get into nursing school in the fall.
9 Sally _____ in a lawyer's office. They didn't pay her a salary, but after six months, they offered her a job.
10 As part of my program, I'm _____ at a design studio. I'm _____ like graphic design.
11 Tim is unemployed, but he is _____ as a salesclerk. I'm sure he'll _____ soon.

2 Choose the correct words to complete the sentences.

1 After she'd been with her company for two years, she got a *job placement / promotion* – she became Sales Manager.
2 Last week, I *took a training course / did an internship* to learn how to use the new database.
3 When the factory closed down last month, all the workers *got fired / were laid off*.
4 She *got fired / resigned* because she stole a computer from the office.
5 My cousin did *an internship / a job* for a year in a television company, but, unfortunately, he didn't get a *promotion / job* at the end of it.
6 Jill has found a new job, so she's *resigned / gotten fired* from her old job.

◀ Go back to page 48

## 6B Work and careers (2)

1 ▶ 6.6 Match the words in **bold** with definitions a–h. Listen and check.

1 I'm **responsible for** digital marketing. ____
2 My company was voted the best **employer** in the region. ____
3 Ian likes traveling. He's had **temporary** jobs in different places. ____
4 Please send a **cover letter** to introduce yourself and say why you're suitable for the position. ____
5 I was **unemployed** for a year before I found a job. ____
6 I work as a waitress, but I'd like a **career** in advertising. ____
7 They pay my **salary** on the first day of every month. ____
8 I work with kids. I love seeing them learn. It's very **rewarding**. ____

a a person or company that employs people
b the occupation you choose for most of your working life
c money you receive for doing your job
d a job that usually lasts a few weeks or months
e a feeling of satisfaction that you've done something useful
f without work
g a document you send with your résumé when you apply for a job
h in charge of

2 Complete the e-mail below with the words and phrases in the box.

> full-time   résumé   permanent   application form   well-paid   varied
> working conditions   stressful   employees   part-time   manager

When I finished college, I got a ¹_____ job in a restaurant, just a few days a week. This gave me time to finish a project-management course and look for a ²_____ job, not a temporary one. The ³_____ in the restaurant were awful, it was too noisy, and we worked very late. The ⁴_____ was terrible too – he always yelled at us.

I thought an office job would be less ⁵_____, so I sent my ⁶_____ to lots of companies. When I saw an ad for a project manager, I filled in the online ⁷_____ and had an interview. I got the job! I love it. No two days are ever the same. It's very ⁸_____ . It's a small company with only ten ⁹_____ . We all have ¹⁰_____ jobs so we work 38 hours a week. It's quite a ¹¹_____ job so I can save a little money every month.

◀ Go back to page 50

144

# VOCABULARY PRACTICE

## 6C Education

**1 A** Match sentences 1–8 with pictures a–h.

1. **A** Did Sally **get a good grade** on the test?
   **B** Yes, she got nine out of ten!
2. I have to **hand in** my essay at 8 a.m., not a minute later. My teacher's very **strict**.
3. Gina has started to **study for** her final exams. She's studying all the grammar they've done in class this year.
4. I used to **get into trouble** a lot in school. I didn't **behave** at all. I used to throw things at other students, and I was often sent to the principal's office.
5. You can't **cheat** on the exam. You can't look at your books or ask anyone to help you with the questions.
6. I might **get a degree** in English and French. I'm good at languages, so I think I should study them in college.
7. It's a good idea to **take notes** during lessons and lectures. If you write things down in your notebook, it helps you to remember them.
8. **A** Did you **get your grades** today? Did you **pass** or **fail**?
   **B** I passed! I got over 60% on all my exams. Sara failed, though.

**B** ▶ 6.10 Look at the words and phrases in **bold** in 1A. Listen and repeat.

**2** ▶ 6.11 Match the words in the box with the definitions. Listen and check.

| principal   term   schedule   professor   graduate |

1. part of a school year             _____
2. a college teacher                 _____
3. the manager of a school           _____
4. a list of the times and days for classes   _____
5. a person who has a college degree _____

**3** ▶ 6.12 Complete the chart with the places in the box. Listen and check.

| high school   middle school   nursery school   elementary school |
| boarding school   public school   private school |

| description | place |
| --- | --- |
| a school for ages 3–5 | 1 _____ |
| a school for ages 6–11 | 2 _____ |
| a school for ages 11–15 | 3 _____ |
| a school for ages 15-18 | 4 _____ |
| a school where you don't have to pay | 5 _____ |
| a school where you have to pay | 6 _____ |
| a school where you study, live, and sleep | 7 _____ |

**4** Complete the sentences below with the correct form of a word from exercises 1, 2, or 3.

1. I'm _____ a degree in math. My _____ are all math experts!
2. Private school is very expensive. It's not free like _____ school.
3. I always used to _____ in school. I never _____ into trouble.
4. I can't go out tonight. I have to _____ for an exam tomorrow.
5. You need a degree to apply for that job. It's only for _____ .

a

b

c

d

e

f

g

h

◀ Go back to page 52

# VOCABULARY PRACTICE

## 7A  Movies

1  ▶ 7.1 Match the words and phrases in the box with definitions 1–10. Listen and check.

| scene  sequel  director  cast  subtitles  soundtrack  special effects  plot  script  main character |
|---|

1 the people who act in a movie  _____
2 the person who makes a movie  _____
3 the story of the movie  _____
4 a movie that continues the story of another movie  _____
5 words written at the bottom of the screen  _____
6 a short section of a movie  _____
7 the spoken words of the movie  _____
8 the music of the movie  _____
9 images that are usually created by computer  _____
10 the most important person in the movie's story  _____

2 A ▶ 7.2 Match the phrases in **bold** in the text with sentences a–g.

*Blade Runner* is one of the most famous science fiction movies ever made. ¹It was <u>directed by</u> Ridley Scott, and ²the main character was <u>played by</u> Harrison Ford. ³The movie is <u>set in</u> Los Angeles in the year 2019, and ⁴it was <u>shot</u> at the Warner Brothers' studio in Hollywood and on location in L.A. The movie is about a police officer who is trying to find a group of dangerous androids. ⁵It's <u>based on</u> a novel called *Do Androids Dream of Electric Sheep?* by Philip K Dick. When ⁶*Blade Runner* was <u>released</u> in 1982, not all of the movie critics liked it, but these days it's a science fiction classic. ⁷It has been <u>dubbed</u> into a lot of different languages, and its sequel, *Blade Runner 2049*, was released in 2017. It stars Harrison Ford, Ryan Gosling, and Ana de Armas.

a The story happens in this place and at this time.  ____
b This book inspired the story in the movie.  ____
c It was filmed in this place.  ____
d This person was the movie director.  ____
e The movie was shown in theaters for the first time.  ____
f This actor had this role in the movie.  ____
g The original spoken words of the movie have been replaced with words in another language.  ____

B Look at the <u>underlined</u> words in 2A. Listen and repeat.

3 ▶ 7.3 Match the types of movies in the box with definitions 1–8. Listen and check.

| action movie  animation  horror movie  romantic comedy  science-fiction movie  thriller  musical  documentary |
|---|

1 an exciting movie, often with a plot about solving a crime  _____
2 a movie set in the future, often about space travel  _____
3 a movie with a plot about an amusing love story  _____
4 a movie that gives facts and information about something  _____
5 a lot of the story is told using songs in this type of movie  _____
6 a frightening movie, often about killers, dead people, or monsters  _____
7 a movie that often has a hero who fights or chases bad people  _____
8 a movie of moving images made by using drawings or models  _____

> **Look!** We shorten the forms of some movie types.
> *I love sci-fi movies.*

◀ Go back to page 58

VOCABULARY PRACTICE

## 7C TV and music

1 ▶ 7.7 Match the types of TV shows in the box with pictures 1–9. Listen and check.

game show   talk show   drama   reality show   cartoon   sitcom   soap opera   the news   talent show

1 _____   2 _____   3 _____
4 _____   5 _____   6 _____
7 _____   8 _____   9 _____

2 ▶ 7.8 Complete sentences 1–6 with the words in the box. Listen and check.

ads   audience   channel   episode   host   series   season

1 Can you change the _____, please? The news is on at 9:00 p.m., and I want to watch it.
2 I'm going to make coffee while the _____ are on, so I don't miss the show.
3 Everyone in the _____ laughed when the host told a joke about the politician.
4 I prefer watching TV _____ to movies. My favorite is *Game of Thrones*. _____ one was the best!
5 I can't stand this _____. He always asks his guests such silly questions.
6 I missed the last _____ of that soap opera. What happened?

3 ▶ 7.9 Complete sentences 1–7 with the words in the box. Listen and check.

band   tracks   playlist   on tour   hits   live (adj.)   album

1 My favorite _____ is *The Best of Jana* by a singer called Jana.
2 Why don't you choose your favorite 50 songs and make a _____ for the party?
3 When I saw Shakira in concert last year, she sang all of her _____, including my favorite song, *Whenever, Wherever*.
4 When we were students, my sister and I were in a _____. I was the singer, and she played the guitar.
5 I love seeing my favorite groups _____ in concert.
6 I can't wait for my favorite singer to go _____. I hope she plays at the stadium in my city.
7 There are 20 _____ on that album.

◀ Go back to page 62

147

## VOCABULARY PRACTICE

### 8A  Sports, places, and equipment

1  ▶ 8.2 Match the words in the box with pictures 1–9. Listen and check.

| ball   bat   skates   goal   net   goggles   racket   stick   helmet |

1 _____   2 _____   3 _____
4 _____   5 _____   6 _____   7 _____   8 _____   9 _____

2  ▶ 8.3 Match the sports with pictures 1–12. Listen and check.

| soccer   diving   basketball   hockey   ice skating   track and field   auto racing   baseball   swimming   volleyball   tennis   football |

1 _____   2 _____   3 _____   4 _____
5 _____   6 _____   7 _____   8 _____
9 _____   10 _____   11 _____   12 _____

3A  ▶ 8.4 Look at words 1–6 in 3B. Listen and repeat.
 B  Match the sports in exercise 2 with the places.

1 court _____   3 rink _____   5 circuit _____
2 field _____   4 pool _____   6 track _____

148                                                                ◀ Go back to page 66

VOCABULARY PRACTICE

## 8B Health and fitness verb phrases

1 ▶ 8.9 Complete the text with the correct form of *get*, *be*, or *have*. Listen and check.

Do you ¹_____ **an unhealthy lifestyle**?

It's very easy these days to ²_____ **bad habits** when it comes to exercise, food, and sleep. If you'd like to ³_____ **a healthy lifestyle**, talk to your doctor and follow the advice below.

- Try to ⁴_____ **exercise** five times a week for at least 30 minutes. Adults need 150 minutes of moderate aerobic activity every week, or 75 minutes of vigorous activity.
- Make sure you ⁵_____ **a balanced diet**. Eat a variety of foods from all five food groups, but limit how much sugar, fat, and salt you eat.
- Even in stressful situations, try not to ⁶_____ **stressed**. Make sure you have enough time to relax. Regular exercise helps reduce stress levels.

- Exercise also helps you lose weight if you ⁷_____ **overweight**, and if you are out of shape, it helps you to ⁸_____ **in shape**.
- If you ⁹_____ **on a diet**, don't try to lose weight too quickly.
- If you ¹⁰_____ **underweight**, aim to eat food that is high in energy, for example, peanut butter on toast or a baked potato with tuna.
- It's important to ¹¹_____ **a good night's sleep**. We all need different amounts of sleep, but most adults need 7–9 hours a night.

2 Complete the sentences with the correct form of the verb phrases in exercise 1.

1 There's a lot of pressure on my job. I often _____ out.
2 My grandmother _____ . She plays tennis regularly and eats healthy food.
3 I try to _____ by eating lots of different foods, especially vegetables, fruit, meat, and fish.
4 I _____ four times a week. I usually go to the gym or go running.

5 Jack was sick for a month and didn't eat much. Now he _____ and has to eat a lot of protein.
6 I have a three-month-old baby who wakes me up every hour, so it's difficult to _____ .
7 No chocolate cake for me, thanks. I _____ . I can only eat low-fat food.

◀ Go back to page 68

## 10B Making nouns from verbs

1 ▶ 10.6 Make nouns from the verbs in the box below and write them in the chart on the right. Listen and check.

| -sion | -ment | -ation | -tion |
|---|---|---|---|
| confusion | | | |

confuse   argue   imagine   govern   inform   protect   achieve
connect   disappoint   decide   educate   organize

2 Complete the second sentences with a noun so they have the same meaning as the first sentences.

1 Antivirus software protects computers from viruses.
Antivirus software offers computers _____ from viruses.
2 Thanks to Sarah for organizing the event so well.
Thanks to Sarah for your great _____ .
3 A lot was achieved in the twentieth century. Walking on the moon is one of the best examples of this.
Walking on the moon was one of the best _____ of the twentieth century.
4 Educating our children is a huge responsibility.
Our children's _____ is a huge responsibility.
5 A large city has to govern effectively. A large city has to have an effective _____ .

6 I went to a concert last week, but I was disappointed.
The concert I went to last week was a _____ .
7 Last night my neighbors were arguing really loudly.
Last night my neighbors were having a really loud _____ .
8 We decided to sell our car and use public transportation instead.
We made the _____ to sell our car and use public transportation instead.
9 The lesson was very difficult, so a lot of people were confused.
There was a lot of _____ because the lesson was very difficult.
10 Nobody informed us why the flight had been canceled.
We didn't receive any _____ about why the flight had been canceled.

◀ Go back to page 86

149

## VOCABULARY PRACTICE

## 9A Food and cooking

1 ▶ 9.1 Match the foods in the box with pictures 1–11. Listen and check.

| chickpeas   steak   lime   yogurt   lentils   asparagus   lamb chop   lobster   squid   skim milk   whole wheat bread |

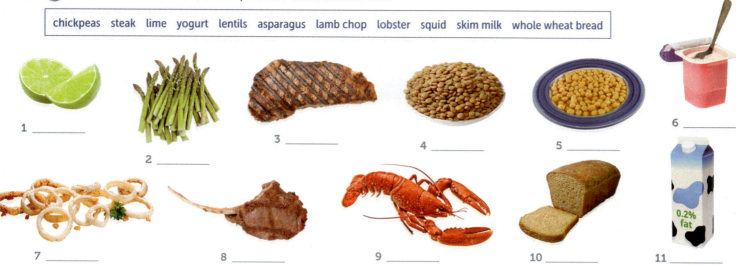

2A ▶ 9.2 Put the words in the box in the correct column of the chart. Add the words from exercise 1. Listen and check.

B Add other food words you know to the chart.

| zucchini   olive oil   garlic   soy sauce   toast   shellfish   avocado |

| seafood | meat | dairy products | legumes | fruit and vegetables | carbohydrates | other |
|---|---|---|---|---|---|---|
|  |  | *yogurt* | *lentils* |  |  |  |
|  |  |  |  |  |  |  |
|  |  |  |  |  |  |  |

3 ▶ 9.3 Look at the pictures. Complete descriptions 1–10 with the words in the box. Listen and check.

| baked   boiled   grated   grilled   homemade   melted   roast   sliced   takeout   fried |

1 _____ egg   2 _____ potato   3 _____ burger   4 _____ beef   5 _____ chicken

6 _____ rice   7 _____ cheese   8 _____ carrot   9 _____ food   10 _____ soup

150

◀ Go back to page 76

# VOCABULARY PRACTICE

## 9C Eating out

**1 A** Read the conversations. Match the phrases in **bold** with definitions a–j.

A Should we ¹**eat out** tonight or get some takeout?
B Let's eat out. I'll ²**reserve a table** at that new place on Main Street.
A Great! I've heard that the food is delicious, and there's a nice ³**atmosphere**, too – it's relaxed, welcoming, and they have good music.
B I hope the ⁴**service** is good, too. I hate rude waiters.

A I'll have the steak.
B How would you like it? ⁵**Rare**? ⁶**Medium**?
A I'll have a ⁷**well-done** steak, please.

A I'm still hungry! Let's ⁸**order** dessert.
B No, I'm tired. Can we just ⁹**get the check**?
A Sure. Do you have any cash so we can ¹⁰**leave a tip**?

a make a reservation for a particular time ____
b when meat is cooked a lot ____
c eat at a restaurant ____
d ask how much the meal is so you can pay ____
e when meat is cooked a little, and it's still red ____

f tell the waiter what you want to eat ____
g the feeling inside the restaurant ____
h when meat is cooked more than a little, but not a lot ____
i how the staff treats the customers ____
j leave a small amount of money for the waiter ____

**B** ▶ 9.7 Look at the words and phrases in **bold** in 1A. Listen and repeat.

**2** ▶ 9.8 Look at the pictures. Match objects 1–10 with words in the box. Listen and check.

| napkin  vinegar  knife  fork  spoon  plate  salt  pepper  bowl  tablecloth |

1 _____   6 _____
2 _____   7 _____
3 _____   8 _____
4 _____   9 _____
5 _____   10 _____

◀ Go back to page 80

151

# VOCABULARY PRACTICE

## 10A Crime

**1 A** Match sentences 1–8 with pictures a–h.

1. The police stopped me because I was driving too fast. I had to pay a $200 _____.
2. A _____ saw a masked man running away from the bank with a bag full of money. Police officers _____ the robber moments later.
3. The _____ was found dead on the dining-room floor.
4. In most countries, it's against the _____ to drive while holding a cell phone.
5. They're building a new _____ in my town with space for 500 criminals.
6. The police aren't sure who committed the crime, but they have released pictures of two _____ .
7. My neighbor's son is appearing in _____ . The police say he stole $75,000.
8. If you leave valuable objects in your car on this street, someone will _____ it and steal them.

**B** ▶ 10.1 Complete the sentences in exercise 1A with the correct form of the words in the box below. Listen and check.

| arrest   break into   court   fine   law   prison   suspects   victim   witness |
|---|

**2** ▶ 10.2 Match the descriptions of crimes 1–5 with the words in the box below. Listen and check.

| theft   murder   robbery   mugging   burglary |
|---|

1. Two people entered a house at night through an open window. They took jewelry and two computers. _____
2. A man attacked me on the street. He made me give him my phone and all my money. _____
3. He walked into the house and killed the man inside. _____
4. Three armed men ran into the bank and told the staff to give them all the money. _____
5. I left my bike at the train station. When I went back, it wasn't there. _____

**3** ▶ 10.3 Complete the chart below with the words in the box. Listen and check.

| robber   burglarize   murderer   thief   mug
| rob   steal   mugger   murder   burglar |
|---|

| crime | verb | criminal |
|---|---|---|
| theft | | |
| murder | | |
| robbery | | |
| mugging | | |
| burglary | | |

a

b

c

d

e

f

g

h

◀ Go back to page 84

**VOCABULARY PRACTICE**

## 11A The natural world

1 ▶ 11.1 Match the words in the box with pictures 1–11. Listen and check.

| sea   canyon   hill   iceberg   coast   desert   field   forest   glacier   jungle   volcano |
|---|

2 ▶ 11.2 Match the words in the box with descriptions 1–8. Listen and check.

| earthquake   flood   hail   hurricane   monsoon   rainbow   storm   tornado |
|---|

1 an arc of colors in the sky  _____
2 strong winds with rain, thunder, and lightning  _____
3 a very strong wind that can destroy towns  _____
4 when an area of normally dry land is covered with water  _____
5 when the ground shakes violently  _____
6 a very strong wind that moves in a circle and can lift cars and houses  _____
7 a season of heavy summer rain in some tropical regions  _____
8 small, hard balls of ice that fall from the sky  _____

◀ Go back to page 94

153

**VOCABULARY PRACTICE**

# 11C Extreme adjectives

1 ▶ 11.5 Read sentences 1–12 and match the extreme adjectives in **bold** to adjectives a–l. Listen and check.

1 It's **boiling** in here. Can I open a window? _____
2 Liam gave me an **enormous** bunch of flowers. I needed three vases for them! _____
3 After running the marathon, the athlete looked absolutely **exhausted**! _____
4 I've been playing soccer in the mud. My clothes are **filthy**. _____
5 Put on a scarf, hat, and gloves – it's **freezing** outside! _____
6 He was **furious** when his neighbor crashed into his car. _____
7 He tells **hilarious** jokes. He's an absolutely fantastic comedian! _____
8 He looked so **miserable** when the other team scored the winning goal. _____
9 I haven't eaten all day – I'm absolutely **starving**. _____
10 He was riding a **tiny** bike. He was much too big for it. _____
11 Your garden is **gorgeous**! You must be really proud of it. _____
12 Lena is a **fantastic** violinist. I'm sure she'll play professionally one day. _____

a very hungry
b very sad
c very small
d very tired
e very good
f very cold
g very big
h very pretty
i very hot
j very angry
k very dirty
l very funny

2 Complete the sentences with an extreme adjective from exercise 1.

1 Simon's just bought an _____ house – it has six bedrooms!
2 I'm _____ because I didn't have time to have lunch today.
3 Sara's feeling _____ because she failed all her exams.
4 You haven't washed your car for ages – it's absolutely _____ !
5 I worked from 7 a.m. to 8 p.m. today, so now I'm _____ !
6 It was snowing and absolutely _____ when we arrived in Moscow last night.
7 My grandfather was _____ when he saw that the boys had broken his window.

8 They didn't have any air conditioning, so it was absolutely _____ .
9 Paul's new girlfriend is _____ . I think she's a model.
10 He has a _____ apartment. It only has one room, plus a little kitchen and bathroom.
11 We just came back from seeing a _____ movie at the theater – we couldn't stop laughing.
12 I just finished reading a _____ book. It's the best book I've read in years!

◀ Go back to page 98

# 12A Phrases with *go* and *get*

1 A Match the words in the box with *go* phrases 1–4.

> a guided tour   traveling   coffee   school   a trip   bed   a walk
> away   hiking   scuba diving   vacation   home   college

1 go _____ _____ _____ _____ _____
2 go to _____ _____ _____
3 go for _____ _____
4 go on _____ _____ _____

B ▶ 12.1 Listen and repeat the phrases in 1A.

2 Match the use of *get* in each sentence below with meanings a–e.

1 Can you get my glasses? They're in the kitchen. _____
2 We spent all day on the beach, and I got bored. _____
3 Chris got our flights online. _____
4 Did you get my e-mail? _____
5 If we don't leave soon, we won't get there on time. _____

a buy
b arrive
c become
d receive
e bring

3 Choose the correct words to complete sentences 1–6.

1 Simon's going *for* / *on* a business trip to Tokyo.
2 There are a lot of tourists in the summer. It *gets* / *goes* really crowded.
3 When we get *at* / *to* Buenos Aires, Silvia's going to meet us at the airport.
4 When I was in Switzerland, we *went* / *got* hiking in the mountains.
5 We climbed a mountain, and I *went* / *got* tired quickly.
6 On our first day in Sydney, we went *to* / *on* a guided tour.

4 Rewrite the underlined parts of sentences 1–5 with a phrase with *go* or *get*.

1 Would you like to drink coffee with me later? _____
2 It becomes very cold here in winter. _____
3 I'll arrive at your house at about ten o'clock. _____
4 I'd love to visit lots of different places around the world for a year. _____
5 I need to buy some more sun cream. _____

◀ Go back to page 102

VOCABULARY PRACTICE

## 12B Air travel

1 ▶ 12.5 Complete the instructions with the correct form of the words and phrases in the box below. Listen and check.

| flight attendant | book a flight | pack | check in | window seat | go through security | departure lounge | land | departure board |
| take off | show your passport | carry-on bag | gate | checked baggage | boarding pass | aisle seat |

### Booking and flying with Go There Airline

On our website you can ¹_____ up to eleven months before the date of travel, and you can ²_____ online for your flight 24 hours before departure time.

Make sure you ³_____ your own bags and suitcases. Don't take any prohibited items.

You're allowed 20 kg. of ⁴_____ , and you can bring one ⁵_____ with you on the plane. Don't forget to bring valid identification! You'll have to ⁶_____ or identity card.

Sometimes there are long lines to ⁷_____ , so make sure you arrive at the airport at least two hours before your flight.

Wait for your flight in the ⁸_____ , where you can get coffee. Don't forget to look at the ⁹_____ to see which ¹⁰_____ your flight leaves from.

When your flight is called, show your ¹¹_____ to the ¹²_____ , and check your seat number. Do you have an ¹³_____ or a window seat?

When you board the plane, find your seat quickly. Fasten your seat belt before the plane ¹⁴_____ . If you have a ¹⁵_____ , enjoy the view!

Ninety-five percent of our flights ¹⁶_____ smoothly and on time. That's one more reason to fly with Go There Airline!

2 Match definitions 1–8 with words and phrases from exercise 1.

1 bags you carry on a plane _____
2 when the plane leaves the ground _____
3 the document you show to get on a flight _____
4 preparing your bags before you fly _____
5 a person who works on a plane _____
6 when the plane returns to the ground _____
7 bags you don't carry on a plane _____
8 buy your tickets to fly _____

◀ Go back to page 104

155

# COMMUNICATION PRACTICE

## 1A  Student A

1  Answer Student B's questions.

2  Ask Student B questions 1–6 using the simple present or present continuous.
   1  What / kind / books / you / usually / read?
   2  Which books / you / read / at the moment?
   3  What / kind / phone / you / have / at the moment?
   4  you / have / a good day / today?
   5  your classmates / seem / happy / right now?
   6  you / own / a pet / at the moment?

## 1C  Student A

1  Read the text quickly. Ask Student B questions to complete the first part of the story. Use the question words in parentheses.

One morning in 2002, John Darwin went canoeing ¹_____ (where). That day, the weather was ²_____ (what like), and the sea was calm, but John didn't come home. When he didn't go to work, ³_____ (who) called the police. A few weeks later, ⁴_____ (what) appeared on the beach. Everyone thought John was dead, and John's wife Anne received ⁵_____ (what) because he had life insurance.

But the story didn't end there because John wasn't really dead. Five years later, he went ⁶_____ (where) and told the police that he had no memory of the past five years. But they didn't believe him. So where had he been?

After he disappeared, John hid in the house next door for years. Then John and Anne bought a house in Panama, and went there. But they had to go back to the UK to get a new visa – not easy for a dead man, so John went to the police station saying he had no memory.

However, a journalist found an online photo of the couple, taken in Panama City in 2006. Soon, everyone found out about their huge lie. Their children knew nothing about the plan and were very angry. In the end, John and Anne both went to prison.

2  Answer Student B's questions about the second part of the story.

## 1D  Student A

1  You're on a train. Follow the instructions in the box to make small talk with Student B.

- Greet Student B and ask if you can sit next to him/her.
- Say something about the train.
- Ask him/her where he/she's going.
- Ask what his/her job is.
- Ask what that involves.
- Respond with a positive comment.
- End the conversation and get off the train.

2  You're in a busy café. Student B makes small talk with you. Respond to his/her comments. Use the information in the box to answer his/her questions.

- You live about half an hour outside the city.
- You're a chef at a hotel downtown. You plan menus and create the meals. You really like making bread.
- Your favorite type of cooking is French.

# COMMUNICATION PRACTICE

## 2A Student A

1 Look at the picture and read the story behind it.

**What a coincidence!**

Neil Douglas, a photographer from Glasgow, was flying to Ireland one night when something very strange happened. He got on the plane and looked for his seat, but he found that a man, Rob Stirling, had already taken it. When Rob looked up at Neil, they were both surprised to see another man with a beard, ginger hair, and blue eyes! Although Neil and Rob are not related, they look exactly like each other. Everyone on the plane was laughing while they took selfies to show their friends.

2 Cover the text and tell Student B the story behind your picture. Use narrative tenses.

3 Look at Student B's picture and listen to the story behind it.

## 2C Student A

1 Make sentences about Joe using prompts 1–4. Use *used to* and the simple present. Student B listens and corrects.

Five years ago, Joe finished college and got a job in a bank.

| In the past | Now |
| --- | --- |
| 1 Joe / stay in bed / 11 a.m. | he / get up / for work / 6 a.m. |
| 2 Joe / always / wear / casual clothes | he / wear / suit and tie |
| 3 Joe / ride / old bike / to college | he / drive / to work |
| 4 Joe / get / takeout / weekend | he / usually / have dinner / expensive restaurants |

2 Read the sentences about Sandra and listen to Student B. Correct Student B's sentences if necessary.

Last year, Sandra won the lottery.

1 Sandra used to live in a small apartment, but now she lives in a huge house with a swimming pool.
2 Sandra didn't use to have a car, but now she usually drives expensive sports cars.
3 Sandra used to be a waitress in a hotel, but now she doesn't work.
4 Sandra used to go to the zoo to see the lions, but now she goes on safaris in Africa.

# COMMUNICATION PRACTICE

## 3A Students A and B

1 Follow the diagram and make plans to do two activities together. Complete the sentences following the prompts in parentheses. Use the activities in the box or your own ideas.

> go to the movies   go out for coffee   have dinner in a restaurant   have a picnic in the park
> go to the beach   go shopping   play tennis   go to a concert

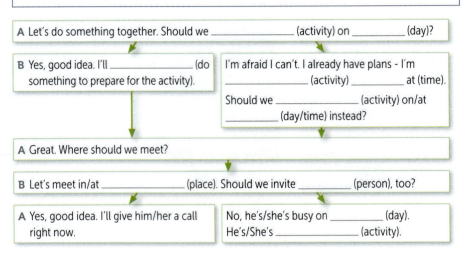

## 3C Student A

1 Ask Student B questions 1–5 about his/her neighbor.
  1 Do you have any nice neighbors?
  2 Where's he from?
  3 What does he do?
  4 Is he married?
  5 Do they have any children?

2 Listen to Student B's questions about one of your neighbors. Respond with an answer a–e, completing the sentence with a relative pronoun.
  a He also has a really noisy sports car _____ wakes me up at 5 a.m. every morning.
  b No, he doesn't. He has a teenage son _____'s also very noisy.
  c Because he has to drive to an office 100 km. away, _____ he works as an accountant.
  d Yes, I do. David, _____ lives on the first floor, is really annoying.
  e Well, first of all, he leaves his garbage bags, _____ smell really bad, in front of my door.

## 3D Student A

1 Tell Student B the three pieces of news in the box. Student B will respond after each piece of news.

> 1 I have some good news. I just started my own photography business.
> 2 Great news! Remember the exam I failed? Actually, I passed!
> 3 I'm afraid I have some bad news for you. You know I'm having financial problems at the moment. Well, I'm sorry, but I can't lend you the money I promised you.

2 Student B will give you three different pieces of news. Listen and respond, using responses a–c.

> a Oh! I'm sorry to hear he's not well. What a shame he can't come!
> b That's wonderful! I'm so happy for you!
> c That's OK. I completely understand.

# COMMUNICATION PRACTICE

## 4A Student A

1 Complete the sentences with *much* or *many*. Then ask Student B the questions.

1 How _____ work do you have at the moment?
2 How _____ coffee do you drink?
3 How _____ free time do you have during the week?
4 How _____ cookies do you eat?
5 How _____ energy do you have on Monday morning?
6 How _____ websites do you usually visit every day?

2 Answer Student B's questions. Use the quantifiers in the box in your answers.

| too much   too many   (not) enough   a lot (of)   lots of   plenty of |
| a little   a few   not much   not many   not any   no   none |

## 4C Student A

1 Look at the information. Ask Student B questions 1–4. Tell Student B if his/her answers are correct.

Buckingham Palace, London
Size: 77,000 sq. m.

Royal Palace, Madrid
Size: 135,000 sq. m.

The White House, Washington, D.C.
Size: 5,000 sq. m.

1 Which building is by far the biggest?
2 Is the White House as big as Buckingham Palace?

2 Look at the pictures. Answer Student B's questions.

the cheetah   the kangaroo   the tiger

Michael Jackson
Record sales: 180 million

Elvis Presley
Record sales: 210 million

Prince
Record sales: 100 million

3 Who was the most successful singer?
4 Was Michael Jackson slightly more successful or much more successful than Prince?

Mark Zuckerberg, Facebook CEO

Beyoncé, singer

Steven Spielberg, director

## 5A Student A

1 Read sentence parts 1–6 to Student B. He/She will complete them. Decide together if the completed sentences make sense.

1 If I have some money left at the end of this month,
2 If I ask a friend to lend me some money,
3 Should we go out for coffee
4 If we take the bus to the mall,
5 I'll wait here with you
6 Unless I have to work late at the office,

2 Listen to Student B. Complete each sentence part with an ending a–f. Decide together if the completed sentences make sense.

a … we'll arrive at 5 o'clock.
b … I'll go out and celebrate.
c … if you have time.
d … tell her to meet me at the theater.
e … you won't pass the exam.
f … when I get home this evening.

159

**COMMUNICATION PRACTICE**

# 5C  Students A and B

**1**  Look at the chart. Do you think these things will happen in the next ten years? Check (✔) your predictions. Compare your ideas in pairs.

**A** *I got 99% on my last exam, and I work really hard, so I think I'm going to speak perfect English in the next ten years! What about you?*
**B** *I don't think I'll speak perfect English in the next ten years. I miss too many classes.*

| In the next ten years … | going to | will definitely | will probably | may/might | probably won't | definitely won't |
|---|---|---|---|---|---|---|
| 1  I / speak perfect English | | | | | | |
| 2  I / run a marathon | | | | | | |
| 3  I / get married and have children | | | | | | |
| 4  someone in my family / move to a different city | | | | | | |
| 5  I / start my own business | | | | | | |
| 6  computers / replace my English teacher | | | | | | |
| 7  my country's soccer team / win the World Cup | | | | | | |

# 5D  Students A and B

**1**  Student A is taking a TV back to the store because the picture isn't clear. Student B is the salesclerk. Follow the diagram to have a conversation.

| Customer (Student A) | | Salesclerk (Student B) |
|---|---|---|
| Politely get the salesclerk's attention. | ⟶ | Offer to help. |
| Explain the problem with your TV. | ⟶ | Offer to check it. |
| Agree and give the salesclerk the TV. | ⟵ | Confirm that there's something wrong with the screen. |
| Say that you'd like a refund. | ⟶ | Ask for the receipt and his/her credit card. |
| Give the salesclerk the receipt and card. | ⟶ | Confirm that the money is back on the card. |

# 6A  Student A

**1**  Ask Student B the questions in conversations 1–3. Circle his/her answers.

1  Have you ever been to the U.S.?    *yes / no*
   Where did you go?    *New York / Washington, D.C.*
   What was it like?    *great / not great*
2  How long have you been a manager?    *since last year / for a year*
   When did you get a promotion?    *last month / three months ago*
   Have you taken any training courses yet?    *yes / no*
3  You don't look well. What's the matter?    *headache / hurt leg*
   Oh no! How did you do it?    *rollerblading / riding my bike*
   Have you been to see a doctor?    *yes / no*

**2**  Listen to Student B's questions. Choose the best answer a–c for each question in conversations 1–3.

1  a  It was a present from my parents.
   b  Yeah, I got it for my birthday.
   c  Only for a couple of days.
2  a  No, I didn't.
   b  Yes, I have.
   c  I met the singer Taylor Swift in a restaurant.
3  a  He left two minutes ago.
   b  To the library, I think.
   c  I'm sorry, he just left.

# 6C  Student A

**1**  Ask Student B questions 1–4.

1  I really like your top. How long have you had it?
2  What's your favorite sports team? How long have you been a fan?
3  Which social networking site do you use the most? How long have you been using it?
4  What TV series are you watching at the moment? How long have you been watching it?

**2**  Listen to Student B's questions. Respond using the present perfect continuous or the present perfect.

# COMMUNICATION PRACTICE

## 7A Student A

1 Ask Student B the trivia questions using the passive in the correct tense. The correct answer is in **bold**.

1 Which sport / play / at Wimbledon in England?
   a **tennis**
   b soccer
   c cricket

2 How many *Harry Potter* movies / make?
   a five
   b **eight**
   c ten

3 What / invent / by Guglielmo Marconi?
   a the television
   b **the radio**
   c the Internet

4 When / The Taj Mahal in India / build?
   a in the 15th century
   b **in the 17th century**
   c in the 19th century

5 Which animals / can / find / on the flag of Bolivia?
   a **an alpaca and a condor**
   b a lion and a swan
   c an owl and a bear

2 Look at the pictures and listen to Student B's questions. Choose the correct answer a–c.

1  a 1789
   b 1889
   c 1989

2  a plants
   b life
   c water

3  a Istanbul
   b Moscow
   c Athens

4  a around 20
   b around 200
   c around 2000

5  a the Great Pyramids at Giza
   b the Pentagon
   c the Great Wall of China

## 7C Student A

1 Ask Student B questions 1–5 using the correct form of *can*, *could*, or *be able to*.

1 _____ you sing well when you were eight years old?
2 Would you like to _____ fly?
3 _____ you watch shows online on your TV?
4 _____ you understand the lyrics of pop songs in English when you were fifteen?
5 Would you like to _____ sing like a famous singer? Who?

2 Answer Student B's questions. Give more information about each answer.

## 7D Student A

1 Student B is a tourist who is lost. You know the town well. Respond to Student B's questions and give directions using the information in the box.

> **The museum.** 10 minutes away on foot. Follow this street until you get to the traffic light. Take a right, and the museum is about 400 m. down that street on the left. It's next to a pizza restaurant.

2 You are in another town and you're lost. Ask Student B for directions to the train station using prompts 1–5.

1 Ask for help politely.
2 Ask for directions to the train station.
3 Ask if it was right or left at the traffic circle.
4 Repeat the route and ask for confirmation.
5 Thank him/her politely.

161

# COMMUNICATION PRACTICE

## 8A Student A

**1** Look at the chart. You think the facts about James Rodríguez are correct but you're not 100% sure. Use statements with tag questions to check the facts with Student B.

| James Rodríguez | |
| --- | --- |
| Sport | Soccer |
| Plays for | Atlético Madrid |
| Nationality | Colombian |
| Born | July 21st, 1991, Cúcuta |
| Height | 1.85 m. |
| Career highlight | Winning the Champions League in 2015 |
| Favorite players | Cristiano Ronaldo, LeBron James |

**2** Look at the facts about Fabiana Claudino in the chart. Student B will check these facts with you. Correct Student B's facts if necessary.

| Fabiana Claudino | |
| --- | --- |
| Sport | Volleyball |
| Nationality | Brazilian |
| Born | January 24th, 1985 |
| Home city | Belo Horizonte |
| Height | 1.93 m. |
| Career highlight | Winning gold in the 2012 Olympic Games |
| Favorite type of movie | Action movies |

## 8C Student A

**1** Read sentences 1–5 to Student B. Listen to his/her replies. Correct the responses if necessary.

1 Don't forget it's your mom's birthday on Saturday.
   Response:  You're right. I have to buy her some flowers.
2 When do I need to be at the airport?
   Response:  You have to be there two hours before the flight.
3 Should I give this banana to the monkey?
   Response:  No! You can't feed the animals in the zoo.
4 It's 6:30. It's time for me to get up!
   Response:  You don't have to get up early today. It's Saturday.
5 Do you have a job interview at eight o'clock tomorrow morning?
   Response:  Yes, I do. I have to go to bed early tonight.

**2** Listen to Student B. Respond using a sentence part 1–5 in column 1 and an ending a–e from column 2.

| 1 | I know. I have to | a | use your camera in the museum. |
| --- | --- | --- | --- |
| 2 | We don't have to | b | change in Miami. |
| 3 | No. You can't | c | dress up in my office. |
| 4 | No, it's not. You have to | d | start going to the gym again. |
| 5 | Thanks, but you don't have to. | e | I can walk. |

## 9A Student A

**1** Ask Student B questions 1–6. Student B will respond. Does the response make sense?

1 Do you like spicy food?
2 What do you feel like doing this weekend?
3 Have you ever tried kangaroo meat?
4 What was the new *Batman* movie like?
5 Hi, Jo. I'm calling you from California!
6 Would you like some more pasta?

**2** Listen to Student B's questions. Choose the correct response a–f.

a Just a glass of water, please.
b Really? What was it like?
c Not really. I feel like staying in.
d She's really funny.
e He's tall, with dark hair.
f Yes, I love it.

COMMUNICATION PRACTICE

## 9C Student A

1 Read sentence parts 1–6 to Student B. He/She will complete them. Decide together if the completed sentences make sense.

  1 My sister is very good at …
  2 It will be very easy for Lisa …
  3 My parents really enjoy …
  4 My friends and I want …
  5 Sam's really worried about …
  6 My colleague promised …

2 Listen to Student B. Complete each sentence part with an ending a–f. Decide together if the completed sentences make sense.

  a … to see her old friend Luke tonight.
  b … trying a new Japanese restaurant he heard about.
  c … get a new car at the moment.
  d … to try that new café by the river.
  e … getting a new cell phone next month.
  f … seeing her old friends from school.

## 9D Student A

1 You and Student B are going to order some takeout. Look at the menu and follow the instructions.

  1 Suggest two dishes to share.
  2 Listen to Student B.
  3 Respond positively to one of his/her suggestions, but not the other. Try to persuade him/her to change his/her mind.
  4 If necessary, agree to disagree and choose a third dish.

**Mimi's takeout menu**

| | |
|---|---|
| Vegetable lasagna | $10.25 |
| Spicy chicken in coconut milk | $11.50 |
| Lamb, mushroom, and spinach stew | $14 |
| Oven-baked zucchini, eggplant, and potato | $10 |
| Spicy beef burger, salad, and French fries | $12.50 |
| Thai green curry with eggplant and mixed peppers | $9 |

## 10A Student A

1 Look at the story. Take turns with Student B and report what the people said. Listen to Student B and complete the missing dialogue.

2 Check your story with Student B. Do you have the same dialogue?

# COMMUNICATION PRACTICE

## 10C  Student A

1  Ask Student B questions 1–4.

  1  If you hit another car in a parking lot, would you ...
    a  leave a note with your name on it to say you're sorry?
    b  wait for the owner and pay for the repairs?
    c  drive away, hoping that nobody saw you?
  2  If you saw somebody stealing food in a supermarket, would you ...
    a  tell the manager?
    b  say nothing?
    c  tell the person to stop?

  3  If there was an important game on TV while you were still at work, would you ...
    a  continue working and not think about it?
    b  leave work a bit early so you could watch part of it?
    c  tell your boss you're sick and watch it at home?
  4  If you found the answers to an important exam, would you ...
    a  give them to your teacher immediately?
    b  study them carefully, but get a few of the answers wrong on purpose?
    c  study them carefully and get all of the answers right?

2  Listen and answer Student B's questions. Explain your decisions.

## 11A  Student A

1  Read facts 1–5 to Student B, completing each sentence with the correct option. Student B will tell you if your answers are correct.

  1  In the summer, you can see the sun for 24 hours a day in some places in *England* / *Norway* / *Australia*.
  2  The first person to climb Mount Everest was from *the U.S.* / *New Zealand* / *the UK*.
  3  Every year *fewer than ten* / *about 100* / *over 1,000* people are killed by sharks.
  4  The strongest hurricane ever had wind speeds of *100* / *320* / *600* kilometers an hour.
  5  Mount Fuji is a volcano in *China* / *South Korea* / *Japan*.

2  Listen to Student B read facts 1–5. The correct answers are in **bold**. Tell Student B if his/her answers are correct.

  1  The largest ocean in the world is the *Atlantic* / **Pacific** / *Indian* Ocean.
  2  Lightning strikes the world *once* / **five times** / *100 times* a second.
  3  Tornadoes are most common **on flat dry land** / *in hot countries* / *near the sea*.
  4  At noon in July and August, the temperature in Riyadh, Saudi Arabia is usually *36* / **43** / *50* °C.
  5  The longest river in the world is the *Mississippi* / **Nile** / *Amazon*.

## 11C  Student A

1  Read problems 1–6 to Student B. He/She will respond.

  1  I got up late. I missed the bus.
  2  I didn't take a map. I got lost.
  3  My car ran out of gas. I had to walk.
  4  I stayed up late last night. I was exhausted this morning.
  5  I didn't have any lunch. I was starving this afternoon.
  6  I parked in front of the station. I got a parking fine.

2  Listen to Student B's sentences. Use the third conditional to respond.

  B  *I was late for a meeting. My boss was furious.*
  A  *If you had arrived on time, your boss wouldn't have been furious.*

## 11D  Student A

1  Student B is going to take a trip this summer. Answer his/her questions using the information in the box.

  > 1  You think California is more interesting.
  > 2  San Francisco is a beautiful city and a good place to stay.
  > 3  Yosemite is a great park for hiking.
  > 4  The cost of food is reasonable. Particularly Mexican food, which is delicious.
  > 5  The weather is always good. September is a good month to go.

2  You want to visit Australia or New Zealand. Ask Student B for recommendations using prompts 1–5.

  1  Ask for a recommendation. Australia or New Zealand?
  2  Ask which city to stay in.
  3  Ask about hiking. Are there any good places?
  4  You don't have much money. What about food?
  5  Best time to go in terms of weather?

COMMUNICATION PRACTICE

## 7D  Student B

1  You are a tourist who is lost. You want to visit the museum. Ask Student A for directions using prompts 1–5.

   1  Ask for help politely.
   2  Ask for directions to the museum.
   3  Ask if it was left or right at the traffic light.
   4  Repeat the route and ask for confirmation.
   5  Thank him/her politely.

2  Student A is a tourist who is lost. You know the town well. Respond to Student A's questions and give directions using the information in the box.

> **The train station.** 5–6 minutes away on foot. Follow this street until you get to the traffic circle. Take a right and go straight ahead, over a bridge. The station is on the left after the bridge.

## 12A  Student A

1  Read the sentences to Student B. Does he/she agree or disagree? Check (✓) the box if he/she agrees.

|   | Student B |
|---|---|
| 1  I love relaxing vacations. | ☐ |
| 2  I don't enjoy camping. | ☐ |
| 3  I don't like spending all day at the beach. | ☐ |
| 4  I'd love to travel around the U.S. | ☐ |
| 5  I can't wait to go on vacation! | ☐ |
| 6  I've already planned my next vacation. | ☐ |

2  Listen to Student B. Look at your responses below. Respond with *so* or *neither* to agree (✓), or *I* + verb to disagree (✗).

|   | Your responses |
|---|---|
| 1  I usually go on vacation in this country. | ✓ |
| 2  I haven't been away this year. | ✓ |
| 3  I can't go away for a whole month. | ✗ |
| 4  I'd love to stay on the coast. | ✗ |
| 5  I didn't like that hotel very much. | ✓ |
| 6  I'm looking forward to getting away. | ✓ |

## 12C  Student A

1  Read the clues below about the building in the photo. Follow the instructions.

   • After each clue, wait for Student B to make deductions.
   • After three clues, Student B can guess the answer.
   • If Student B's guess is wrong, give him/her the extra clue.

The Taj Mahal

**Clue 1:** It's not in the U.S.
**Clue 2:** It was built in the 17th century, in memory of a princess.
**Clue 3:** Both the interior and the exterior are beautifully decorated.
**Extra clue:** It's in India.

2  Look at the picture and the list of buildings and follow the instructions.

   • Listen to Student B's clues. After each clue, make deductions about which building it is.
   • After you hear three clues, give your answer.
   • If you're wrong, you can hear one more clue. Guess again.

| | |
|---|---|
| The Great Wall of China | The Statue of Liberty |
| The Taj Mahal | The Great Pyramid of Giza |
| Machu Picchu | Big Ben |

165

# COMMUNICATION PRACTICE

## 1A  Student B

1  Ask Student A questions 1–6 using the simple present or present continuous.
   1  What / kind / clothes / you / usually / wear / on the weekend?
   2  What / you / wear / today?
   3  What / you / think about / right now?
   4  What / you / think about / modern art?
   5  you / enjoy / studying English?
   6  you / enjoy / today's English class?

2  Answer Student A's questions.

## 1C  Student B

1  Read the text quickly. Answer Student A's questions about the first part of the story.

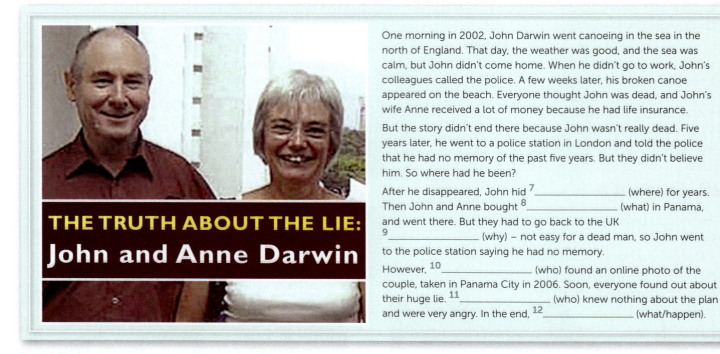

One morning in 2002, John Darwin went canoeing in the sea in the north of England. That day, the weather was good, and the sea was calm, but John didn't come home. When he didn't go to work, John's colleagues called the police. A few weeks later, his broken canoe appeared on the beach. Everyone thought John was dead, and John's wife Anne received a lot of money because he had life insurance.

But the story didn't end there because John wasn't really dead. Five years later, he went to a police station in London and told the police that he had no memory of the past five years. But they didn't believe him. So where had he been?

After he disappeared, John hid [7]_____ (where) for years. Then John and Anne bought [8]_____ (what) in Panama, and went there. But they had to go back to the UK [9]_____ (why) – not easy for a dead man, so John went to the police station saying he had no memory.

However, [10]_____ (who) found an online photo of the couple, taken in Panama City in 2006. Soon, everyone found out about their huge lie. [11]_____ (who) knew nothing about the plan and were very angry. In the end, [12]_____ (what/happen).

2  Ask Student A questions to complete the second part of the story. Use the question words in parentheses.

## 1D  Student B

1  You're on a train. Student A makes small talk with you. Respond to his/her comments. Use the information in the box to answer his/her questions.

   • You're going for an interview in New York.
   • You're an arts administrator. At the moment, you work for a small art gallery, but you'd like to work for a big gallery in New York.
   • Your work involves taking care of the gallery's business and planning events. You love modern art and the world of art.

2  You're in a busy café. Follow the instructions in the box to make small talk with Student A.

   • Greet Student A and ask if you can sit next to him/her.
   • Say something about the café.
   • Ask if he/she lives near the café.
   • Ask about his/her job.
   • Ask another question about his/her job.
   • Make a positive comment about something he/she says.
   • End the conversation and leave the café.

# COMMUNICATION PRACTICE

## 2A Student B

1 Look at the picture and read the story behind it.

**What a coincidence!**

In the summer of 2007, Michael Dick, a carpenter from London, was looking for his 31-year-old daughter, Lisa. He had lost touch with her ten years earlier when she had moved to the small town of Sudbury, about 100 km. away. Michael contacted a local newspaper there, and they wrote an article about his search for Lisa. They took a photo of him and his two other daughters. Lisa, who didn't even live in Sudbury any more, saw the newspaper article. She was shocked to see that she was actually in the photo, just a few meters behind her father and sisters!

2 Look at Student A's picture and listen to the story behind it.

3 Cover the text and tell Student A the story behind your picture. Use narrative tenses.

## 2C Student B

1 Read the sentences about Joe and listen to Student A. Correct Student A's sentences if necessary.

Five years ago, Joe finished college and got a job in a bank.

1 Joe used to stay in bed until 11 a.m., but now he gets up for work at 6 a.m.
2 Joe always used to wear casual clothes, but now he wears a suit and a tie.
3 Joe used to ride an old bike to college, but now he drives to work.
4 Joe used to get takeout on the weekend, but now he usually has dinner at expensive restaurants.

2 Make sentences about Sandra using prompts 1–4. Use *used to* and the simple present. Student A listens and corrects.

Last year, Sandra won the lottery.

| In the past | Now |
|---|---|
| 1 Sandra / live / small / apartment | she / live / huge house / swimming pool |
| 2 Sandra / not have / a car | she / usually / drive / expensive / sports cars |
| 3 Sandra / be / waitress / hotel | she / not work |
| 4 Sandra / go / zoo / to see / lions | she / go / on safaris / Africa |

167

# COMMUNICATION PRACTICE

## 3C Student B

**1** Listen to Student A's questions about one of your neighbors. Respond with an answer a–e, completing the sentence with a relative pronoun.

**a** Yes, he is. His wife, _____'s an elementary school teacher, is named Jenny. She's lovely, too.

**b** Yes, they have a daughter called Tamsin, _____ boyfriend is a professional soccer player.

**c** Yes, I do. Samuel, _____ lives on the second floor, is really friendly. We get along well.

**d** He comes from Avalon, _____ is a small town in California.

**e** He's a computer technician. He works for a company called FIX-IT, _____ repairs computers.

**2** Ask Student A questions 1–5 about his/her neighbor.

**1** Do you have any bad neighbors?

**2** Why is he such a bad neighbor?

**3** What else does he do to annoy you?

**4** Why does he leave so early?

**5** Does he live on his own?

## 3D Student B

**1** Student A will give you three different pieces of news. Listen and respond using responses a–c.

> **a** That's a relief! Congradulations!
> **b** Oh. That's a shame. Thank you for telling me.
> **c** Wow! That's fantastic news!

**2** Tell Student A the three pieces of news in the box. Student A will respond after each piece of news.

> **1** I have some bad news. You know my sister just started college. Well, she needs a laptop. I'm afraid I can't give you my old laptop after all. I'm really sorry.
> **2** I have great news! Our restaurant's had an excellent review in a national newspaper!
> **3** I'm afraid I have some bad news about Joe. He needs an operation, so he can't come on vacation with us.

## 4A Student B

**1** Answer Student A's questions. Use the quantifiers in the box in your answers.

> too much   too many   (not) enough   a lot (of)   lots of   plenty of
> a little   a few   not much   not many   not any   no   none

**2** Complete the sentences with *much* or *many*. Then ask Student A the questions.

**1** How _____ friends do you have on social media?

**2** How _____ sleep do you usually get a night?

**3** How _____ pairs of shoes do you own?

**4** How _____ TV do you watch?

**5** How _____ energy do you have on Friday evening?

**6** How _____ time do you have to see friends?

COMMUNICATION PRACTICE

## 4C Student B

1 Look at the pictures. Answer Student A's questions.

The White House, Washington, D.C.

Buckingham Palace, London

Royal Palace, Madrid

2 Look at the information. Ask Student A questions 1–4. Tell Student A if his/her answers are correct.

the tiger
Top speed: 65 km./h

the cheetah
Top speed: 110 km./h

the kangaroo
Top speed: 70 km./h

1 Which is the fastest of the three animals?
2 Is the kangaroo slightly faster or much faster than the tiger?

Prince

Michael Jackson

Elvis Presley

Steven Spielberg, director
Worth: $3.5 billion

Mark Zuckerberg, Facebook CEO
Worth: $55 billion

Beyoncé, singer
Worth: $265 million

3 Who is by far the wealthiest of the three famous people?
4 Is Beyoncé as wealthy as Steven Spielberg?

## 5A Student B

1 Listen to Student A. Complete each sentence part with an ending a–f. Decide together if the completed sentences make sense.

a ... I always promise to pay it back immediately.
b ... when class finishes?
c ... I'll probably buy some new shoes.
d ... until the bus comes.
e ... I'll be home at about 7 o'clock this evening.
f ... it will be much quicker than walking.

2 Read sentence parts 1–6 to Student A. He/She will complete them. Decide together if the completed sentences make sense.

1 Unless you study harder,
2 Come and see me next week
3 If the train isn't late,
4 If Kate calls,
5 As soon as I graduate,
6 I'll give you a call,

## 6A Student B

1 Listen to Student A's questions. Choose the best answer a–c for each question in conversations 1–3.

1 a To Washington, D.C.
  b I had a great time.
  c Yes, I went there last year.
2 a About three months ago.
  b Yes, I have – I've been on two courses.
  c Since last year.
3 a I was riding my bike, and I fell off.
  b No, I haven't. It's not that bad.
  c I've hurt my leg.

2 Ask Student A the questions in conversations 1–3. (Circle) his/her answers.

1 That's a nice laptop. Is it yours?    yes / no
  How long have you had it?    a short time / a long time
  Who gave it to you?    grandparents / parents
2 Have you ever met anyone famous?    yes / no
  Who did you meet?    an actor / a singer
  Did you speak to her?    yes / no
3 Hello. Is Michael there?    yes / no
  Do you know where he went?    to the library / to work
  When did he leave?    don't know / two minutes ago

# COMMUNICATION PRACTICE

## 6C Student B

1  Listen to Student A's questions. Respond using the present perfect continuous or the present perfect.

2  Ask Student A questions 1–4.
   1  Why did you decide to learn English? How long have you been learning it?
   2  What's your favorite gadget? How long have you had it?
   3  What's your favorite singer or band? How long have you been listening to their music?
   4  What's your favorite café or restaurant? How long have you been going there?

## 7A Student B

1  Look at the pictures and listen to Student A's questions. Choose the correct answer a–c.

a  tennis
b  soccer
c  cricket

a  five
b  eight
c  ten

a  the television
b  the radio
c  the Internet

a  in the 15th century
b  in the 17th century
c  in the 19th century

a  an alpaca and a condor
b  a lion and a swan
c  an owl and a bear

2  Ask Student A the trivia questions using the passive in the correct tense. The correct answer is in **bold**.

1  When / the Eiffel Tower / build?
   a  1789
   b  **1889**
   c  1989

2  What / recently / discover / on the planet Mars?
   a  plants
   b  life
   c  **water**

3  In which city / Europe and Asia / connect / by a bridge?
   a  **Istanbul**
   b  Moscow
   c  Athens

4  How many babies / born / in the world every minute?
   a  around 20
   b  **around 200**
   c  around 2000

5  What can / see / from the International Space Station?
   a  the Great Pyramids at Giza
   b  the Pentagon
   c  **the Great Wall of China**

## 7C Student B

1  Answer Student A's questions. Give more information about each answer.

2  Ask Student A questions 1–5 using the correct form of *can*, *could*, or *be able to*.
   1  When you were eight years old, _____ you watch any TV shows that you wanted?
   2  Which musical instrument would you like to _____ play?
   3  Would you like to _____ sing like an opera singer?
   4  _____ you watch TV shows on your smartphone?
   5  _____ you ever _____ see your favorite band in concert?

**COMMUNICATION PRACTICE**

# 8A  Student B

1   Look at the facts about James Rodríguez in the chart. Student A will check these facts with you. Correct Student A's facts if necessary.

2   Look at the chart. You think the facts about Fabiana Claudino are correct but you're not 100% sure. Use statements with tag questions to check the facts with Student A.

| James Rodríguez | |
|---|---|
| Sport | Soccer |
| Plays for | Real Madrid |
| Nationality | Colombian |
| Born | July 12th, 1991, Cúcuta |
| Height | 1.80 m. |
| Career highlight | Winning the Champions League in 2016 |
| Favorite players | Cristiano Ronaldo, LeBron James |

| Fabiana Claudino | |
|---|---|
| Sport | Volleyball |
| Nationality | Brazilian |
| Born | January 24th, 1986 |
| Home city | Rio de Janeiro |
| Height | 1.90 m. |
| Career highlight | Winning gold in the 2016 Olympic Games |
| Favorite type of movie | Romantic comedies |

# 8C  Student B

1   Listen to Student A. Respond using a sentence part 1–5 in column 1 and an ending a–e from column 2.

| 1 You're right. I have to | a feed the animals in the zoo. |
|---|---|
| 2 You have to | b go to bed early tonight. |
| 3 No! You can't | c be there two hours before the flight. |
| 4 You don't have to | d buy her some flowers. |
| 5 Yes, I do. I have to | e get up early today. It's Saturday. |

2   Read sentences 1–5 to Student A. Listen to his/her replies. Correct the responses if necessary.

1 You look like you're out of shape these days.
  Response:   I know. I have to start going to the gym again.
2 Why don't you wear a suit to work?
  Response:   We don't have to dress up in my office.
3 Am I allowed to take a photo?
  Response:   No. You can't use your camera in the museum.
4 Is the flight to New York direct?
  Response:   No, it's not. You have to change in Miami.
5 Should I drive you to the station?
  Response:   Thanks, but you don't have to. I can walk.

# 9A  Student B

1   Listen to Student A's questions. Choose the correct response a–f.

a It was really exciting!
b That's great! What's the weather like there?
c No, I haven't. What's it like?
d Should we go to the movies?
e No, thanks. I'm full.
f Yes, I do. I eat everything!

2   Ask Student A questions 1–6. Student A will respond. Does the response make sense?

1 What's Tina like?
2 Would you like something to drink?
3 We went to that new Italian restaurant last night.
4 What does Ian look like?
5 Do you like orange juice?
6 Do you want to go out tonight?

# 9C  Student B

1   Listen to Student A. Complete each sentence part with an ending a–f. Decide together if the completed sentences make sense.

a ... to be on time for the meeting.
b ... to make new friends when she goes to college.
c ... to go to the beach this summer.
d ... being late for his interview.
e ... making new friends.
f ... going abroad on vacation.

2   Read sentence parts 1–6 to Student A. He/She will complete them. Decide together if the completed sentences make sense.

1 On Saturday, I'd really like ...
2 Nicholas suggested ...
3 I'm thinking about ...
4 We can't afford to ...
5 Maria's looking forward to ...
6 Maria wants ...

171

COMMUNICATION PRACTICE

## 9D Student B

1  You and Student A are going to order some takeout. Look at the menu and follow the instructions.

   1 Listen to Student A's suggestions.
   2 Respond negatively. Suggest two alternative dishes.
   3 Listen to Student A. Change your mind if you want, or agree to disagree. Choose a third dish if necessary.

**Mimi's takeout menu**

| | |
|---|---|
| Vegetable lasagna | $10.25 |
| Spicy chicken in coconut milk | $11.50 |
| Lamb, mushroom, and spinach stew | $14 |
| Oven-baked zucchini, eggplant, and potato | $10 |
| Spicy beef burger, salad, and French fries | $12.50 |
| Thai green curry with eggplant and mixed peppers | $9 |

## 10A Student B

1  Look at the story. Take turns with Student A and report what the people said. Listen to Student A and complete the missing dialogue.

2  Check your story with Student A. Do you have the same dialogue?

## 10C Student B

1  Listen and answer Student A's questions. Explain your decisions.

2  Ask Student A questions 1–4.

   1 If you saw a colleague stealing paper at work, would you …
      a say nothing?
      b tell your colleague to put it back?
      c tell your boss?
   2 If a friend gave you a horrible sweater for your birthday, would you …
      a say you already have one just like it, and exchange it for something else?
      b say thanks, smile, but never wear it?
      c say you don't like it?
   3 If a stranger asked to borrow your cell phone, would you …
      a say, "Sorry, I don't have one"?
      b say, "Sorry, I'm in a hurry"?
      c lend it to him/her?
   4 If your friend left her Facebook page open on your computer, would you …
      a close it because it's private?
      b update her status with something funny?
      c read her private messages?

# COMMUNICATION PRACTICE

## 11A  Student B

1  Listen to Student A read facts 1–5. The correct answers are in **bold**. Tell Student A if his/her answers are correct.

  1  In the summer, you can see the sun for 24 hours a day in some places in *England* / ***Norway*** / *Australia*.

  2  The first person to climb Mount Everest was from *the U.S.* / ***New Zealand*** / *the UK*.

  3  Every year ***fewer than ten*** / *about 100* / *over 1,000* people are killed by sharks.

  4  The strongest hurricane ever had wind speeds of *100* / ***320*** / *600* kilometers an hour.

  5  Mount Fuji is a volcano in *China* / *South Korea* / ***Japan***.

2  Read facts 1–5 to Student A, completing each sentence with the correct option. Student A will tell you if your answers are correct.

  1  The largest ocean in the world is the *Atlantic* / *Pacific* / *Indian* Ocean.

  2  Lightning strikes the world *once* / *five times* / *100 times* a second.

  3  Tornadoes are most common *on flat dry land* / *in hot countries* / *near the sea*.

  4  At noon in July and August, the temperature in Riyadh, Saudi Arabia is usually *36* / *43* / *50* °C.

  5  The longest river in the world is the *Mississippi* / *Nile* / *Amazon*.

## 11C  Student B

1  Listen to Student A's sentences. Use the third conditional to respond.

  **A** *I got up late. I missed the bus.*
  **B** *If you hadn't gotten up late, you wouldn't have missed the bus.*

2  Read problems 1–6 to Student A. He/She will respond.

  1  I was late for a meeting. My boss was furious.

  2  I didn't take the garbage out. It smelled bad this morning.

  3  I didn't take an umbrella. I got wet.

  4  I forgot to text Dan. He didn't know about the party.

  5  I didn't lock my bike. It was stolen.

  6  I turned off my freezer. There was a flood in my kitchen.

## 11D  Student B

1  You want to visit California or Florida. Ask Student A for recommendations using prompts 1–5.

  1  Ask for a recommendation. California or Florida?

  2  Ask which city to stay in.

  3  Ask about hiking. Are there any good places?

  4  You don't have much money. What about food?

  5  Best time to go in terms of weather?

2  Student A is going to visit Australia or New Zealand. Answer his/her questions using the information in the box.

  1  You think New Zealand is more interesting.

  2  Christchurch is a beautiful city and a good place to stay.

  3  South Island is a great place for hiking.

  4  The cost of food is reasonable. Particularly the pies.

  5  The weather can be wet. January is a good month to go.

## 12A  Student B

1  Listen to Student A. Look at your responses below. Respond with *so* or *neither* to agree (✔), or *I* + verb to disagree (**X**).

| Your responses | |
| --- | --- |
| 1  I love relaxing vacations. | ✔ |
| 2  I don't enjoy camping. | ✔ |
| 3  I don't like spending all day at the beach. | **X** |
| 4  I'd love to travel around the U.S. | ✔ |
| 5  I can't wait to go on vacation! | ✔ |
| 6  I've already planned my next vacation. | **X** |

2  Read the sentences to Student A. Does he/she agree or disagree? Check (✔) the box if he/she agrees.

| | Student A |
| --- | --- |
| 1  I usually go on vacation in this country. | ☐ |
| 2  I haven't been on vacation this year. | ☐ |
| 3  I can't go away for a whole month. | ☐ |
| 4  I'd love to stay on the coast. | ☐ |
| 5  I didn't like that hotel very much. | ☐ |
| 6  I'm looking forward to getting away. | ☐ |

COMMUNICATION PRACTICE

## 12C Student B

1 Look at the picture and the list of buildings and follow the instructions.
   - Listen to Student A's clues. After each clue, make deductions about which building it is.
   - After you hear three clues, give your answer.
   - If you're wrong, you can hear one more clue. Guess again.

| The Great Wall of China | The Statue of Liberty |
| The Taj Mahal | The Great Pyramid of Giza |
| Machu Picchu | Big Ben |

2 Read the clues below about the building in the photo. Follow the instructions.
   - After each clue, wait for Student A to make deductions.
   - After three clues, Student A can guess the answer.
   - If Student A's guess is wrong, give him/her the extra clue.

Machu Picchu

**Clue 1:** It's not in Europe.
**Clue 2:** It was built in the 15th century and is made of stone.
**Clue 3:** Its name means "old peak."
**Extra clue:** It's in Peru.

# IRREGULAR VERBS

| Infinitive | Simple past | Past participle |
|---|---|---|
| be | was, were | been |
| beat | beat | beaten |
| become | became | become |
| begin | began | begun |
| bite | bit | bitten |
| break | broke | broken |
| bring | brought | brought |
| build | built | built |
| buy | bought | bought |
| catch | caught | caught |
| choose | chose | chosen |
| come | came | come |
| cost | cost | cost |
| do | did | done |
| draw | drew | drawn |
| dream | dreamt/dreamed | dreamt/dreamed |
| drink | drank | drunk |
| drive | drove | driven |
| eat | ate | eaten |
| fall | fell | fallen |
| feel | felt | felt |
| find | found | found |
| fly | flew | flown |
| forbid | forbade | forbidden |
| forget | forgot | forgotten |
| forgive | forgave | forgiven |
| get | got | gotten |
| give | gave | given |
| go | went | gone, been |
| grow | grew | grown |
| have | had | had |
| hear | heard | heard |
| hide | hid | hidden |
| hit | hit | hit |
| hold | held | held |
| hurt | hurt | hurt |
| keep | kept | kept |
| know | knew | known |
| learn | learned | learned |

| Infinitive | Simple past | Past participle |
|---|---|---|
| leave | left | left |
| lend | lent | lent |
| let | let | let |
| lie | lay | lain |
| lose | lost | lost |
| make | made | made |
| mean | meant | meant |
| meet | met | met |
| pay | paid | paid |
| put | put | put |
| read /riːd/ | read /red/ | read /red/ |
| ride | rode | ridden |
| ring | rang | rung |
| rise | rose | risen |
| run | ran | run |
| say | said | said |
| see | saw | seen |
| sell | sold | sold |
| send | sent | sent |
| shut | shut | shut |
| sing | sang | sung |
| sit | sat | sat |
| sleep | slept | slept |
| speak | spoke | spoken |
| spend | spent | spent |
| stand | stood | stood |
| steal | stole | stolen |
| stick | stuck | stuck |
| swim | swam | swum |
| take | took | taken |
| teach | taught | taught |
| tell | told | told |
| think | thought | thought |
| throw | threw | thrown |
| understand | understood | understood |
| wake | woke | woken |
| wear | wore | worn |
| win | won | won |
| write | wrote | written |

# Richmond

58 St Aldates
Oxford
OX1 1ST
United Kingdom

Printed in Mexico
**ISBN:** 978-84-668-2796-6
© Richmond / Santillana Global S.L. 2017
Reprinted, 2018

All rights reserved. No part of this book may be reproduced, stored in a retrieval system or transmitted in any form by any means, electronic, mechanical, photocopying, recording, or otherwise, without the prior permission in writing of the Publisher.

**Publishing Director:** Deborah Tricker
**Publisher:** Simone Foster
**Media Publisher:** Sue Ashcroft
**Content Developer:** Stephanie Bremner
**Editors:** Peter Anderson, Debra Emmett, Helen Ward, Tom Hadland, Eleanor Clements, Ruth Cox, Fiona Hunt, Kate Mellersh
**Americanization:** Deborah Goldblatt
**Proofreaders:** Bruce Wade, Tas Cooper, Shannon Neill
**Design Manager:** Lorna Heaslip
**Cover Design:** This Ain't Rock'n'Roll, London
**Design & Layout:** Lorna Heaslip, Oliver Hutton, ColArt Design
**Photo Researcher:** Magdalena Mayo
*Learning Curve* video: Mannic Media
**Audio Production:** Eastern Sky Studios
**App Development:** The Distance

**We would also like to thank the following people for their valuable contribution to writing and developing the material:**
Alastair Lane, Bob McLarty, Brigit Viney, Pamela Vittorio (Video Script Writer), Belen Fernandez (App Project Manager), Eleanor Clements (App Content Creator)

**We would like to thank all those who have given their kind permission to reproduce material for this book:**

**Illustration:**
Simon Clare; Dermot Flynn c/o Dutch Uncle; Guillaume Gennet c/o Lemonade; John Goodwin; The Boy FitzHammond c/o NB Illustration; Douglas Strachan at Strachangray Creative

**Photos:**
*J. Jaime; S. Enríquez;* 123RF; ALAMY/WENN Ltd., PhotoAlto sas, AF archive, HO Images, Chronicle, BSIP SA, B Christopher, Lev Dolgachov, Morey Milbradt, Richard Levine, Kevin Su, Rob Watkins, epa european pressphoto agency b.v., cineclassico, Aflo Co. Ltd., Mark Eden, Photo Japan, REUTERS, Mark phillips, Peterforsberg, Jorge Peréz, ilpo musto, Design Pics Inc, ZUMA Press, Inc., Glasshouse Images, MBI, TGSPHOTO, CoverSpot Photography, Entertainment Pictures,

Allstar Picture Library, Tewin Kijthamrongworakul, Tribune Content Agency LLC, Pictorial Press Ltd, Caryn Becker; BBC; BNPS (BOURNEMOUTH NEWS & PICTURE SERVICE) Rachel Adams, Steve Way; GETTY IMAGES SALES SPAIN/ Photodisc/Thinkstock, Photos.com Plus, Thinkstock; GTRESONLINE; I. PREYSLER; ISTOCKPHOTO/Getty Images Sales Spain; JOHN FOXX IMAGES; REX SHUTTERSTOCK/ FOX/Genre Movies, Page Images, Sipa Press, Silverhub, Galvan/AP, Ray Tang; SHUTTERSTOCK/Rex; SHUTTERSTOCK NETHERLANDS,B.V.; SOUTHWEST NEWS; wikipedia/ Ed g2s; Michael Parsons; Pedroromero2; Neil Douglas; Rockford Register Star and rrstar.com; COAST Collective Architecture Studio; Amos Magliocco/Eric Nguyen; courtsey of Vic Armstrong; Carroll County Sheriff; Project Monsoon, School of the Art Institute of Chicago; SERIDEC PHOTOIMAGENES CD; ARCHIVO SANTILLANA; GETTY IMAGES SALES SPAIN/ Westend61; ISTOCKPHOTO; ARCHIVO SANTILLANA

**Cover Photo:** iStockphoto/Getty Images Sales Spain

**Texts:**
p.48 Adapted from 'Fabrice Muamba: how I went from professional footballer to journalist' by Hannah Friend, Guardian Professional, 11 June 2014. Copyright Guardian News & Media Ltd 2016.

p.16 Adapted from 'Meet Steve Way - England's unlikeliest athlete for the Commonwealth Games' by Sean Ingle, theguardian.com, 31 May 2014. Copyright Guardian News & Media Ltd 2016.

**We would like to thank the following reviewers for their valuable feedback which has made Personal Best possible. We extend our thanks to the many teachers and students not mentioned here.**
Brad Bawtinheimer, Manuel Hidalgo, Paulo Dantas, Diana Bermúdez, Laura Gutiérrez, Hardy Griffin, Angi Conti, Christopher Morabito, Hande Kokce, Jorge Lobato, Leonardo Mercato, Mercilinda Ortiz, Wendy López

The Publisher has made every effort to trace the owner of copyright material; however, the Publisher will correct any involuntary omission at the earliest opportunity.

Printed in Mexico by Corporativo Prográfico S.A de C.V. Calle Dos Núm. 257, Bodega 4,Col. Granjas San Antonio, C.P. 09070 Del. Iztapalapa, Mexico, Mexico city. in December 2017.